SCIENCESAURUS®

A STUDENT HANDBOOK

GREAT SOURCE®

HOUGHTON MIFFLIN HARCOURT
Supplemental Publishers

Acknowledgments

Reviewers

Kathy Adair
Science Facilitator
Hurst-Euless-Bedford ISD
Hurst, Texas

Shernett Alexander
Curriculum Specialist,
Elementary Science
St. Lucie County School District
Fort Pierce, Florida

Dr. Stephen A. Anderson
Principal
Amerman Elementary School
Northville, Michigan

Joyce Thornton Barry
Science Chair, K–12
Plainview-Old Bethpage CSD
Plainview, New York

Taunya Brown
Science Facilitator
Wenatchee School District
Wenatchee, Washington

Marilyn Cook
Teacher
Port Aransas ISD
Port Aransas, Texas

Michelle Ferro
Science Coordinator
West Melbourne Elementary
School for Science
Brevard County, Melbourne,
Florida

Carolyn J. Herringshaw
Third Grade Teacher
Culver School District
Culver, OR

Heather W. Kemp
Teacher
Jefferson County Public Schools
Louisville, Kentucky

Barbara Langley
Math / Science Coach
Osceola School District
Kissimmee, Florida

Paula Nelson-Shokar
Science Supervisor
Miami-Dade County Public
Schools
Miami, Florida

Maxine Rosenberg
Science Education Consultant
Newton, Massachusetts

Dr. Kenneth Russell Roy
Science Safety Compliance
Specialist
National Safety Consultants
Vernon, Connecticut

Kitty Rutherford
Teacher
Wake County Public Schools
Raleigh, North Carolina

Nadine A. Solomon
Elementary Math and Science
Specialist
Arlington Public Schools
Arlington, Massachusetts

Richard Sturgeon
Teacher, Biology and Earth/
Space Sciences
Glastonbury High School
Glastonbury, Connecticut

Jennifer W. Taylor
Science Resource Teacher, K–8
Volusia County
Daytona Beach, Florida

Lauri Zabinski
Math and Science Resource
Teacher K–5
Challenger Elementary
Tamarac, Florida

Credits

Writing and Editing: Science House Publishing Services: Sarah Martin, Fran Needham, Linda Thornhill, Molly Wetterschneider, Linda Blumenthal, Rebecca Calhoun, Laura Prescott; Great Source: Marianne Knowles
Design: PUMPKiN PIE DESIGN; Great Source: Marcus McLaurin
Production Management: PUMPKiN PIE DESIGN; Great Source: Katherine Beinder
Cover Design: PUMPKiN PIE DESIGN
National Science Teachers Association: Tyson Brown
Photo and Illustration credits start on page 478.

International Standard Book Number: 978-0-669-01434-1 (hardcover)
5 6 7 8 9 0   0868   14 13 12

International Standard Book Number: 978-0-669-01508-9 (softcover)
5 6 7 8 9 0   0868   14 13 12 11
4500361426

Table of Contents

Almanac 342

Yellow Pages 389

How This Book Is Organized

ScienceSaurus® is a book about science. Science has two parts: *knowing* and *doing*. You can use *ScienceSaurus* to look up something that you want to know. For example, you can use it to find out how many planets there are in our solar system. You can also use *ScienceSaurus* to look up something you want to do. For example, you can use it to find out how to read a thermometer.

Topics and Sections

ScienceSaurus has seven big topics. Each topic has smaller sections. All of these are listed in the Table of Contents on pages iii–v.

98

Animals

Have you ever been to a zoo? What did you see there? Monkeys? Lions? Maybe you petted baby goats.

Monkeys, lions, and goats look and act very different, but they have something in common. They are all animals. You are an animal, too.

...is a living thing that cannot make its own ...ds must eat plants or other animals to live. ...s can move around from place to place. ...t easier for animals to find food.

...e nearly everywhere on land or in water. ...n flat, grassy places. Monkeys live high up ...h live in lakes, rivers, or the ocean. Birds ...where do people live?

78

Life Science

Where do you think they're going?

iii

Table of Contents

You'll also find the smaller sections listed on the first page of each big topic.

Looking at the Pages

Here's a page from *ScienceSaurus*. Let's look at all the parts.

These letters show you how to **pronounce** important science words.

Physical Science   285

Friction and Motion

Friction (FRIK shun) is a force that slows objects down. It is produced when objects rub together. The rougher the objects are, the more friction there is between them.

The road rubs against your bike tires. This slows down your bike. You must pedal your bike to keep it moving. Friction can be helpful, too. Brakes use friction to stop your bike.

You can skate on ice. There is not much friction between your skates and the smooth ice. That's why you can glide easily across the ice. But ice skates won't work on pavement. Pavement is rough. There would be too much friction.

∧ There is very little friction between ice skates and smooth ice.

The **colored band** along the top of the page tells you which topic you are in. Each topic has its own color. Red is the color for Physical Science.

Did you know? tells you things you might not already know about the topic you're reading about. It is one of the special features you'll find on the pages.

Did you know?
Friction produces heat energy. When you rub your hands together, they get warmer.

See Also
Forces Cause Motion pages 282–283
Producing Heat page 278

See Also tells you where you can go to find out more information about the topic you are reading about.

Here are two other special features:

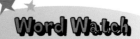

Word Watch
The word *quake* means *to shake*. During an earthquake people can often feel the ground shake.

Word Watch gives you more information about science words.

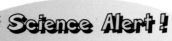

Science Alert!
Spiders are arthropods, but they are not insects. Insects have six legs. Spiders have eight legs. Insects have three body parts. Spiders have two body parts.

Science Alert! tells you about things you need to pay special attention to. Some Science Alerts are about safety. Most are about things that might be different from what you expect.

Almanac

What is an almanac? An almanac is a collection of general information. The almanac in *ScienceSaurus* has information you will need to study science.

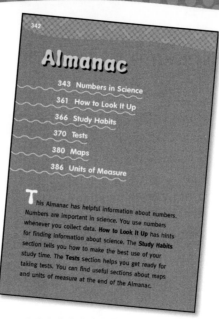

This Almanac has helpful information about numbers. Numbers are important in science. You use numbers whenever you collect data. **How to Look It Up** has hints for finding information about science. The **Study Habits** section tells you how to make the best use of your study time. The **Tests** section helps you get ready for taking tests. You can find useful sections about maps and units of measure at the end of the Almanac.

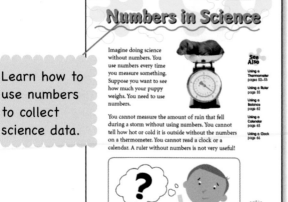

> Learn how to use numbers to collect science data.

Numbers in Science

Imagine doing science without numbers. You use numbers every time you measure something. Suppose you want to see how much your puppy weighs. You need to use numbers.

You cannot measure the amount of rain that fell during a storm without using numbers. You cannot tell how hot or cold it is outside without the numbers on a thermometer. You cannot read a clock or a calendar. A ruler without numbers is not very useful!

> Learn how to look up science information.

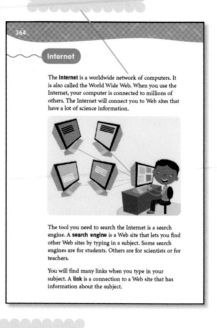

Internet

The **Internet** is a worldwide network of computers. It is also called the World Wide Web. When you use the Internet, your computer is connected to millions of others. The Internet will connect you to Web sites that have a lot of science information.

The tool you need to search the Internet is a search engine. A **search engine** is a Web site that lets you find other Web sites by typing in a subject. Some search engines are for students. Others are for scientists or for teachers.

You will find many links when you type in your subject. A **link** is a connection to a Web site that has information about the subject.

Short-Answer Tests

Short-answer tests ask you to write down information. Your answer may be a word, a phrase, or a sentence. Be sure to write your answers in complete sentences if the directions tell you to.

1. What are four things that plants need? Plants need air, water, light, and nutrients.
2. What is pitch? Pitch describes how high or low a sound is.
3. Name three kinds of fossil fuels. Three kinds of fossil fuels are coal, oil, and natural gas.

Think about your answer before you start writing. You might want to write down some notes before making a whole sentence. For the first question, you might make a list of all the things plants need first. Then you can make the list into a sentence and write it on the lines.

> Learn how to prepare for science tests.

Yellow Pages

This part of *ScienceSaurus* has four parts:

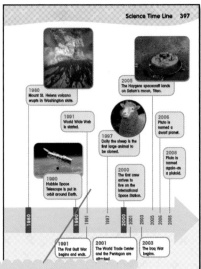

The **Science Time Line** shows you some big events in science history.

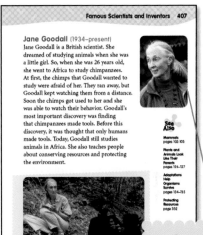

You can read about the lives of **Famous Scientists and Inventors.**

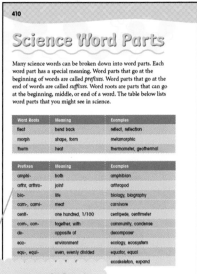

Science Word Parts help you understand science words.

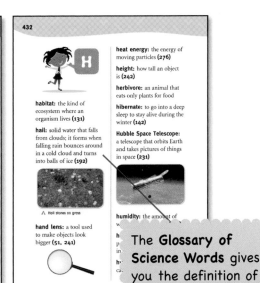

The **Glossary of Science Words** gives you the definition of science words used in this book and in other science books.

How to Use This Book

There are three ways to find information about a topic in *ScienceSaurus*.

1 **Look in the Table of Contents**
Look for big subjects, like *space* or *energy,* in the Table of Contents. The Table of Contents is at the front of the book.

2 **Look in the Index**
Look for smaller subjects, like *caterpillars* or *craters,* in the Index. The Index is at the very back of the book.

3 **Look in the Glossary**
Use the Glossary to find the definition of a science word. The Glossary is at the back of the book, before the Index.

This number tells you the page where you'll find the word.

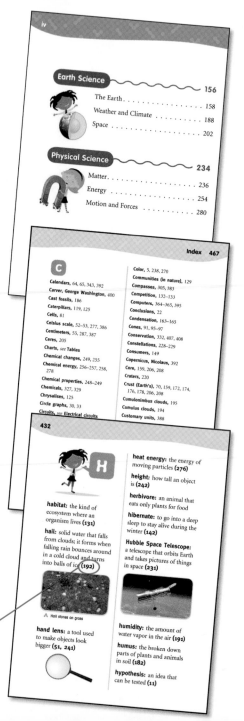

How to Use *sci*LINKS®

Let's say you want to learn more about a topic you read about in *ScienceSaurus*. *Sci*LINKS can help by showing you Web sites on the Internet that have more information.

You'll see *sci*LINKS on many pages of this book. Here's what each one tells you:

The **keyword** tells you the science topic of this *sci*LINK.

The **URL** tells you the online address of the *sci*LINKs Web site.

Keyword: Clouds
www.scilinks.org
Code: GSS23075

The **code** tells you what to type in at the *sci*LINKs Web site.

Here's how to use

1. **Go to** the *sci*LINKS Web site by typing the URL www.scilinks.org.

2. **Click on** "Register" to set up a user name and password. Log in. (Ask your teacher for help if you need it.)

3. **Type in** the *sci*LINK code for the keyword you want. You will see a list of links.

4. **Pick** a site you want to visit. Click on the link for that site. The link will take you to the site.

5. **Close** the window when you are done with that site. Then click on another link to visit another site.

Doing Science

What does it look like?

Nature is full of mysteries. What are stars made of? How do mountains form? When do bats sleep? These are questions answered by science. **Science** is the study of the natural world. A person who studies science is a **scientist.**

Science Is Observing

Your senses let you observe things. To **observe** (ahb ZURV) means to gather information using your senses. Seeing, hearing, smelling, tasting, and touching are senses.

An **observation** (ahb zur VAY shun) is something you notice with your senses. A cat plays with a toy. What observations can you make? One observation is that the cat hits the toy. Another observation is the color of the cat's fur.

Can you observe if the cat is happy? Not really. An observation is something you can be sure about using your senses.

Scientists observe things using their senses, just like you do. A scientist may observe that it rains more near the ocean than in the desert. The scientist wants to know why. Maybe it's because the ocean has so much water. Maybe it's because the desert is so hot. The scientist makes more observations and writes them down to find out why.

Careful observations are the beginning of all science. A scientist may observe geese flying south in September. The scientist may guess that the geese are flying south for the winter. Is the scientist's guess an observation? No, it isn't. The geese might be flying to a nearby pond.

See Also

Precipitation
page 192

When the Seasons Change
page 142

∧ Where are these geese going? You can't observe that until they land!

How to Observe

See Also

Arthropods
pages 114-115

Behaviors for Getting Food
page 140

Gravity and Motion
page 284

Suppose you watch a spider build a web. What can you observe? You might begin by asking yourself questions. *What color is the spider? How big is it? What shape is the web? How big is the web?*

Color, size, and shape are observations. You can ask other questions, like *Can it move? What is it doing?* The spider can move. It is building a web. These are observations.

Some observations can be made by counting things. You can count the number of legs on a spider. You can count the number of petals on a flower. What are some other things you can count?

You can ask questions that begin *What happens if…?* For example, you could ask *What happens if I drop this ball?* Then you observe what happens. The ball falls when you let go.

You also can make observations by comparing things. You might say *This soap smells like lemons. An airplane is bigger than a car.*

Here are some examples of observations you can make.

Things You Can Observe

Observation	Examples
Color	A banana is yellow. Joe's hair is brown.
Shape	A wheel is round. Paper is flat.
Odor	Popcorn smells buttery. The air smells like flowers.
Taste	The lemon is sour. The cookie is sweet.
Sound	A bee buzzes. Thunder booms.
How it feels	Glass is smooth. Rabbit fur is soft.
Size	The tree is tall. The river is wide and long.
How many	A spider has eight legs. There are five kittens.
Movement	A frog jumps. A worm crawls.

Using Tools to Observe

See Also

Using Science Tools
pages 50–67

Observing Matter
pages 240-241

Measuring Matter
pages 242-243

Measuring Temperature
page 277

Suppose you want to answer the question, *How long is my pencil?* You need a tool to make this observation. A **tool** helps you make observations that go beyond your senses.

You can use tools to measure (MEZH ur) things. To **measure** means to answer the question *How much?* A **measurement** (MEZH ur munt) tells how much there is of something.

Some tools make small things look bigger. You can use a hand lens to look at things like ants or seeds. A microscope (MY kruh skohp) helps you see things that are very small. A telescope (TEL uh skohp) lets you see things that are far away, like planets and stars.

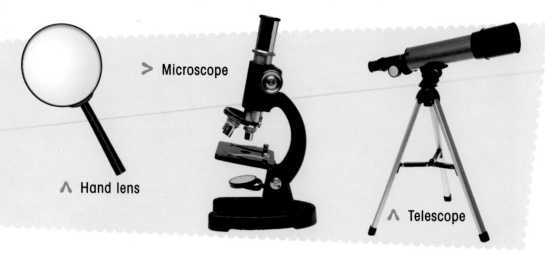

> Microscope

∧ Hand lens

∧ Telescope

Tools let you compare observations. Using a tool, you can measure the temperature indoors and the temperature outdoors. Then you can compare the two temperatures.

Observations Lead to Questions

Imagine you are on a hike. The trail takes you by a pond. You observe a log floating in the pond. Later, you observe a twig floating in a puddle. A log and a twig are both made of wood. You start to wonder. *What makes wood float?* Your observations have led you to a question.

Your question leads you to find out what makes wood float. You observed that big logs and tiny twigs both float. You decide that size probably does not matter. Does the kind of wood matter? You can test different kinds of wood to answer this question.

Doing an Investigation

Keyword:
Scientific
Investigation
www.scilinks.org
Code: GSS23005

One way to find an answer to a question is to do what scientists do. Scientists do investigations (in ves tih GAY shunz). An **investigation** is a way to find out the answer to a question.

Scientists follow these steps when they do an investigation. Pages 10–25 of this book will tell you more about each step.

Not every investigation has all these steps. Sometimes you can answer a question just by making observations.

See Also

Ask a Question
page 10

Make a Hypothesis
page 11

Make a Plan
pages 12–16

Steps in an Investigation	
1	Ask a question.
2	Make a good guess about the answer to your question.
3	Plan your investigation.
4	Collect the materials you need.
5	Do your investigation. Record your observations.
6	Look at your results.
7	Figure out what your results mean.
8	Share your results with other people.
9	Ask more questions.

Here's one example of an investigation. Suppose you wonder whether a ball will roll different distances on different surfaces. You have an idea. You think the ball will roll farther on a smooth tile floor than on a rough carpet. You can do an investigation to see if your idea is correct.

You roll a ball on the floor and then on the carpet. You compare how far the ball rolls each time. You could measure the distance the ball rolled each time.

Science Alert!

Results can be a little different each time you do the same investigation. It's a good idea to repeat an investigation a few times. That way, you'll know you didn't make a mistake. You'll know your results are correct.

Ask a Question

See Also

Measuring Temperature
page 277

Many observations lead to a question. The question might ask *What, How, When, Where,* or *Why.*

Good science questions have clear answers. You observe that it is sunny outside. You might ask *Is it warm out today?* That question doesn't have a clear answer. "Warm" means different things to different people. A good science question is *What is the temperature outside?* You can do an investigation to answer the question.

Sometimes you can't answer a question with your own investigation. You have to look up the answer. Read the questions below. You can answer the flower question by investigating. You have to look up answers for the volcano and bat questions.

∧ Why do volcanoes erupt?

∧ Where are seeds made in a flower?

∧ When do bats sleep?

Make a Hypothesis

You have observed that your dog eats all her Dog Yum dog food every day. You think your dog likes Dog Yum better than any other kind of dog food, but you don't know for sure. You decide to investigate this question: *What kind of dog food does my dog like best?*

See Also

Doing an Investigation
pages 8–9

Is that a good science question? No, it isn't. How would you know if your dog likes the food? How would you know which food she likes best? You can't observe or measure "like" and "best."

You know your dog eats all of her Dog Yum. You don't know if she will eat all of another kind of dog food. You decide to change the question: *What kind of dog food will my dog eat the most of?* You can observe the answer to this question. You can measure how much dog food your dog eats.

Now you can make a hypothesis (hy PAHTH ih sis). A **hypothesis** is an idea that can be tested. You can test your hypothesis by doing an investigation.

> Your hypothesis is *My dog will eat more Dog Yum than another kind of dog food.*

Make a Plan

Your hypothesis is *My dog will eat more Dog Yum than another kind of dog food.* You want to test your hypothesis. You plan to compare Dog Yum with Barko dog food.

You decide to give your dog one cup of food each time you feed her. After she eats for 5 minutes, you'll measure the food left in the bowl. If she eats all or most of the food, you'll know she likes it. If she leaves a lot of food in the bowl, you'll know she doesn't like it.

You need to do three things to make a good plan.

How to Plan for an Investigation

1   Make a list of materials you will need.

2   Write down the steps you will follow.

3   Make a place to write your observations.

Science Alert !

Sometimes, your teacher will make the plan for you. Follow the plan exactly. If you make your own plan, be sure to have your teacher or another adult check it to make sure it is safe.

List the Materials

Make a list of all the materials you need for your
investigation. Your list might look like this.

See Also

Doing an Investigation
pages 8–9

Make a Plan
page 12

Write the Steps
page 14

Make a Place to Write Observations
page 15

Materials
Dog Yum dog food
Barko dog food
measuring cup
food bowl
clock
pencil and paper

You might decide to make your materials list at the
same time you write your steps. Your steps give you a
clue about the materials you need.

In this investigation, one of
the steps is to time your dog
while she eats. You need a
clock for that step.

You have to give your
dog the same amount of
food each time. You also
have to measure the dog
food that is left over. You
need a measuring cup for
those steps.

Write the Steps

Write down all the steps you will follow in your investigation. The steps might look like this.

Steps to Follow

Day 1

1. Measure one cup of Dog Yum.
2. Pour Dog Yum into the food bowl.
3. Give my dog 5 minutes to eat.
4. Measure how much Dog Yum is left over at the end of 5 minutes.
5. Write down how much Dog Yum is left over.
6. Clean up.

Day 2

1. Measure one cup of Barko.
2. Pour Barko into the food bowl.
3. Give my dog 5 minutes to eat.
4. Measure how much Barko is left over at the end of 5 minutes.
5. Write down how much Barko is left over.
6. Clean up.

Make a Place to Write Observations

Look at your list of steps. What observations will you make? Knowing this will help you decide what to write down.

In this investigation, you will measure the amount of Dog Yum food that your dog leaves in the bowl. The next day, you will do the same thing for Barko food. You will need to write down the amount of food that is left over each day.

You could write the amounts in a table like this one.

Food My Dog Likes

Food	Amount of Food Left Over
Dog Yum	
Barko	

See Also

Tables
pages 28–29

The dog food investigation is simple. You have one dog and two kinds of food. How does this work when you have more things in your investigation?

> Remember to make a place to write things down *before* you start your investigation.

See Also

What Do Plants Need?
pages 86-87

Choose a Variable to Test

You know plants get soil, water, and sunlight outdoors. Maybe plants need all those things. How can you tell? You can do an investigation.

Soil, sunlight, and water are variables (VAYR ee uh bulz) in your investigation. A **variable** is something in an investigation that can change. When you do an investigation, you have to test only one variable at a time. The dog food investigation has one variable. The plant investigation has three. How can you be sure you are testing only one variable?

Suppose you will work with two classmates. Your group decides to test sunlight. Your hypothesis is *Plants in sunlight grow taller than plants in the dark.*

You'll get two plants. You'll put one of your plants in a sunny place. You'll put one plant in a dark place. Sunlight is the only variable that you will change.

See Also

Measuring Liquids
pages 58–61

The plants have to be the same kind and the same size. They have to be in the same kind of pot and the same kind of soil. You'll have to give them the same amount of water. Here is a plan for your investigation.

Plant Investigation		
	In sunlight	**In the dark**
When to measure	Monday and Friday	Monday and Friday
When to water	Monday and Friday	Monday and Friday
Amount of water	50 mL	50 mL
Place	Sunny window	Dark closet

Collect the Materials

Look at your plan. A good plan lists what materials you will need. You'll need these materials for the plant investigation.

See Also

Using a Ruler
page 55

- two plants in pots
- something to measure water
- water
- a ruler to measure the plants
- a place to write down observations
- masking tape and a pencil to make labels

∧ Your group will need a sunny place and a dark place for all your plants.

You'll need to label your pots with your name. That way, you'll know which plants are yours. Also label the pots *In sunlight* and *In the dark* so you can tell the plants apart later.

Write Down Your Observations

See Also

Science Is Observing
pages 2–3

Tables
pages 28–29

Using a Ruler
page 55

Follow the steps in your investigation. Use a ruler to measure how tall each plant is. Observe what the plants look like. Are they green and healthy? Do they look droopy and unhealthy?

A table is a good way to keep track of your observations. You will need space to write down your data (DAY tuh). **Data** is the information you collect in an investigation. Data can include dates and measurements. In this investigation, you will measure how tall your plants are.

You might want to draw pictures of your observations. The pictures do not have to be perfect. They just need to show what you observed.

⋀ When you draw the plants, include the labels on the pots. The labels will help you remember what the pictures show. The labels will also help other people understand your pictures.

You could use a table to write your observations. The table might look like this.

How the Plants Grew

Day and Date	Plant in Sunlight		Plant in the Dark	
	How tall	What it looks like	How tall	What it looks like
Monday May 5	9 cm		9 cm	
Friday May 9	11 cm		9 cm	
Monday May 12	12 cm		9 cm	
Friday May 16	14 cm		9 cm	

Look at the Data

Look at the table on page 19. It shows the data from the plant investigation. Do you see any patterns? The plant in sunlight grew. It was taller at the end of the investigation than at the beginning. It was taller than the plant grown in the dark.

Friday May 16	14 cm		9 cm	

∧ Plant grown in sunlight and plant grown in the dark.

See Also

Organizing Data
page 26

Seeing Patterns in Data
pages 34–35

You can see these patterns because you organized the data. There is space in the table to write down the dates and measurements. There is enough space to draw pictures of the plants.

Planning is very important! Good planning makes it easier to keep track of your observations. Good observations make it easier to see patterns in data.

Sometimes it is easier to see a pattern if you graph the data. A graph is a way to show data in picture form. The graph on this page shows the data from the plant investigation. The bars show how tall the plants were on the days they were measured.

See Also

Bar Graphs
page 32

The red bars show the measurements of the plant in sunlight. That plant grew taller.

The blue bars show the measurements of the plant in the dark. That plant didn't grow taller.

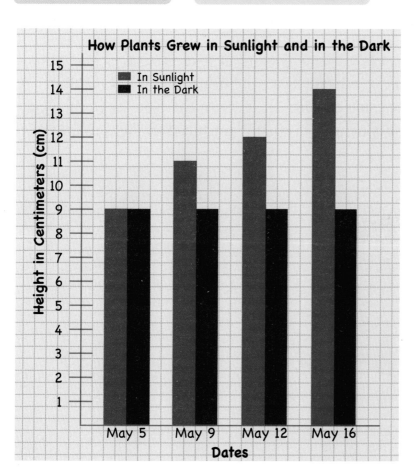

Draw Conclusions

Look at the plant data in the graph on page 21. Is there a pattern in the data? What does the graph show? It shows that the plant in sunlight grew taller than the plant in the dark.

See Also

Make a Hypothesis page 11

Is this what you thought would happen? Compare the results of your investigation with your hypothesis. Your hypothesis was *Plants in sunlight grow taller than plants in the dark.* Your investigation showed that your hypothesis was correct.

You can now make a conclusion (kuhn KLOO zhun). A **conclusion** explains the pattern that you see in the data. Your conclusion is that plants need sunlight to grow.

These results do not tell you anything about the importance of soil or water. You did not test those variables. You kept them the same for both plants.

Sometimes a hypothesis is not correct. Look back at pages 11–15. Your hypothesis was *My dog will eat more Dog Yum than another other kind of dog food.* You gave her Dog Yum one day. The next day, you gave her Barko. Look at the data from the investigation.

Food My Dog Likes

Food	Amount of Food Left Over
Dog Yum	none
Barko	none

Your dog ate all the Dog Yum *and* all the Barko. There was no food left over either day. Can you conclude that your dog likes Dog Yum better than Barko? No, you can't. Your dog seems to like both foods.

Was your hypothesis wrong? Yes, it was. Did your investigation fail? No, it didn't. You learned something. Now you know that your dog likes another kind of food besides Dog Yum.

Next, you can test other kinds of dog food. Maybe your dog will like another kind even better than Dog Yum and Barko. Or maybe you'll find out that your dog likes any kind of dog food!

Share Your Results

Scientists share information about their investigations. They explain how they did an investigation. Then other scientists can try the same investigation. If many scientists get the same results, they can be sure the results are correct.

Scientists give written and oral reports. You can share your ideas in reports, too. You can give an oral report. You can make a poster. You can draw pictures and graphs on your poster.

This is a poster for the plant investigation.

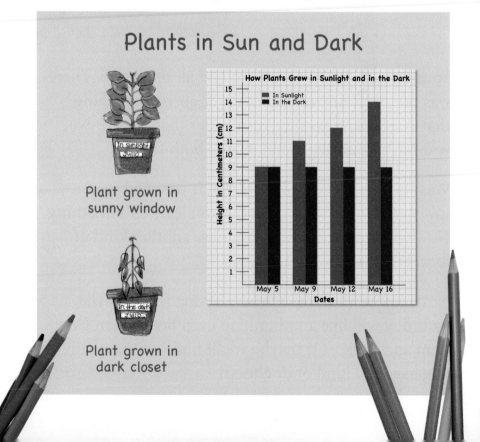

Plants in Sun and Dark

Plant grown in sunny window

Plant grown in dark closet

How Plants Grew in Sunlight and in the Dark

Ask More Questions

An investigation might lead to more questions. Suppose a scientist finds that some kinds of bats sleep during the day. The scientist has answered a *When* question.

Answering the *When* question could lead the scientist to ask a *What* question.

> ### What do bats do at night?

The scientist investigates this question. She finds that bats come out at night to hunt moths and other insects.

Next, the scientist wants to answer a *How* question.

> ### How do bats find insects in the dark?

The scientist does another investigation. She finds that bats use sounds to find insects.

See Also

Mammals
pages 102-103

Behaviors for Getting Food
page 140

Sound Energy
pages 260-265

> A bat makes clicking sounds as it flies around. The sounds bounce off objects. The bat hears the sounds that bounced. It can tell the size and shape of the object. It can tell whether the object is moving. That's how the bat finds insects in the dark.

Organizing Data

You might collect a lot of data in an investigation. You need a way to organize your data. Organizing data helps you look for patterns. It lets you compare things easily.

See Also

Using a Thermometer
pages 52–53

Suppose you investigate how the outdoor temperature changes while you're in school one day. You measure the temperature every hour. You write the temperatures and times on note paper like this.

58°F 8:00 A.M.
1:00 P.M. 72°F
11:00 A.M. 65°F
12:00 noon 68°F
60°F 9:00 A.M.
3:00 P.M. 71°F
2:00 P.M. 74°F
10:00 A.M. 62°F

You should plan how to organize the data *before* you start an investigation. Here's a good way to organize the data.

∧ How did the temperature change during the day? You can't tell. You didn't organize the data.

Time	Temperature (°F)
8:00 A.M.	58
9:00 A.M.	60
10:00 A.M.	62
11:00 A.M.	65
12:00 noon	68
1:00 P.M.	72
2:00 P.M.	74
3:00 P.M.	71

< Can you see how the temperature changed during the day? Yes, you can. How did it change?

Charts and Tables

Tables are a good way to organize data from observations or an investigation. A **table** has rows and columns. Rows go across. Columns go up and down. Tables are also called charts.

See Also

Seasons and Weather
pages 196-197

Tally Charts

A **tally chart** shows how many of something you counted. Suppose you want to find out which season of the year your classmates like best. You mark their answers in a tally chart like this.

The first column names the things you are counting.

Make one tally mark on the chart for each thing you count. When you get to 5, draw a slash through the 4 tally marks. Then you can count the tally marks by fives.

Count the number of tally marks in each row. Write that number in the last column.

Season	Tally	Number
Spring	///	3
Summer	~~////~~ ////	9
Fall	////	4
Winter	//	2

Which season do your classmates like best? A tally chart makes it easy to find the answer!

Tables

A table has spaces for writing dates, measurements, and other data. It also can have spaces for drawing pictures.

See Also

Measuring Liquids
pages 58–61

Water Moves Around Earth
pages 162–165

Changing States
pages 246-247

Suppose you want to find out if heat makes water evaporate faster. You design an investigation. You'll put two measuring cups outdoors. The cups will be the same size and the same shape. You'll put one cup in sunlight and the other cup in shade. You'll fill each cup with water to the 250 mL line. You'll observe the amount of water in the cups every hour.

You can make a table like this one to record the data.

You need a column of spaces to write the amount of water left in the cup in sunlight.

You need another column of spaces to write the amount of water left in the cup in shade.

Give your table a title.

Decide when you will collect data. Write those times in the first column.

Amount of Water in Each Cup

Time	Cup in Sunlight	Cup in Shade
10:00 A.M.		
11:00 A.M.		
12:00 noon		
1:00 P.M.		
2:00 P.M.		

Use the table to write down the amount of water in each cup. Find the time in the first column. Look across that row. Write down the amount of water in each cup. Make sure you write the data in the correct column.

Here is the table with all the data filled in.

Amount of Water in Each Cup		
Time	Cup in Sunlight	Cup in Shade
10:00 A.M.	250 mL	250 mL
11:00 A.M.	200 mL	225 mL
12:00 noon	150 mL	200 mL
1:00 P.M.	100 mL	175 mL
2:00 P.M.	50 mL	150 mL

Compare the amounts of water in the two cups. Did the same amount of water evaporate from both cups? No. More water evaporated from the cup in sunlight. Does sunlight make water evaporate faster? Yes, it does.

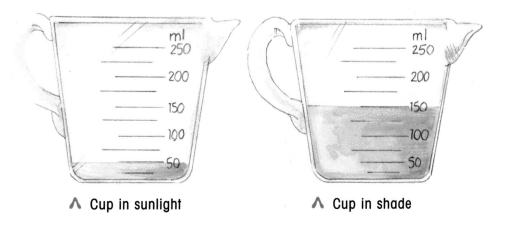

∧ Cup in sunlight   ∧ Cup in shade

Graphs

You use a table to organize data. Then you can show the data in a picture. A picture that shows data is called a **graph** (GRAF). There are different kinds of graphs.

Suppose you ask your classmates to vote on their favorite kind of cookie. You find that 12 students like chocolate chip cookies best, and 4 students like peanut butter cookies best. Here are three different kinds of graphs for the data.

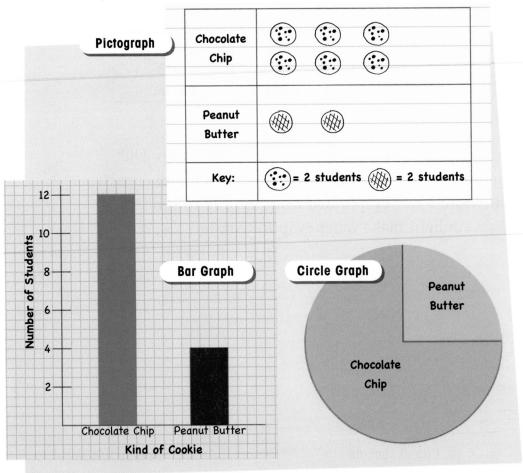

Pictographs

You investigated your classmates' favorite seasons. You recorded the data in a table like the one on page 27. You can show the data in a pictograph (PIK tuh graf). A **pictograph** has pictures instead of numbers.

See Also

Seasons and Weather
pages 196-197

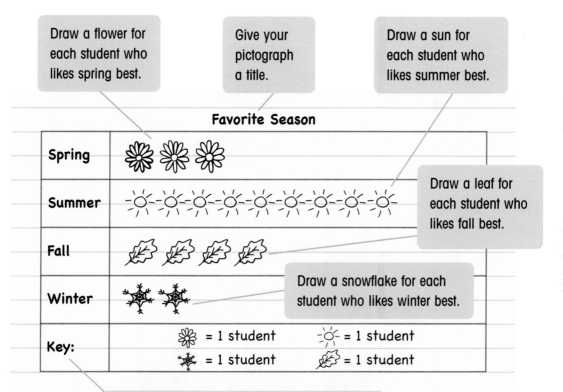

Draw a flower for each student who likes spring best.

Give your pictograph a title.

Draw a sun for each student who likes summer best.

Favorite Season

Spring	
Summer	
Fall	
Winter	
Key:	

Draw a leaf for each student who likes fall best.

Draw a snowflake for each student who likes winter best.

= 1 student   = 1 student
= 1 student   = 1 student

A pictograph has a key. The key tells what each picture stands for. In this pictograph, each picture stands for one student.

If your class has a lot of students, let each picture stand for two or three students. That way, you won't need to draw as many pictures.

See Also

Leaves
Page 88

Bar Graphs

You can show data in a bar graph. A **bar graph** shows the same kind of data for different things.

Suppose you collected leaves on a hike. You have 12 oak leaves, 15 maple leaves, and 6 ash leaves. The data you want to graph is the number of each kind of leaf.

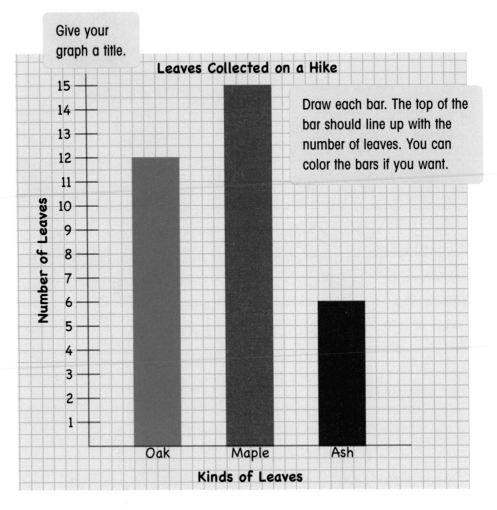

Give your graph a title.

Leaves Collected on a Hike

Draw each bar. The top of the bar should line up with the number of leaves. You can color the bars if you want.

Number of Leaves

Oak Maple Ash

Kinds of Leaves

The sizes of the bars show the number of leaves you collected. The tallest bar is the bar for maple leaves. The graph shows that you collected the most maple leaves.

Circle Graphs

A **circle graph** shows parts of a whole. A circle graph is also called a *pie chart*. It looks like a pie that has been cut into pieces. Use fractions or percents to make a circle graph.

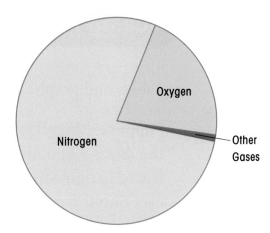

∧ This circle graph shows the gases in air.

Suppose three fourths of your classmates like rock music best, and one fourth like country music best. You could make a circle graph to show the data.

See Also

Fractions
pages 348-351

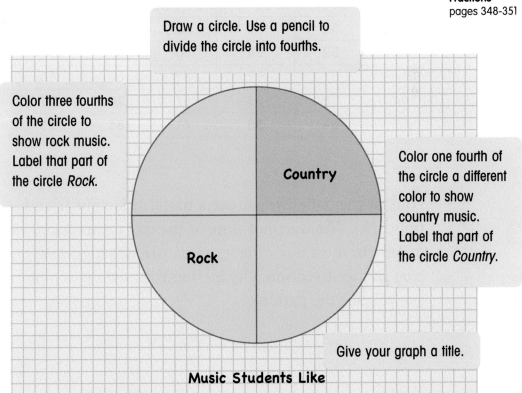

Draw a circle. Use a pencil to divide the circle into fourths.

Color three fourths of the circle to show rock music. Label that part of the circle *Rock*.

Color one fourth of the circle a different color to show country music. Label that part of the circle *Country*.

Give your graph a title.

Music Students Like

Seeing Patterns in Data

See Also

Look at the Data
page 20

Using a Thermometer
pages 52–53

Tables and graphs can help you see patterns in data.

Suppose a friend tells you that the warmest time of the day is 12:00 noon. You want to find out if your friend is right. You measure the temperature outdoors every hour from 11:00 in the morning until 3:00 in the afternoon. You do this for five days. You organize your data in a table like this.

Day	Outdoor Temperature (°F)				
	11:00 A.M.	12:00 noon	1:00 P.M.	2:00 P.M.	3:00 P.M.
Monday	55	60	62	65	59
Tuesday	52	54	60	66	62
Wednesday	57	62	67	64	60
Thursday	58	63	67	70	71
Friday	54	58	61	65	59

Look at the data. Do you see a pattern? Is your friend right? No. The warmest time of the day wasn't 12:00 noon. On most days, the temperature was highest at 2:00 in the afternoon. Organizing your data in a table lets you see the pattern.

Suppose you collected weather data for two weeks.
You recorded if it was sunny, cloudy, or rainy each day.
This graph shows the data you recorded.

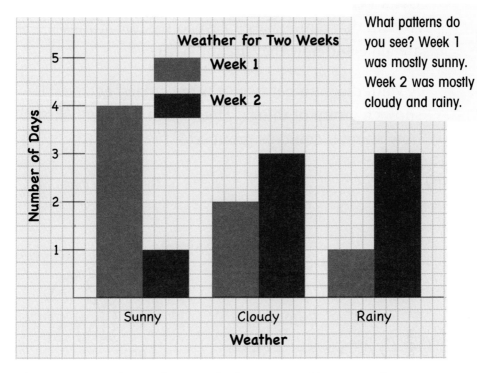

Weather for Two Weeks

Week 1

Week 2

Number of Days

Sunny   Cloudy   Rainy

Weather

What patterns do you see? Week 1 was mostly sunny. Week 2 was mostly cloudy and rainy.

There is something the graph does *not* tell you. It does not tell you *which days* were sunny or cloudy or rainy.

You could use a tally chart to keep track of sunny days, cloudy days, and rainy days. Then you could use the numbers on the tally chart to make the bar graph.

See Also

Tally Charts
page 27

Venn Diagrams

Use a **Venn diagram** to sort things into groups.
A Venn diagram makes it easy to see how things
are alike and how they are different.

A Venn diagram has two or more circles. Each circle
shows a group of things. These Venn diagrams show
how animals could be grouped.

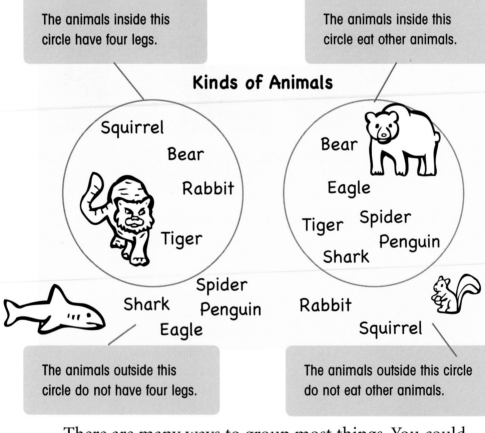

The animals inside this circle have four legs.

The animals inside this circle eat other animals.

Kinds of Animals

Squirrel

Bear

Rabbit

Tiger

Bear

Eagle

Tiger   Spider

Penguin

Shark

Spider

Shark   Penguin

Eagle

Rabbit

Squirrel

The animals outside this circle do not have four legs.

The animals outside this circle do not eat other animals.

There are many ways to group most things. You could
group animals by where they live. What other groups
can you think of?

Some animals fit in both groups. To show that, draw the circles so they overlap. The animals that fit in both groups go where the circles overlap. The Venn diagram would look like this.

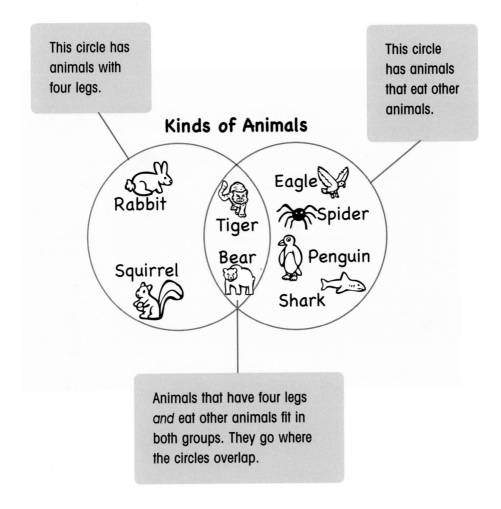

This circle has animals with four legs.

This circle has animals that eat other animals.

Kinds of Animals

Rabbit

Tiger

Eagle

Spider

Bear

Penguin

Squirrel

Shark

Animals that have four legs *and* eat other animals fit in both groups. They go where the circles overlap.

You can sort almost anything with a Venn diagram. Rocks, leaves, and kinds of music are examples. Can you think of other things? How could you sort each kind of thing?

Working Safely

Investigations can be fun. But if you're not careful, you can hurt yourself. Always work safely in science class. Here are some tips for how to be safe.

Tips for Safe Investigations

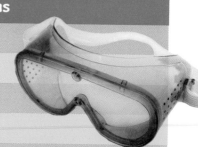

Follow all directions.

Always get permission to do an investigation.

Ask for help if you are not sure what to do.

Never fool around during an investigation.

Always use science tools the way you are supposed to.

Keep your work area neat and clean.

Always wear the correct safety equipment.

Know what to do in an emergency.

Never taste anything in a science investigation unless your teacher tells you to.

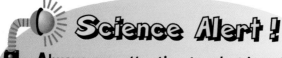

Science Alert!

Always pay attention to what is going on around you. Tell your teacher if you see something that isn't safe.

Follow Directions

Always pay attention in science class. Follow your teacher's directions exactly. Check with your teacher if you are not sure what to do.

Your teacher might give you directions that are written. Read all the directions before you begin. Your teacher might give you directions out loud. Write down everything your teacher tells you.

Follow the steps of an investigation in the correct order. Do not skip steps. The last step might be to clean up. Always follow that step.

You might work with other students. Each member of your group has a different job. Your teacher might assign jobs. Do the job you are assigned. Make sure the other students know their jobs. Do your part to work together safely.

Always stop work right away if your teacher tells you to.

Keyword: Safety
in the Science
Classroom
www.scilinks.org
Code: GSS23010

Handle with Care!

See Also

Using Science Tools
pages 50–67

You use different kinds of tools to do science investigations. Rulers, hand lenses, and thermometers are examples of science tools you will use. These tools are safe if you handle them correctly.

Here are some important safety rules for handling science tools.

Safety Rules for Using Science Tools

Handle tools carefully. Do not do anything that might damage them.

Make sure tools are clean before you use them. Clean the tools again after you use them.

Put tools away where they belong when you are finished using them.

Do not use other students' tools unless you have their permission.

Any tool can hurt you if you handle it the wrong way. Use tools only the way they should be used.

To stay healthy, you wash your hands before you eat. You also need to wash your hands after science lessons to stay healthy. You might handle pond water or soil in an investigation. Pond water and soilmight have germs in them. You should wash your hands after handling these materials.

Wash your hands with soap and water. Rub your hands together while you count to 10.

Rinse off all the soap and dirt.

Dry your hands with a paper towel. Throw the towel into the trash can.

Keep your hands away from your face when you handle science materials. Do not wipe your hands on your clothes.

A Safe Work Space

Keep your work space clean and neat. This will make your investigation go smoothly. It will keep you or a classmate from being hurt.

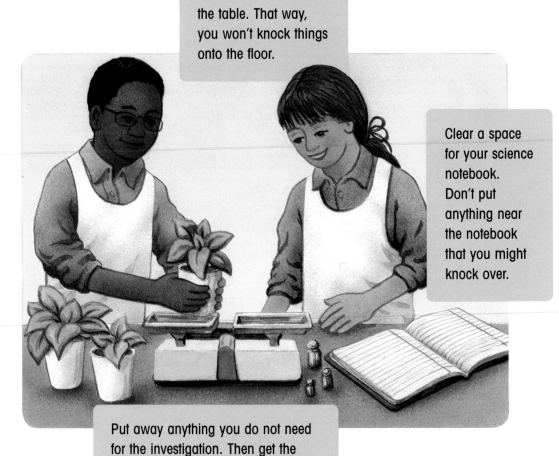

Work in the center of the table. That way, you won't knock things onto the floor.

Clear a space for your science notebook. Don't put anything near the notebook that you might knock over.

Put away anything you do not need for the investigation. Then get the tools and materials you will need. Organize the tools and materials neatly so they are easy to find.

Clean the table when you finish the investigation.

When you stand up, push in your chair.

Be careful around electric cords. Do not put anything on top of them. Make sure they do not cross areas where people walk.

Check the floor near and under your table. Make sure there is nothing that someone could trip over.

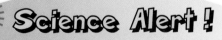

Science Alert!

If you spill something, tell your teacher right away. Follow your teacher's directions for cleaning up spills.

Dress to Be Safe

You dress for safety when you ride a bike. You wear a helmet to protect your head. Maybe you wear knee pads to protect your knees.

It is important to dress for safety in science class, too. The students in this picture are dressed to be safe. They are wearing safety goggles and lab aprons. The girl's long hair is tied back. The next page has more tips for dressing safely.

Tips for Dressing Safely in Science Class

Do not wear loose or baggy clothes.

Roll up long sleeves.

Wear shoes with closed toes. Do not wear sandals.

Take off jewelry.

Store your coat, hat, and gloves away from your work area.

Tie back your hair if it is long.

Cover cuts on your hands with bandages.

Wear lab gloves if you need them. Do not wear latex (LAY teks) gloves if you are allergic (uh LUR jik) to them.

Wear a lab apron if you need it.

Wear safety goggles when you use materials that could hit your eyes or get into your eyes.

Make sure your safety goggles are clean before you put them on. Dirty goggles can spread an eye infection.

Be Safe Outdoors

Wear the right clothes when you investigate outdoors. Here's how to dress safely before you go out.

Cover as much of your skin as you can. This will protect you from bug bites, scratchy plants, and sunburn.

Wear a hat with a brim. A hat shades your eyes and face. It keeps you cool, too.

Wear long sleeves.

Wear long pants.

Wear sunscreen and bug spray. Wash them off as soon as you go back inside.

Wear socks and sturdy shoes.

• Know what these plants look like. Never touch them.

∧ Poison ivy

∧ Poison oak

∧ Poison sumac

• Stay with the group. Keep the adult leader in sight. Never go off alone.

• Watch your step. Tree roots or rocks can trip you.

• Never drink water from streams, ponds, or puddles.

• Never put any part of a wild plant into your mouth.

• When you go back inside, check your shoes, socks, and clothes for ticks. Tell your teacher if you find a tick. Let your teacher remove it.

> Some ticks are *very* small. A deer tick is about the size of this dot. •

Emergency!

Accidents can happen even when you are careful. An accident can cause an emergency. You need to know what to do. You need to do it quickly.

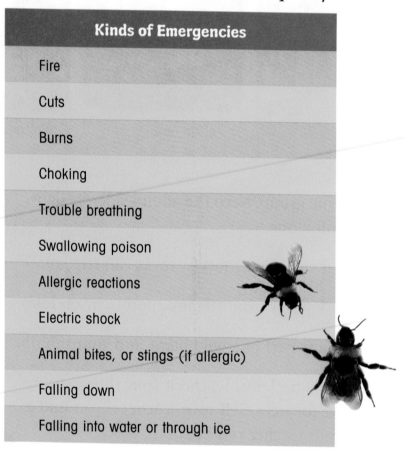

Kinds of Emergencies
Fire
Cuts
Burns
Choking
Trouble breathing
Swallowing poison
Allergic reactions
Electric shock
Animal bites, or stings (if allergic)
Falling down
Falling into water or through ice

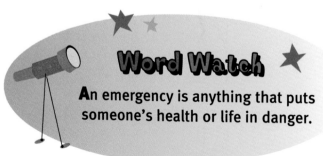

Word Watch

An emergency is anything that puts someone's health or life in danger.

What to Do in an Emergency

Know what to do in an emergency. Here are some ways to be prepared.

Know the answers to these questions
Where are the emergency exits in your school?
How do you call for help?
Where can adults find the emergency equipment?

When an Emergency Happens
Stay calm.
Tell your teacher or another adult right away.
Do whatever your teacher tells you to do.
Stay out of the way unless someone asks you to help.

SCiLINKS.
NSTA

Keyword: Safety
in the Science
Classroom
www.scilinks.org
Code: GSS23010

Using Science Tools

See Also

Science Is Observing
pages 2-3

Your senses let you observe some things. You can observe things like color and size with your senses. Sometimes your senses are not enough. You need a tool.

Different science tools do different things. You can use some tools to see tiny things. A hand lens makes it easier to see a tiny thing, like an ant.

Other tools let you make measurements. You can guess how long something is. You can guess how much there is of something. You can guess how hot or cold it is outside. Tools let you measure how long, how much, and how hot or cold.

It's hot outside!

It is? I thought it was cold!

Using a Hand Lens

You observe many things in science class. You might watch ants in an ant farm. You might look at flowers, shells, or rocks. You can use a hand lens to see things better. A **hand lens** makes things look bigger.

How to Use a Hand Lens

Hold the hand lens between your eye and the object. Move the hand lens slowly back and forth until you can see the object clearly.

Science Alert !

Never use a hand lens to look at the sun. Never let sunlight shine through a hand lens onto something.

Using a Thermometer

See Also

Temperature
page 190

Measuring
Temperature
page 277

A **thermometer** (thur MAHM ih tur) measures temperature (TEM pur uh chur). **Temperature** tells how hot or cold something is.

Temperature is measured in units called **degrees.** People measure temperature with two different temperature scales. People in the United States use the **Fahrenheit** (FAR un hyt) **scale** to measure temperature. People in other countries use the **Celsius** (SEL see us) **scale** to measure temperature. Scientists use the Celsius scale, too. The thermometer in the picture has both scales marked on it.

This is the Fahrenheit scale. It measures in degrees Fahrenheit. Degrees Fahrenheit is written as °F. The temperature shown on the thermometer is 50°F.

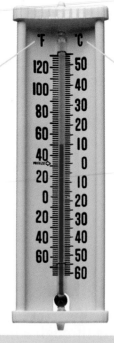

This is the Celsius scale. It measure in degrees Celsius. Degrees Celsius is written as °C. The temperature shown on the thermometer is 10°C.

The two scales measure the same temperature. They just use different numbers.

A thermometer has red liquid inside a glass tube. When the temperature gets warmer, the red liquid moves up the tube. When the temperature gets cooler, the red liquid moves down the tube.

The numbers on this thermometer are 10°C apart. Each line stands for 2°C.

Find the top of the red liquid. Find the mark on the thermometer next to it. Read the temperature next to that mark. In this picture, the top of the red liquid is two lines above 20°C. The temperature is 24°C.

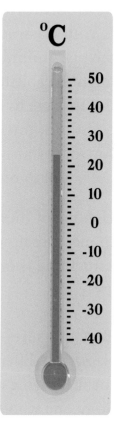

°C

50
40
30
20
10
0
-10
-20
-30
-40

∧ Some thermometers show the temperature in numbers. Be sure to look for °C or °F next to the number.

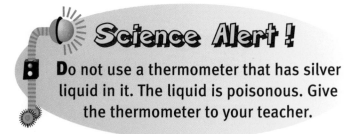

Science Alert !

Do not use a thermometer that has silver liquid in it. The liquid is poisonous. Give the thermometer to your teacher.

Measuring Length

See Also

Measuring Matter
pages 242-243

Distance
page 287

How long is an earthworm? How far is it to your classroom from the playground? You might be able to guess the answers to these questions. You can be sure of the answer if you use a tool to measure.

Use one of these tools to measure how long something is or how far away it is.

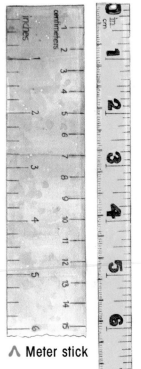

∧ Ruler

∧ Meter stick

∧ Tape measure

Tape measures come in different sizes. The different sizes are good for measuring different things. Someone who sews clothes uses a shorter tape measure. A carpenter uses a longer tape measure. Someone who builds driveways uses a very long tape measure.

Using a Ruler

Use a ruler to measure short lengths. You can measure things like your pencil or a leaf with a ruler.

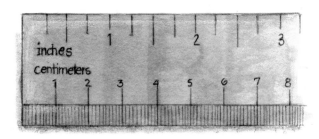

Many rulers have two scales. One scale is in inches. An **inch** is the customary unit for measuring short lengths. People in the United States use inches. The other scale is in metric (MET rik) units. Scientists use metric units. A **centimeter** (SEN tuh mee tur) is the metric unit for measuring short lengths. The abbreviation for *centimeter* is *cm.* Centimeters are divided into **millimeters** (MIL uh mee turz). There are 10 millimeters in 1 centimeter.

How to Use a Ruler

Suppose you want to measure a leaf.

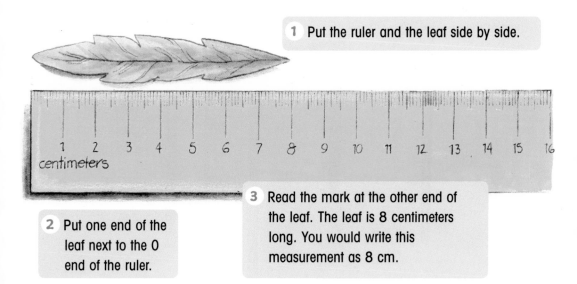

1 Put the ruler and the leaf side by side.

2 Put one end of the leaf next to the 0 end of the ruler.

3 Read the mark at the other end of the leaf. The leaf is 8 centimeters long. You would write this measurement as 8 cm.

Using a Meter Stick

Suppose you want to measure how tall a bookcase is. A ruler would be hard to use. It isn't long enough. A meter stick is a better tool for measuring longer lengths.

Many meter sticks have two scales. One scale is in inches. A meter stick is about 40 inches long. There are 36 inches in a yard. A **yard** is the customary unit for measuring longer lengths. People in the United States use yards. The other scale is in metric units. A **meter** (MEE tur) is the metric unit for measuring longer lengths. Scientists use meters. The abbreviation for *meter* is *m*.

How to Use a Meter Stick

Suppose you want to measure how tall your desk is.

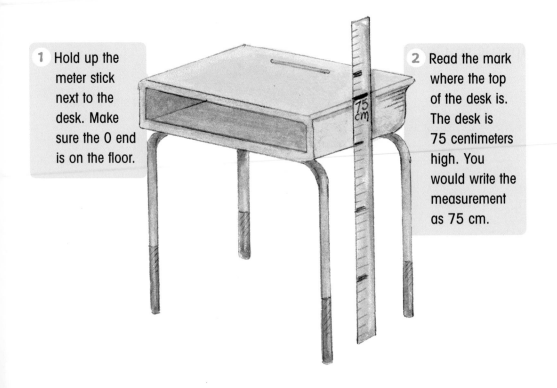

1 Hold up the meter stick next to the desk. Make sure the 0 end is on the floor.

2 Read the mark where the top of the desk is. The desk is 75 centimeters high. You would write the measurement as 75 cm.

Using a Tape Measure

Use a tape measure to measure longer lengths or distances. Many tape measures have two scales. One scale is in yards. **Yards** are the customary unit for measuring longer lengths. The other scale is in meters. **Meters** are the metric unit for measuring longer lengths. Make sure to use the side of the tape measure that has the units you want.

See Also

Distance
page 287

How to Use a Tape Measure

Suppose you want to measure how far it is from your classroom to the cafeteria. You will need another student to help you. You will also need a piece of chalk.

1 Have the other student stand at the door to your classroom. The student should hold the 0 end of the tape measure on the floor.

2 Unroll the tape measure all the way. Make a chalk mark where the tape ends. Write down the measurement.

3 Pick up the tape measure. Have the other student hold the 0 end on the chalk mark you made. Stretch the tape measure all the way again. Make another chalk mark. Write down the measurement again.

4 Keep marking the floor and moving the tape measure until you reach the cafeteria door. Add all the measurements to get the distance to the cafeteria.

Measuring Liquids

Suppose you want to know how much milk is in a glass. How can you find out? You can measure the volume (VAHL yoom) of the milk. **Volume** is the amount of space that something takes up.

Use one of these tools to measure volume.

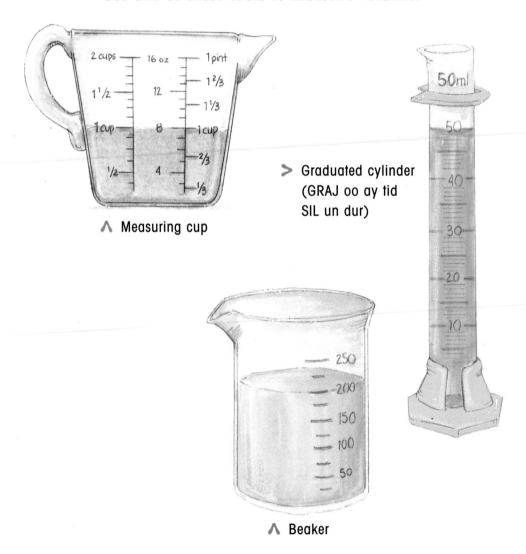

∧ Measuring cup

> Graduated cylinder (GRAJ oo ay tid SIL un dur)

∧ Beaker

Using a Measuring Cup

You can use a measuring cup to measure liquids. Measuring cups come in different sizes. Use smaller measuring cups to measure smaller volumes. Use larger measuring cups to measure larger volumes.

Most measuring cups have two scales. One scale is in ounces and cups. The ounce and the cup are the customary units for measuring small volumes. People in the United States use customary units. The other scale is in metric units. Scientists use metric units. The **liter** (LEE tur) is the metric unit for measuring volume. The abbreviation for *liter* is *L*. Liters are divided into **milliliters** (MIL uh lee turz). The abbreviation for *milliliters* is *mL*. There are 1,000 milliliters in a liter.

How to Use a Measuring Cup

Suppose you want to measure one cup of water.

1 Decide how much water you want to measure. You will measure 1 cup.

2 Pour water into the measuring cup until it reaches the line for 1 cup.

Using a Beaker

You can use a beaker to measure liquids. Beakers come in different sizes. Use a smaller beaker to measure smaller volumes. Use a larger beaker to measure larger volumes.

Beakers have one scale. It is in metric units. The metric unit for measuring smaller volumes is the **milliliter** (MIL uh lee tur). The **liter** (LEE tur) is the metric unit for measuring larger volumes. Scientists use beakers to measure the volume of liquids. They use *mL* to stand for *milliliter.* They use *L* to stand for *liter.*

How to Use a Beaker

Suppose you want to measure 200 mL of water.

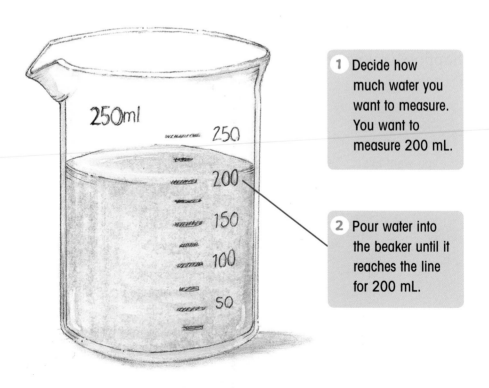

1 Decide how much water you want to measure. You want to measure 200 mL.

2 Pour water into the beaker until it reaches the line for 200 mL.

Using a Graduated Cylinder

Scientists use graduated cylinders to measure small volumes of liquid. A graduated cylinder measures more exactly than a beaker does.

Graduated cylinders have one scale. It is in metric units. The metric unit for measuring smaller volumes is the **milliliter** (MIL uh lee tur), or *mL* for short.

How to Use a Graduated Cylinder

Suppose you want to measure 50 mL of water.

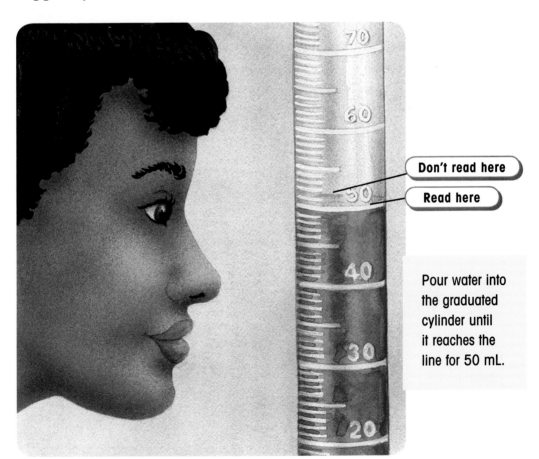

Don't read here

Read here

Pour water into the graduated cylinder until it reaches the line for 50 mL.

Using a Balance

See Also

Measuring Matter
pages 242-243

A lump of clay has more matter than a wad of paper of the same size. The clay has more mass. **Mass** is the amount of matter in something.

A **balance** (BAL uns) measures mass. You can use a balance to compare the masses of two objects. You can also use a balance to measure the mass of one object.

Comparing Masses

This picture shows a balance being used to compare the masses of two objects. Can you tell which object has more mass?

How to Compare Masses

Keyword:
Balances
www.scilinks.org
Code: GSS23020

1 Check the pointer before you put anything on the balance. Make sure the pointer is on the 0 mark. If it is not, ask your teacher for help.

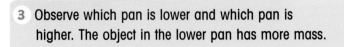

2 Put an object in each pan.

3 Observe which pan is lower and which pan is higher. The object in the lower pan has more mass.

Measuring Mass

You can use a balance to measure the mass of an object. You need a balance that comes with known masses. Known masses are small metal objects that are marked with metric units.

The metric unit for measuring small masses is the **gram.** The metric unit for measuring large masses is the **kilogram** (KIL uh gram). There are 1,000 grams in a kilogram. The known masses are marked to show grams.

How to Measure Mass

Suppose you want to measure the mass of a rock.

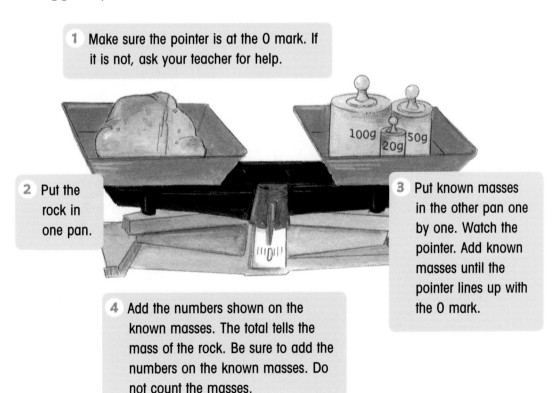

1 Make sure the pointer is at the 0 mark. If it is not, ask your teacher for help.

2 Put the rock in one pan.

100g   20g   50g

3 Put known masses in the other pan one by one. Watch the pointer. Add known masses until the pointer lines up with the 0 mark.

4 Add the numbers shown on the known masses. The total tells the mass of the rock. Be sure to add the numbers on the known masses. Do not count the masses.

Measuring Time

See Also

Time
page 288

How many days does it take for a tadpole to become an adult frog? How many times does your heart beat in a minute? You can answer these questions if you have tools that measure time.

Many different tools measure time. Choose the right tool for your question. You need one tool to measure a short amount of time. You need a different tool to measure a long amount of time.

Use one of these tools to measure time.

∧ Calendar   ∧ Clock   ∧ Stopwatch

Using a Calendar

How long does it take a robin's egg to hatch? The answer is a number of days. Use a calendar to measure days.

How to Use a Calendar

The name of the month and the year are shown here.

The days of the week are written in a row across the top. The first day in the row is Sunday.

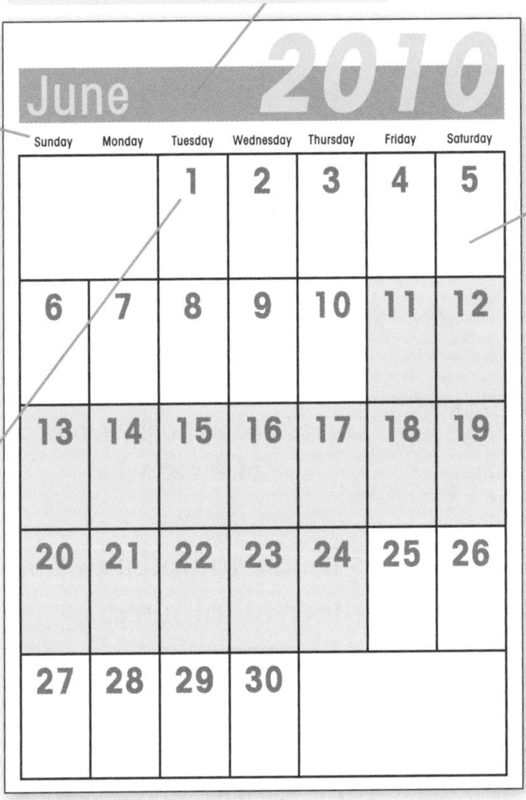

The first day of the month can fall on any day. This calendar shows that June 1 is on Tuesday in 2010.

June 2010

Sunday	Monday	Tuesday	Wednesday	Thursday	Friday	Saturday
		1	2	3	4	5
6	7	8	9	10	11	12
13	14	15	16	17	18	19
20	21	22	23	24	25	26
27	28	29	30			

Each box stands for one day. The boxes are numbered. June has 30 days, so there are 30 boxes.

Each row is one week. A week has seven days.

You can use a calendar to show how many days it takes for something to happen. The colored days on this calendar show how long it takes a robin's egg to hatch. How many days does it take? How many weeks is that?

Using a Clock

How long do you sleep each night? The answer will be a number of hours. Use a clock to measure hours.

How to Use a Clock

The hour hand is on the 8. The minute hand is on the 12. It is 8 o'clock. Time for bed!

The hour hand is on the 7. The minute hand is on the 12. It is 7 o'clock. Time to get up!

Count the number of hours from 8 o'clock until 7 o'clock. How many hours did you sleep?

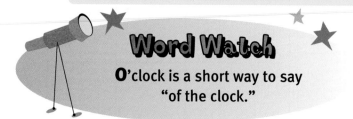

Word Watch

O'clock is a short way to say "of the clock."

How long does it take to boil a pot of water? The answer is a number of minutes.

This shows how many minutes it took for the water to boil. How many minutes did it take?

Each small mark stands for one minute. There are 60 minutes in one hour.

Using a Stopwatch

How long will a ball roll across the floor before it stops? The answer will be in seconds and parts of a second. You need a stopwatch to answer this question.

See Also

Time
page 288

How to Use a Stopwatch

Press the **RESET** button so you see 0:00₀₀ on the stopwatch.

When the ball starts rolling, press the **START/STOP** button.

When the ball stops rolling, press the **START/STOP** button.

The two numbers on the left are minutes. The two middle numbers are seconds. The two numbers on the right are parts of a second. The ball rolled for 6 seconds.

You can use a stopwatch to count the number of times your heart beats in one minute. You can use it to time how long it takes you to run 50 meters. Can you think of some other ways to use a stopwatch?

Science and Technology

See Also

Temperature
page 190

Humidity
page 191

Do you like to watch TV? Do you listen to music on CDs or an MP3 player? Do you like to play video games? Do you eat food cooked on a stove? Do you ride on a bus? You can do these things because of technology (tek NAHL uh jee). **Technology** is any tool that people find useful.

You use technology for fun. People also use technology to learn about the natural world. Scientists send weather balloons high into the air. Weather balloons are technology. They carry tools that collect data. The tools are technology. They measure air temperature. They also measure the amount of moisture in the air. These measurements help scientists predict weather patterns.

∧ Scientists send hundreds of weather balloons into the air every day. The tools fall back to Earth. Scientists collect the tools and use them again.

Keyword: Science and Technology
www.scilinks.org
Code: GSS23025

People use technology to solve problems. Power plants that make electricity are technology. Power plants put pollution into the air. Air pollution harms people and the environment. Wind turbines and dams make electricity without putting pollution into the air. Wind turbines and dams are technology.

See Also

Energy from Dams
page 322

Energy from Wind
page 323

Pollution
pages 325-331

Engineers (en juh NEERZ) are people who design technology. Engineers and scientists work together to learn about the natural world. Together, they solve problems. They create technology such as weather balloons, wind turbines, dams, and many other tools.

The tools that you use in science class are technology, too.

Technology Helps Scientists

Technology helps scientists make observations about the natural world. Microscopes are one kind of technology. The first microscopes let scientists see tiny living things they could never see before. They saw living things made of only one cell. They saw germs that cause diseases.

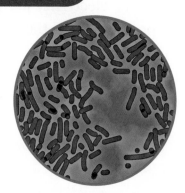

∧ Bacteria are too tiny to see with your eyes, even with a hand lens. You can only see them with a microscope.

Powerful telescopes let scientists see far out into space. Scientists can use their observations of to make maps of space.

Technology lets scientists "see" inside Earth, too. Some tools measure tiny movements deep under ground. These measurements tell scientists about changes deep in Earth's crust. The tools also help scientists predict earthquakes.

See Also

Is It Alive?
pages 81-82

Structure of Earth
page 159

Earthquakes
page 172

Telescopes
pages 230–231

Observing Matter
pages 240-241

∧ This powerful telescope lets scientists see stars that are too faint to see with your eyes.

Satellites (SAT l yts) are an important technology. A **satellite** is something that orbits in space around Earth. Scientists send satellites into space to take pictures of Earth. They use the pictures to make maps of Earth's surface.

The maps show deserts and forests. Scientists compare maps that were made in different years. They can see that deserts are getting bigger and forests are getting smaller. These changes are a problem for people, animals, and plants.

Satellite pictures also show that parts of the ocean are getting warmer. Tiny ocean organisms are dying because they cannot live in warmer water. These organisms are food for animals that live in the ocean. When the tiny organisms die, the animals do not have as much food. The tiny organisms also help keep the ocean water healthy. The oceans are in trouble without these tiny organisms.

See Also

Food Chains
pages 152-153

Food Webs
pages 154-155

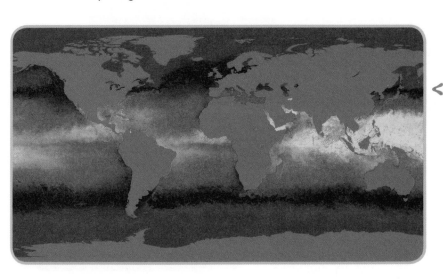

< This is a satellite picture of Earth's oceans. Warm parts of the ocean are shown in red. Cool parts are shown in blue.

Technology Helps All People

Do your clothes have zippers and buttons? Zippers and buttons are technologies that help you get dressed. A can opener is technology that helps you get food.

How did you get to school today? Probably in a bus or car. Cars, buses, boats, trains, and planes carry people all around the world. People count on these technologies every day.

You need satellites as much as scientists do. Satellites use signals to send information around the world. Televisions, radios, cell phones, and the Internet use satellites to work.

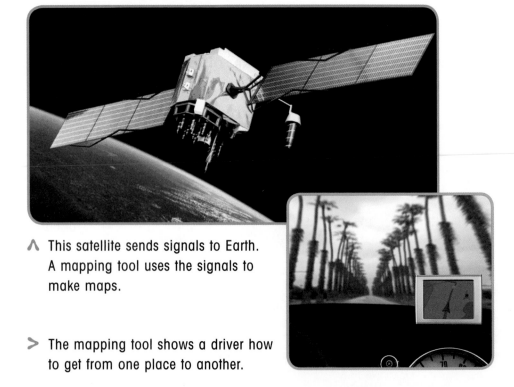

∧ This satellite sends signals to Earth. A mapping tool uses the signals to make maps.

> The mapping tool shows a driver how to get from one place to another.

Maybe you know someone who broke an arm or leg. The person probably had an X ray taken to show where the break was. X-ray machines take pictures of bones. X-ray machines are technology.

Doctors also use technology to take pictures of the brain and heart. They use technology to study the chemicals in your blood and make sure you are healthy.

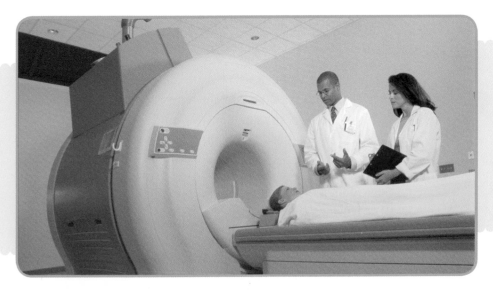

∧ This machine takes pictures of things inside a person's body.

The population of the world is getting bigger. More food is needed to feed all the people. Farmers use technology to grow more crops in the same space. Chemicals make crops grow better. Some chemicals give plants more of the nutrients they need. Other chemicals kill weeds, insects, and plant diseases that destroy crops. But chemicals can harm the environment, too. Scientists use technology to develop crops that do not need as many chemicals to grow better.

SC*LINKS.*
N S T A
Keyword: Science
and Technology
www.scilinks.org
Code: GSS23025

Designing Technology

Keyword:
Scientific
Investigation
www.scilinks.org
Code: GSS23005

Engineers go through many steps to design new technology. Here are some steps an engineer might follow. The next pages give examples of the steps.

1 Explain the Problem
Every technology is meant to solve a problem. Step 1 is to figure out what the problem is.

2 Design a Solution
Next, think of a way to solve the problem. Maybe you need to change the way you do something. Maybe you need to design a new tool.

3 Build the Technology
Make the tool you designed.

4 Decide If It Works
Does the new tool solve the problem? Test it to see if it works. If the tool does not work, design a different one. Engineers often test many different ideas before they choose the best solution.

5 Is It Worth It?
Decide if the cost is worth it. Is the technology too expensive? Does it harm the environment?

6 Share
Tell other people what you did.

Explain the Problem

The first step in designing technology is to figure out the problem. Railroad refrigerator cars must keep things cool for long distances. Thick, heavy pads were used to line the walls of the cars. The pads were supposed to keep things cool, but there was a problem. The pads did not hold together very well.

Design a Solution

Engineers began looking for a new technology to hold the thick pads together. They had this idea. Put glue on strips of cellophane (SEL uh fayn). Then wrap the sticky tape around the pads to hold them together.

 Did you know ?

Sometimes, ideas for new technology come from nature. Engineers studied the sticky feet of tree frogs. They used their findings to design a new kind of tape. The tape can be peeled off easily and used again on something else. It works just like the frogs' feet!

Build the Technology

Engineers made a sticky tape for the refrigerator pads. They tested the tape on the pads.

Decide If It Works

The tape tore easily. Glue didn't go on the strips evenly. The tape wasn't good enough to use on the refrigerator pads.

Then engineers observed that the tape was good for sealing packages and fixing torn paper. Millions of people use the tape today. You probably use it yourself!

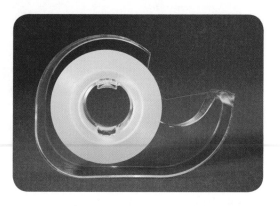

Technology cannot solve every problem. Some problems are too complicated. People might live where they cannot get the technology. Some problems do not have technology solutions.

Is It Worth It?

Some technologies cost so much that people can't afford them. One example is the hybrid car. Hybrid cars run on gasoline and on electricity from a special battery. Hybrid cars were very expensive at first. Not many people could buy them. Newer technology has made hybrid cars less expensive today.

Does the technology hurt the environment? Dams do not cause air pollution, but they change the environment. Water floods the land behind the dam. People and animals have to find other homes, and plants die. Are dams worth it?

See Also

Oil
page 318

Energy from Dams
page 322

Share What You Did

Give an oral report or written report to tell what you did. Other people might have the same problem. They might have tried things you didn't think of. You all could put your ideas together to solve the problem.

Life Science

Take a deep breath. Ahhhh.... Feel the air in your lungs. You need air to stay alive. What about plants? Do they breathe? This is a question for a person who studies life science. **Life science** is the study of living things. A **living thing** is something that is alive.

To the movies?

Living Things

Think about a sunny day at the park. Children toss a ball back and forth on the grass. A turtle suns itself on a log. Fish splash in the pond. Birds sing in the trees. What do the children, grass, fish, birds, and trees have in common? They are all living things.

∧ How many living things can you name in the picture?

There are many different kinds of living things. A living thing is called an **organism** (OR guh niz um). You see organisms every day. Maybe you see robins on the way to school. Perhaps you have seen flies buzzing around trash. Robins and flies are organisms. You are an organism, too!

Is It Alive?

Some of the things in a park are alive. Other things are nonliving. **Nonliving** means they are not alive. Soil, rocks, and the water in a pond are nonliving. What about leaves on the ground? The leaves came from a tree. They used to be alive, but they are not alive any more.

How can you tell if something is alive or not? All living things share the same basic things.

Living things are made of tiny parts called **cells.**

Living things need energy to stay alive. **Energy** is something that living things use to live, grow, and move. Living things get energy from food.

Living things respond (rih SPAHND) to things around them. A turtle dives into the water when there is danger. A dog barks when the doorbell rings. The turtle and the dog respond to things around them.

< A plant has millions of cells.

∧ Animals get energy from the food they eat.

Living things **reproduce** (ree pruh DOOS) to make more living things. New living things start small and then grow. To grow means to get bigger. You started out as a tiny baby. You have grown bigger.

See Also

Life Cycle of Amphibians page 123

Living things also develop (dih VEL up) as they grow. To develop means to change. Some kinds of living things get new body parts as they develop.

∧ A frog starts out as a tadpole.

∧ It changes into an adult frog.

Living things do not stay alive forever. At some point, they die. A tree dies and becomes a fallen log. Trees and other living things reproduce before they die. They make more living things to take their place.

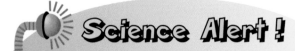

Science Alert!

Something is not living just because it grows. Icicles grow longer, but icicles are not living. Something must show all the features of a living thing to be alive.

Kinds of Living Things

What kinds of fruit do you like? Maybe you like oranges or grapes. Or maybe you like apples. There are lots of different kinds of fruit.

Grocery stores group fruit so you can easily find the kind you like. To group things is to **classify** (KLAS uh feye) them.

There are many different kinds of living things on Earth. Some are huge, like elephants. Some are tiny, like the germs that cause a sore throat. Scientists classify organisms to make it easier to study them.

Plants and animals are two main groups of organisms. How can you tell if something is a plant or an animal? A **plant** uses energy from sunlight to make food. An animal cannot make its own food like a plant does. An **animal** must eat plants or other animals for food.

See Also

Plants
pages 85–97

Animals
pages 98–127

Granny Smith Apples   Macintosh Apples   Red Delicious Apples

Florida Oranges

The chart lists ways to tell plants and animals apart.

Plants	Animals

• cannot move from place to place on their own	• can move from place to place on their own
• make their own food	• eat other living things
• reproduce with seeds or spores	• reproduce with eggs or have live birth

There are other organisms besides plants and animals. Most of them are too small to be seen without a microscope.

See Also

Plants
pages 85–97

Animals
pages 98–127

Plants

How many kinds of plants can you think of? Trees and grass are plants. So are bushes and shrubs. A **plant** is a living thing that makes its own food and cannot move from place to place on its own. Plants use their leaves to make their own food.

Some plants grow on land. Other plants grow in water. Maybe you've seen lily pads on a pond. The round, green pad is a leaf. The rest of the plant is under water.

Keyword: Plants
www.scilinks.org
Code: GSS23030

∧ The round leaves of water lilies float on the water. The leaves make food for the plant.

See Also

Leaves
page 88

Producers
page 148

What Do Plants Need?

Plants need many things to stay alive. The most important things are water, air, and sunlight. Plants use these three things to make food. Plants need the energy in the food to grow and develop. To grow means to get bigger. To develop means to change.

Plants also need space. Big plants need more space than small plants. Most trees cannot grow in a pot. There isn't enough space!

Soil is another thing that most plants need. Soil supports the plant. Soil also has water and nutrients (NOO tree unts). **Nutrients** are materials that plants use to grow and develop. Nutrients are different from food. They do not provide energy like food does.

How much sunlight a plant gets is important. A plant cannot make food if there is too little sunlight. It may stop growing and die. Too much sunlight may burn a plant's leaves.

How much water a plant gets is also important. Too much water makes the leaves turn yellow and drop off. A plant without leaves cannot make food. Too little water makes a plant wilt. A wilted plant cannot make food either.

Soil can also make a difference in how a plant grows. Many plants grow well in rich soil that has a lot of nutrients. Grasses like rich soil. Other plants grow well in loose, sandy soil. Sandy soil does not hold a lot of water or nutrients. Cactuses grow well in sandy soil.

∧ This healthy plant got the right amount of sunlight and water.

∧ This wilted plant did not get enough water.

Plant Parts

Plants have different parts that help them get the things they need to survive.

Leaves

Leaves make food for the plant. Leaves use sunlight to turn gases and water into food.

Leaves have different shapes. Some leaves are very wide. This shape lets them collect a lot of sunlight. Maple trees have wide leaves. Plants that live where it is dry often have leaves that are long and thin. This shape helps the plant save water. Pine and fir trees have leaves shaped like needles.

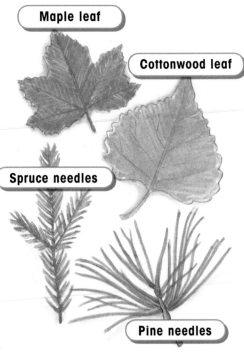

Maple leaf

Cottonwood leaf

Spruce needles

Pine needles

When you eat salad, you are eating the leaves of a lettuce plant. People use leaves to make medicines, too. Maybe you have rubbed aloe vera (AL oh VEER uh) on a sunburn. The juice in the leaf can help heal the burn.

Roots

Plants need water and nutrients to live. A plant's **roots** take in water and nutrients from the soil. The roots also support the plant and hold it in the soil.

Some plants have fibrous (FY brus) roots. Fibrous roots have lots of branches. Grasses have fibrous roots. Other plants have a thick taproot. A taproot stores food and water for the plant. Carrots and beets are taproots that you can eat.

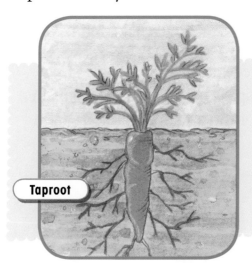

Taproot

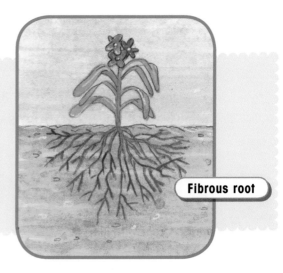

Fibrous root

Plants that grow in dry places have roots that grow near the soil surface. The roots can collect water and nutrients more easily there.

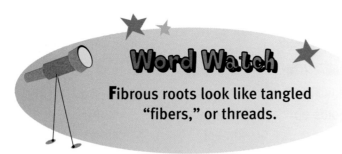

Word Watch

Fibrous roots look like tangled "fibers," or threads.

See Also

Plant Parts
Work Together
page 92

See Also

Plant Parts
Work Together
page 92

Stems

A **stem** supports the plant. It holds the leaves up toward the sun. Stems also move water, food, and nutrients around inside the plant.

Some stems store food and water for the plant. A celery stalk is a stem that stores food and water. The fleshy part of a cactus is a stem.

Plants in shade may have very long stems. The stems grow long to reach the sunlight. That way, the leaves can collect the sunlight they need to make food.

Some of your favorite vegetables are probably stems. Celery is a stem. So is asparagus. People use stems in other ways, too. Stems of the bamboo plant are used to make furniture.

∧ A tree trunk is a thick, woody stem.

∧ A sunflower stem holds up the flower.

∧ Celery is a stem you can eat.

∧ A cactus stem is thick and stores water.

Flowers and Cones

Some plants use flowers to **reproduce,** or make new plants. A **flower** has petals and is often colorful. Other plants make new plants using cones. A **cone** has scales and is not colorful.

Flowers make a powdery material called **pollen** (PAHL un). So do some kinds of cones. Seeds are made when pollen moves from one part of a flower to another. Seeds are also made when pollen moves from one kind of cone to another. A **seed** contains a baby plant and stored food. **Fruit** forms around the seed of a flowering plant.

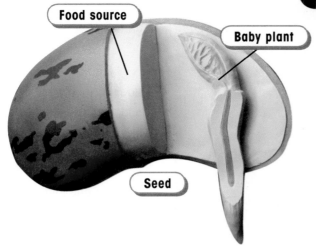

Food source

Baby plant

Seed

See Also

Plants with Flowers
page 94

Plants with Cones
page 95

Plant Parts Work Together

See Also

Leaves
page 88

Roots
page 89

Stems
page 90

The leaves, roots, and stems of a plant work together to help the plant get what it needs to live and grow. The picture shows how the plant parts work together.

Leaves take in gases from the air. They use sunlight to turn the gases and water into food for the plant.

Stems carry water and nutrients from the roots to other parts of the plant. They carry food from the leaves to other parts of the plant. The plant uses the nutrients and food to grow and develop.

Roots take in water and nutrients from the soil. The water and nutrients move from the roots up the stem and into the leaves.

Plant Life Cycles

Plants change during their lives. They start small and grow larger. They **reproduce,** or make more plants. Finally, they die. The changes that a plant goes through during its life are its **life cycle.**

All plants look like the parent plant they came from. An oak tree grows from an acorn. The new oak tree looks like the parent oak tree that made the acorn. There will be some differences. The new oak tree may grow taller than its parent tree. The branches won't grow exactly the same way.

How a plant looks depends on where it grows, too. A plant that grows where there is little rain may be small and have few flowers. If the same kind of plant gets a lot of rain, it may be large with lots of flowers.

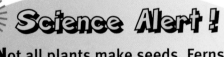 **Science Alert!**

Not all plants make seeds. Ferns and mosses make spores. Like seeds, spores grow into new plants.

 See Also

Flowers and Cones page 91

Plants with Flowers

The life cycle of a plant with flowers starts with a seed. The seed changes and grows into a plant. When the plant is grown, it makes new seeds. Then the cycle starts again.

Life cycle of a bean plant

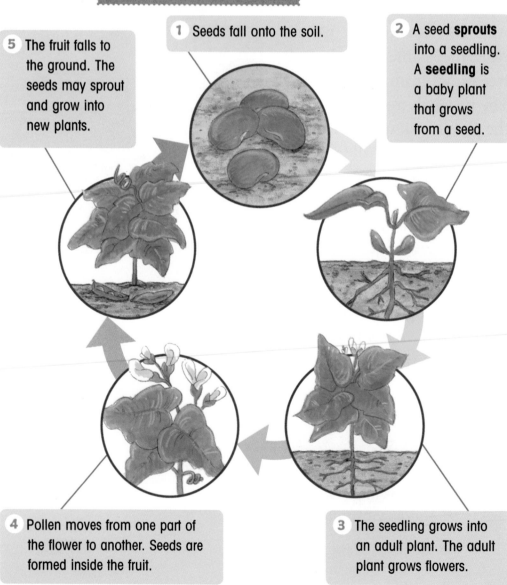

1 Seeds fall onto the soil.

2 A seed **sprouts** into a seedling. A **seedling** is a baby plant that grows from a seed.

5 The fruit falls to the ground. The seeds may sprout and grow into new plants.

4 Pollen moves from one part of the flower to another. Seeds are formed inside the fruit.

3 The seedling grows into an adult plant. The adult plant grows flowers.

Plants with Cones

Not all plants have flowers. A **conifer** (KAHN uh fur) is a plant that has cones. Cones have seeds inside. The life cycle of a conifer starts with a seed. The seed grows into a tree. The adult tree makes new seeds. Then the cycle starts again.

See Also

Flowers and Cones
page 91

Life cycle of a conifer

1 Seeds fall onto the soil.

5 The cones open, and seeds fall to the ground. The seeds may sprout and grow into new trees.

2 A seed sprouts into a seedling.

4 The small cones make pollen. Pollen falls onto the large cones. The large cones form seeds.

3 The seedling grows into an adult tree. The adult tree forms large and small cones.

Classifying Plants

Scientists classify plants in order to study them. To **classify** (KLAS uh feye) means to put into groups. Plants in the same group have similar characteristics, or **traits** (TRAYTS).

Scientists look at plant parts to classify the plant. For example, some plants reproduce using flowers. Other plants use cones. Scientists classify plants by whether the plants use flowers or cones to reproduce. Plants that reproduce using spores are classified in another group.

Leaf shape is another trait used to classify plants. Are the leaves long and thin, or broad and flat? Do they have rough or smooth edges?

Stems can be used to classify plants. Some plants have woody stems. Other plants have soft stems.

∧ Trees have woody stems.

∧ Tomato plants have soft stems.

This chart lists some ways to classify plants.

Classifying Plants

Plant Part	What Kind It Is	What It Looks Like
Flower or Cone	Flower	
	Cone	
Leaf	Spear leaf	
	Broad leaf	
Stem	Woody stem	
	Soft stem	
Root	Taproot	
	Fibrous root	

See Also

Leaves
page 88

Roots
page 89

Stems
page 90

Flowers and
Cones
page 91

Animals

Have you ever been to a zoo? What did you see there? Monkeys? Lions? Maybe you petted baby goats.

Monkeys, lions, and goats look and act very different, but they have something in common. They are all animals. You are an animal, too.

An **animal** is a living thing that cannot make its own food. Animals must eat plants or other animals to live. Most animals can move around from place to place. This makes it easier for animals to find food.

Animals live nearly everywhere on land or in water. Lions live in flat, grassy places. Monkeys live high up in trees. Fish live in lakes, rivers, or the ocean. Birds live on land or on water. Where do people live?

What Do Animals Need?

There are many different kinds of animals. All animals need the same things.

Animals need nutrients (NOO tree unts) to live and grow. Animals also need energy. Animals get energy and nutrients from the food they eat. They get food by eating plants or other animals.

∧ Frogs live near water or in wet places.

Animals need water to drink and air to breathe. Air has oxygen (AHKS uh jun) in it. Animals need oxygen to live and grow.

Different kinds of animals need different amounts of water, food, and air. Desert animals don't need much water. Their bodies hold water.

∧ This lizard lives in the desert, where there is little water.

Animals need space to live and raise their young. Animals also need shelter. **Shelter** protects animals from heat, cold, and danger.

Animals with Backbones

Scientists classify animals into two main groups. The two groups are animals with backbones and animals without backbones. A **backbone** is a row of bones along an animal's back.

The backbone is part of an animal's skeleton (SKEL ih tn). The **skeleton** is made up of all the bones in the animal's body. The skeleton supports the body. It also protects the soft parts inside the body.

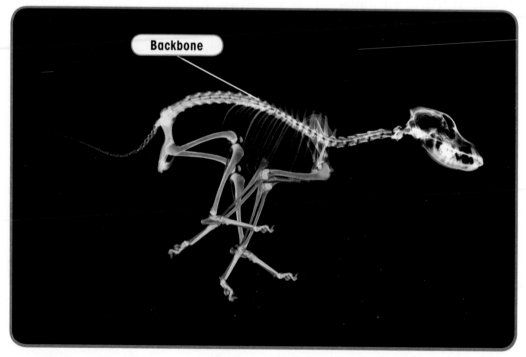

Backbone

∧ This picture shows a dog's skeleton. The picture was taken with an X-ray machine.

Scientists classify animals with backbones into five groups.

Animals with Backbones

Group	Features
Mammals	• have hair or fur • mothers nurse their young with milk • breathe air with lungs • babies grow inside the mother
Birds	• have feathers and wings • have two legs and a beak • breathe air with lungs • hatch from eggs
Reptiles	• live on land or in water • have dry, scaly skin • have four legs or no legs • breathe air with lungs • hatch from eggs
Amphibians	• live in water when they are young and on land when they are adults • have moist, smooth skin • young breathe air with gills • adults breathe air with lungs and through their skin • hatch from eggs
Fish	• live in water • have slippery scales • have fins • breathe air with gills • hatch from eggs

See Also

Mammals
pages 102–103

Birds
pages 104–105

Reptiles
pages 106–107

Amphibians
pages 108–109

Fish
pages 110–111

Mammals

See Also

Life Cycle of Mammals
page 120

Do you have a pet cat or dog? Maybe squirrels live in your neighborhood. All these animals are mammals (MAHM ulz). A **mammal** is an animal that nurses its young with milk.

Mammals grow and develop inside the mother. They are born live. Mammal mothers have body parts that make milk for their young.

> Mammals nurse their young with milk.

All mammals have hair or fur. Hair or fur protects a mammal and keeps it warm. The hair on your head helps keep you warm.

Mammals use lungs to breathe air. **Lungs** are sacs inside the body that take in air. Mammals use the oxygen in air to live and grow.

Mammals have teeth for biting and chewing their food. A cat has sharp teeth for tearing meat. A beaver has large front teeth for chewing wood.

∧ Tiger

∧ Beaver

Most kinds of mammals live on land. Bears, mice, and humans live on land. Whales are mammals that live in the ocean. Whales need air. They have to come to the surface to breathe.

Bats are mammals that can fly. They come out at night to hunt for food. They use their sense of hearing to find their food. They catch and eat flying insects.

Did you know?

Some kinds of bats don't eat insects. They eat fruit. Some of these bats fly around in the daytime. They hang from tree branches and sleep at night.

Birds

All **birds** have feathers and wings. These structures allow them to fly. Birds also fluff their feathers to stay warm.

Birds have streamlined bodies. This shape helps them fly quickly through the air. Birds can smooth their feathers to keep their streamlined shape.

Birds have light, hollow bones. This reduces a bird's weight so it can fly.

Birds have two legs for walking. Some birds perch on tree branches. They can curl their toes around a branch to keep from falling off.

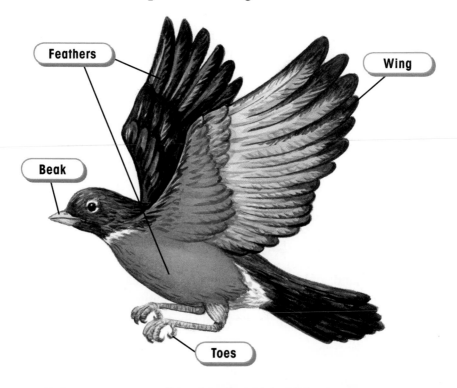

Feathers

Wing

Beak

Toes

Birds have lungs for breathing, like you do. When you run, you breathe harder. Your lungs take in more air this way. The oxygen in air gives you the boost you need. Instead of breathing harder, birds have extra structures in their lungs. The structures take in extra air.

See Also

Life Cycle of Birds
page 121

Mother birds lay eggs that have a hard shell. The shell protects the growing bird inside. The baby bird then hatches from the egg. The parents usually take care of the babies until they can fly.

Birds spend most of their lives on land. They fly to get from one place to another.

Did you know?

Not all birds can fly. Penguins can't fly, but they are very good swimmers. They use their wings like flippers. Ostriches can't fly, but they can run very fast with their large, powerful legs.

Reptiles

SCi LINKS.
NSTA
Keyword:
Reptiles
www.scilinks.org
Code: GSS23035

Turtles, lizards, and snakes are reptiles (REP tylz). A **reptile** has skin covered with dry scales. The skin is thick for protection. It keeps the body from drying out. Have you seen a turtle pull its head into its shell? The shell gives the turtle added protection.

Most reptiles live on land, but many live in or near water. Sea turtles live in the ocean. Freshwater turtles live in lakes and rivers.

∧ Turtle

Reptiles use lungs to breathe. Reptiles that live in water must swim to the surface to breathe.

A reptile's body temperature changes when the air temperature changes. Have you seen lizards or turtles sunning themselves? They use the sun to warm their bodies. To cool off, a lizard may crawl under a rock. A turtle may dive into the water.

∧ Lizard

∧ Snake

Most kinds of reptiles have four legs for walking on land. Sea turtles have flippers in place of legs. Snakes do not have legs. They bend their bodies to pull themselves along the ground.

See Also

Life Cycle of Reptiles
page 122

Reptiles hatch from eggs. The eggs have a leathery shell for protection. The shell is not hard like a bird's egg.

Most kinds of reptiles dig a hole and then lay their eggs in it. They cover up the eggs to protect them. Then they leave the eggs.

∧ Alligator nest

∧ Snake eggs hatching

When young reptiles hatch, they look just like their parents. They can take care of themselves right away.

Amphibians

See Also

Life Cycle of Amphibians
page 123

Are there spring peepers where you live? The peepers are frogs calling to each other. Frogs and toads are amphibians (am FIB ee unz). An **amphibian** lives in water when it is young and on land when it is an adult.

Amphibians lay eggs in water or wet places. The eggs are like jelly. They do not have shells.

Young amphibians develop in the water. They use gills to breathe. They have tails for swimming. They grow and develop into adults. Then they live on land.

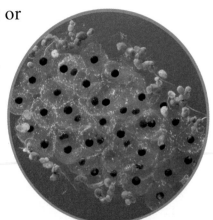

∧ Frog eggs

∧ A young amphibian has a tail and feathery gills.

Adult amphibians have lungs to breathe air. They breathe through their skin, too. The skin is thin enough for air to pass through it. It is also wet and smooth.

Adult amphibians breathe air, but they often live near water to keep their skin wet.

∧ Bullfrog

∧ Toad

∧ Salamander

Adult amphibians have four legs. They use their legs to move around. Frogs and toads use their hind legs to jump. Frogs make long jumps. Toads make short hops.

Adult salamanders (SAL uh man durz) have a tail. Adult frogs and toads do not have tails.

Fish

All **fish** have gills and live in water their whole lives. A **gill** is a structure for breathing under water. Gills take in oxygen from the water.

Most fish are covered with hard, slippery scales. The scales protect the fish. They also let the fish move easily through the water.

Fish have fins for swimming. The powerful tail fin pushes the fish through the water. Fish use their side fins to steer. Fish have streamlined bodies. The streamlined shape lets them swim easily through water.

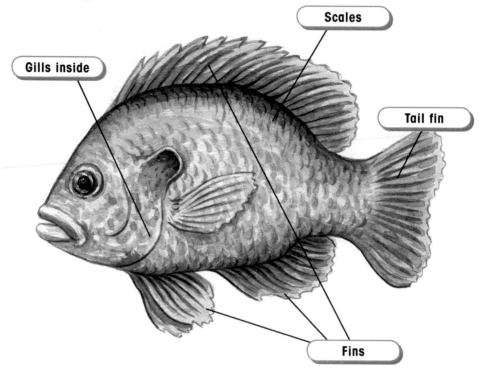

Scales

Gills inside

Tail fin

Fins

Fish hatch from eggs. The eggs do not have a shell.
The mother fish lays eggs and leaves them.

**See
Also**

**Life Cycle
of Fish**
page 124

**Body Parts for
Breathing Air**
page 137

Fish live in salt water or fresh water. Saltwater fish live
in the ocean. Tuna, sharks, and clown fish are saltwater
fish. Freshwater fish live in lakes and rivers. Catfish are
freshwater fish. Maybe you have a pet goldfish. A
goldfish is a freshwater fish.

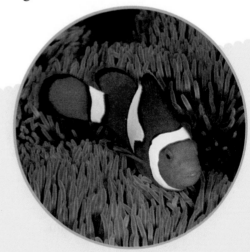

∧ Clown fish live in the ocean.

∧ Catfish live at the bottom of rivers.

Animals Without Backbones

Keyword: Insects
www.scilinks.org
Code: GSS23040

There are many kinds of animals without backbones. Insects do not have backbones. Insects are usually small. Other animals without backbones are much larger than insects. Animals without backbones live on land and in water.

Animals without backbones move around in different ways. Insects and spiders have legs for walking, running, jumping, and climbing. Some insects have wings for flying.

∧ Spiders live on land, but some kinds of spiders can dive under water.

∧ Octopuses can swim.

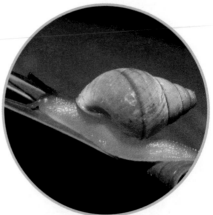

∧ Snails make a slime trail to glide on.

Animals without backbones breathe in different ways. Sea stars, crabs, and lobsters have gills. Earthworms breathe through their skin. Insects have tiny holes in their bodies. Air moves through the holes into the body.

∧ Sea star

∧ Earthworm

Most animals without backbones lay eggs. Young hatch from the eggs. The young may look like the parents. Young grasshoppers look like their parents. Many other young animals without backbones look very different from their parents. Young dragonflies look very different from adult dragonflies.

< Grasshoppers are insects.

Arthropods

Most animals without backbones are arthropods (AHR thruh pahdz). An **arthropod** is an animal with jointed legs. Jointed legs let an arthropod move around easily.

Arthropods have a hard outer covering called an **exoskeleton** (ek soh SKEL ih tn). *Exo* means "outside of." An exoskeleton is on the outside of the animal's body. The exoskeleton protects the soft body parts inside.

Most arthropods have two or three body sections. They have a head, a middle part, and a tail part. In some kinds of arthropods, the middle part and tail part are joined to make one part.

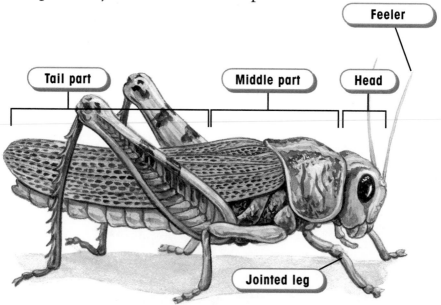

Feeler

Tail part

Middle part

Head

Jointed leg

∧ A hard exoskeleton covers all the body parts of an arthropod.

Centipedes (SEN tuh peedz) and millipedes (MIL uh peedz) are arthropods. They have lots of legs. They burrow in the ground or hide under rocks.

∧ Millipede

Crabs and lobsters live in the ocean. They have thick exoskeletons for protection. Crayfish live in fresh water. Crabs, lobsters, and crayfish have large claws. They use the claws to protect themselves and grab food.

∧ Crab

∧ Crayfish

Most arthropods are insects. Insects have feelers on their head. They use their feelers to smell and feel things. Many insects have wings and can fly.

Many kinds of spiders make silk threads to spin webs. They use their webs to catch food.

Science Alert !

Spiders are arthropods, but they are not insects. Insects have six legs. Spiders have eight legs. Insects have three body parts. Spiders have two body parts.

Extinct Animals

You have seen pictures of dinosaurs, but you have never seen a live dinosaur. Dinosaurs lived a long time ago. They are not around any more.

∧ Tyrannosaurus rex

Dinosaurs and other animals that are not around any more are extinct (ik STINGKT). **Extinct** means there are none alive.

How do we know about extinct animals if there are none around? Scientists know about extinct animals from studying fossils (FAHS ulz). A **fossil** is a body part of an animal that lived a long time ago. A fossil can be a whole animal. Most of the time, it is just a bone or a shell.

Scientists put together the fossil bones of dinosaurs to learn what the animals looked like. Sometimes, they can figure out what a dinosaur ate. A dinosaur with big, sharp teeth would have eaten meat.

∧ These scientists are taking dinosaur leg bones out of rock.

Have you ever made shapes by pressing an object into clay? When you took the object out of the clay, the object's shape stayed in the clay.

Some fossils are made that way, too. A body part is covered with mud. The mud hardens. The body part dissolves, but its shape stays in the mud. Then the mud turns into rock.

Sometimes an insect or other small animal is trapped in tree sap. The animal dies. The sap hardens with the animal inside. The animal becomes a fossil.

∧ This fossil shows what the shell looked like.

∧ You can see the spider inside the hardened tree sap.

Some animals do not leave fossils behind. Soft animals that did not have bones or a shell may not leave a fossil. Scientists do not know as much about these animals.

Endangered Animals

Some kinds of animals today are in danger of becoming extinct. Animals that might become extinct are called **endangered** (en DAYN jurd) animals.

Sperm (SPURM) whales are endangered animals. People once hunted sperm whales. People killed so many sperm whales that they almost became extinct. Today, it is against the law to hunt sperm whales.

∧ Manatees

Manatees (MAN uh teez) are endangered animals, too. Manatees live in rivers and bays along the coast of Florida. Laws protect manatees, but many are injured or killed each year when they are hit by speeding motorboats. People are also building towns and roads in areas where manatees live. This destroys the manatees' habitat. Scientists are worried that manatees could become extinct.

Animal Life Cycles

All animals follow a pattern during their lives. They are born. They grow up. They develop as they grow. They become adults. An **adult** is an animal that is all grown up. Adult animals can reproduce. To **reproduce** means to make more living things of the same kind. Finally, animals grow old and die. The pattern from birth to death is called the animal's **life cycle.**

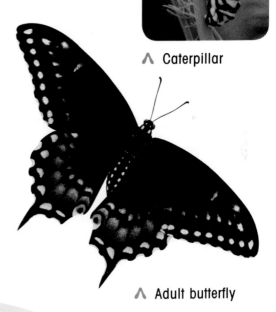

∧ Caterpillar

Each animal group has its own kind of life cycle. Some animal babies look like their parents. A puppy looks like a small dog. Other animal babies look very different from their parents. A caterpillar is a young butterfly or moth, but it does not look like the adult insect.

∧ Adult butterfly

Science Alert!

A caterpillar looks like a worm, but it is an insect. Here is one way to tell the difference. Caterpillars have legs. Worms do not have legs.

Life Cycle of Mammals

See Also

Mammals
pages 102–103

A baby mammal grows inside its mother. It is born live. Its mother nurses it with milk after it is born. A baby mammal looks like its parents, but it is much smaller.

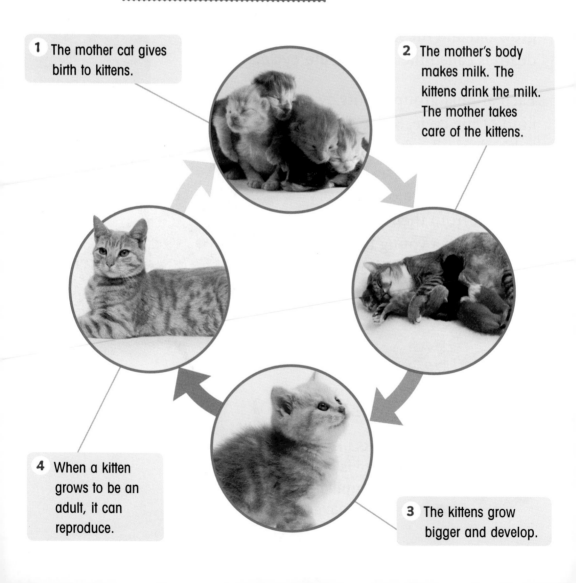

Life cycle of a cat

1 The mother cat gives birth to kittens.

2 The mother's body makes milk. The kittens drink the milk. The mother takes care of the kittens.

3 The kittens grow bigger and develop.

4 When a kitten grows to be an adult, it can reproduce.

Life Cycle of Birds

Birds lay eggs with a hard shell. They sit on the eggs to keep them warm. A baby bird grows inside each egg. The egg hatches, and the baby comes out. The baby looks like its parents, except that it is smaller. Its feathers may be a different color, too. The baby still looks like a bird.

See Also

Birds
pages 104–105

Life cycle of a bird

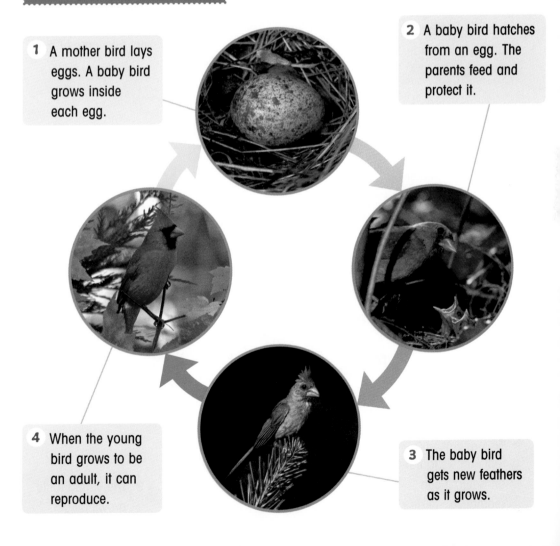

1 A mother bird lays eggs. A baby bird grows inside each egg.

2 A baby bird hatches from an egg. The parents feed and protect it.

3 The baby bird gets new feathers as it grows.

4 When the young bird grows to be an adult, it can reproduce.

Life Cycle of Reptiles

See Also

Reptiles
pages 106–107

Reptiles lay eggs with a leathery shell. Baby reptiles develop inside the eggs. They hatch and come out of the eggs. The babies look like their parents. The babies grow to be adults. They lay eggs, just as their parents did.

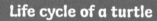

Life cycle of a turtle

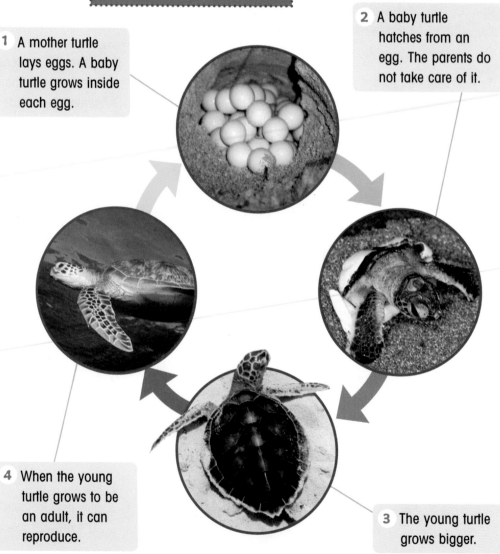

1 A mother turtle lays eggs. A baby turtle grows inside each egg.

2 A baby turtle hatches from an egg. The parents do not take care of it.

4 When the young turtle grows to be an adult, it can reproduce.

3 The young turtle grows bigger.

Life Cycle of Amphibians

Amphibians lay eggs that do not have a shell. Young amphibians do not look like their parents. They change form as they develop. Young amphibians have body parts for living in water. Adult amphibians have body parts for living on land.

See Also

Amphibians
pages 108–109

Life cycle of a frog

1 A mother frog lays eggs in the water. A tadpole develops inside each egg.

2 A tadpole hatches from an egg. It has gills and a tail. It does not have legs. The parents do not take care of it.

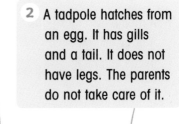

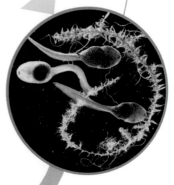

3 The tadpole changes as it grows. The gills and tail disappear. Lungs and legs develop.

4 The adult frog lives on land near water. It can reproduce.

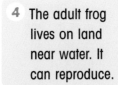

Life Cycle of Fish

See Also

Fish
pages 110–111

Fish lay eggs that do not have a shell. Baby fish develop inside the eggs. The eggs hatch, and the tiny fish come out. The young fish grow and develop into adults.

Life cycle of a fish

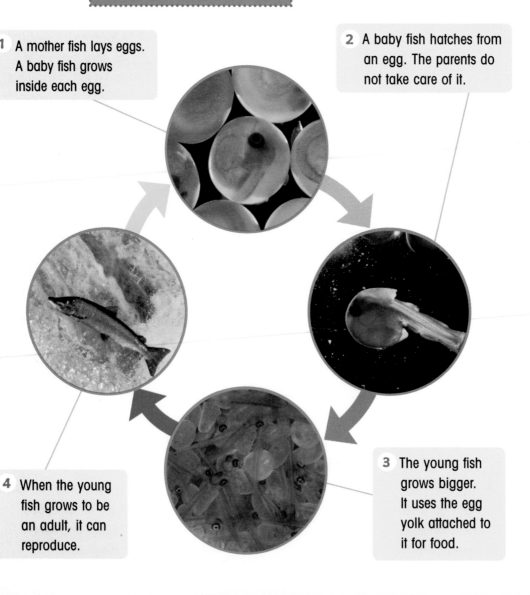

1 A mother fish lays eggs. A baby fish grows inside each egg.

2 A baby fish hatches from an egg. The parents do not take care of it.

3 The young fish grows bigger. It uses the egg yolk attached to it for food.

4 When the young fish grows to be an adult, it can reproduce.

Life Cycle of Insects

Most kinds of insects change form during their life cycle. A **caterpillar** (KAT ur pil ur) is a young insect. A caterpillar is also called a **larva** (LAHR vuh).

See Also

Arthropods
pages 114–115

The larva changes into a **pupa** (PYOO puh). A butterfly pupa has a hard covering called a **chrysalis** (KRIHS uh lis). A moth pupa has a soft covering called a **cocoon** (kuh KOON). The pupa changes into an adult butterfly or moth. Then it breaks out of the covering.

Life cycle of a butterfly

1 A butterfly lays eggs on a plant.

2 A caterpillar hatches from an egg. It eats plants and grows.

3 The caterpillar changes into a pupa. The pupa does not eat. It does not look like it is alive. But inside the chrysalis, its wings are forming.

4 A butterfly breaks out of the chrysalis. The adult butterfly has wings and legs. It can reproduce.

Plants and Animals Look Like Their Parents

Have you ever wondered why a puppy looks like a dog and not like a cat? Or why an acorn grows into an oak tree and not a rose bush? New plants and animals look like the parents that produced them. The new plants and animals are called **offspring.**

Parents pass their traits to their offspring. A **trait** (TRAYT) is a feature that is passed from parent to offspring. A bear gets its large teeth and huge paws from its parents. Large teeth and huge paws are traits of a bear.

Plants pass on their traits, too. A pine tree gets its woody trunk and needles from its parents. A cactus gets its sharp spines from its parents.

∧ What traits did the mother horse pass on to her baby?

Some things are not passed from parents to their offspring. Do you remember learning how to ride a bike? Someone had to teach you. You were not born knowing how to ride a bike. Many young animals have to learn things, too.

∨ Young chimps have to learn how to use a stick to get termites to eat.

∧ Bear cubs have to learn how to catch fish for food.

Have you ever cut yourself by accident? Maybe the cut left a scar. You will not pass the scar to your offspring. Only traits that you were born with can be passed on to your offspring.

Environments and Ecosystems

Have you ever seen a forest? You can see many living things in the forest. You can see many nonliving things, too.

See Also

Is It Alive?
pages 81–82

Soil
pages 182–185

Temperature
page 190

All the living and nonliving things make up the environment (en VEYE run munt). A living thing's **environment** is all the things around it. Plants and animals are part of the environment. Water, rocks, soil, and air are, too. Even sunlight and temperature are part of the environment.

Ecosystems

An **ecosystem** (EE koh sis tum) is all of the living and nonliving things found in one place. The living and nonliving things interact with each other.

A forest is one kind of ecosystem. A forest has lots of trees. Rain, sunlight, and rich soil make the trees grow. The trees give food and homes to many different kinds of animals. The trees also drop leaves on the ground. The dead leaves become part of the soil.

All the living things in an ecosystem form a **community** (kuh MYOO nih tee). A community is made up of many different populations (pop yuh LAY shunz). A **population** is all of the organisms of the same kind living in a place. All of the gray squirrels that live in a forest are one population. All of the oak trees in the forest are another population.

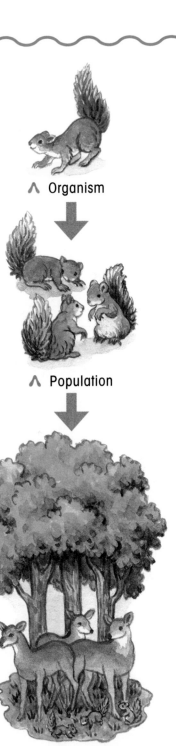

∧ Organism

∧ Population

∧ Community

Kinds of Ecosystems

See Also

Climate
page 198–201

Different ecosystems have different kinds of living and nonliving things. This chart tells what kinds of living and nonliving things you could find in different ecosystems.

Kinds of Ecosystems

Ecosystem	Living Things	Nonliving Things
Forest	oak tree, maple tree, fern, toad, squirrel, deer, fox, raccoon	thick layer of soil, medium rainfall, medium temperatures
Desert	creosote bush, cactus, Gila monster, jackrabbit, rattlesnake, coyote	dry and sandy soil, very little rain, hot temperatures
Grassland	grasses, cottonwood tree, elm tree, bison, prairie dog, antelope, coyote	thick layer of rich soil, little rainfall, medium temperatures

The kind of ecosystem where an organism lives is called its **habitat** (HAB ih tat). A plant or animal that lives in one habitat might not be able to live in another habitat. An organism can live only where it can get everything it needs. Different living things get what they need in different ways.

SCI LINKS
NSTA
Keyword:
Habitats
www.scilinks.org
Code: GSS23045

Kinds of Ecosystems

Ecosystem	Living Things	Nonliving Things
Ocean	algae, coral, shrimp, fish, sea turtle, dolphin	salt water, no soil, warm temperatures in shallow water, cool temperatures in deeper water
Tundra	mosses, lichen, small plants, caribou, arctic fox, snowshoe hare	thin layer of soil over frozen ground, very little rain, cold temperatures
Wetland	reed, water lily, willow tree, insects, duck, minnow, water snake	fresh water, thick layer of wet soil, medium temperatures

Competing for Resources

See Also

What Do Plants Need?
pages 86–87

What Do Animals Need?
pages 99–100

Material Resources
pages 310–315

Soil
pages 182–185

Have you ever taken care of a pet fish? A fish has a few basic needs. It needs clean water in its tank. The water must have oxygen in it. The water can't be too warm or too cold. You have to feed the fish. You also cannot put too many fish in the same tank. A fish needs space. If you do not meet the fish's needs, it might die.

Wild organisms also have needs. They get these needs from their habitat. Something that an organism needs from its habitat is called a **resource** (REE sors). Food, air, and water are resources. Space and shelter are resources, too. Sunlight is a resource that plants need.

∧ Water is an important resource for plants and animals.

A habitat might have only enough resources for some of the organisms there. Then, the organisms have to **compete** for resources. When organisms compete, they struggle with each other. If some organisms cannot get what they need, they have to move away. If they do not find a new habitat with enough resources, they will die.

Wolves compete for food. Wolves that are stronger win the fight. When there is not enough meat, the stronger wolves get to eat it. The weaker wolves go hungry. If they cannot find more meat, they might die.

Plants compete for resources, too. They compete for nutrients, water, sunlight, and space. When you plant a garden, the plants compete for resources. If weeds grow, you have to pull them out. That way, weeds will not use the resources.

Adaptations Help Organisms Survive

Keyword:
Adaptations of
Animals
www.scilinks.org
Code: GSS23050

Animals and plants have parts that help them survive. A hard, thick shell helps protect a turtle from danger. The hard bark of a tree keeps some animals from eating it.

Animals and plants also have behaviors (bih HAYV yursz) that help them compete for resources. A **behavior** is something that an organism does. A cheetah can run very fast to chase its food. Running fast is a behavior. Plants bend toward sunlight. This behavior helps plants grow.

A body part or behavior that helps an organism survive is called an **adaptation** (ad ap TAY shun). Organisms have adaptations that help them survive in their habitats.

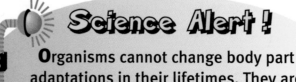

Science Alert!

Organisms cannot change body part adaptations in their lifetimes. They are born with them. Organisms *can* change behavior adaptations.

Some habitats can be very hard to live in. A tundra is cold. A desert is hot and dry. Adaptations help organisms survive in these places. Thick fur helps an animal stay warm in a cold place. Resting in the shade helps an animal stay cool in a hot place. Storing water helps a plant live in a dry place.

Adaptations also help living things get resources. Many animals live in places where there is very little food in winter. To stay alive, some animals store food before winter comes. If young plants sprout right next to the parent plants, there might not be enough space for them to grow. Some plants make seeds that can travel to another place with more space.

Animals and plants have ways to keep safe from animals that would eat them. Some organisms have body parts that protect them. Other organisms have behaviors that help them hide or get away.

< This insect looks like a leaf. That helps it hide from other animals that might eat it.

Body Parts Are Adaptations

Body parts help organisms meet their needs. The parts can have special shapes, colors, or sizes. Large, strong legs help an animal run and jump. Big ears let an animal hear other animals coming closer.

∧ Kangaroos have large back legs. They use their legs to hop very fast.

∧ Monkeys have hands with thumbs. Their hands can hold food and tree branches.

∧ Penguins' wings are shaped like flippers. Their wings let them swim very fast to catch fish.

∧ Ducks have webbed feet that push them through the water. Their feet act like paddles.

Body Parts for Getting Food

Many animals have body parts that help them get food. A giraffe's long neck lets it reach leaves on tall trees. An elephant can grab bushes and tree branches with its trunk.

< A pelican has a beak with a large pouch. It can scoop up fish and carry them.

> A butterfly has a long mouth part. It can reach deep into flowers to drink nectar.

Body Parts for Breathing Air

All animals have to breathe air. They need the oxygen in air. Many animals get air with lungs or gills. Insects have holes in their body coverings that take in air. All these adaptations help animals breathe in their habitats.

See Also

Reptiles
pages 106–107

Fish
pages 110–111

< Sea turtles live in ocean water, but they need to breathe air. Their lungs let them stay under water for hours. Then they go up to the surface to breathe air again.

> Fish have gills that take in oxygen from the water. This adaptation lets them breathe under water.

Body Parts for Staying Safe

Some organisms have body coverings that keep them safe from danger. These adaptations help them hide or fight enemies.

∧ A porcupine has sharp quills on its body. The quills stick any animal that tries to attack it.

∧ This toad's skin looks like tree bark. This hides the toad from animals that might try to eat it.

< The eastern newt has poisonous skin. Any animal that eats the newt might get sick. The newt's bright color warns other animals to stay away.

Body Parts of Plants

Plants have special body parts, too. Adaptations help plants get nutrients, spread their seeds, and store water. Some adaptations protect plants from being eaten by animals.

See Also

What Do Plants Need?
pages 86–87

Plant Life Cycles
pages 93–95

< A Venus flytrap lives in a habitat that has very poor soil. The plant cannot get all its nutrients from soil. It gets some nutrients from insects. Its leaves are an adaptation that traps insects and digests them.

∧ A dandelion has light, fluffy seeds. Wind blows the seeds far away from the parent plant. This gives the new plants more space to grow.

∧ A cactus has sharp spines that protect it from animals that try to eat it. It also has a thick stem that lets it store water in the dry desert where it lives.

Behaviors Are Adaptations

Having special body parts is only part of survival. What an organism does with its body parts is also important. Adaptations can be ways of doing things.

Behaviors for Getting Food

Some behaviors help organisms get food. A spider spins a web to catch insects. A loon dives under the water to catch fish.

> Some crows make tools out of sticks. They use the sticks to reach insects in holes.

> Some bats eat insects that move around at night. The bats sleep during the day and hunt at night.

∧ A baby kangaroo knows how to crawl into its mother's pouch when it is born. It gets milk there.

Behaviors for Staying Safe

Some behaviors help organisms stay safe from animals that would eat them.

Many animals live in large groups. In a group, each animal is protected from enemies. If the animal was all alone, an enemy could attack it easily.

∧ Fish swim in groups called *schools*.

∧ Zebras move in groups called *herds*.

Prairie dogs live in large groups. They dig holes under the ground. Prairie dogs stand up on their back legs to look for enemies. When one prairie dog sees danger, it makes a noise and runs into a hole. All the other prairie dogs run into the holes to hide.

∧ This prairie dog is watching for danger.

When the Seasons Change

Winter is cold and snowy in some places. It's hard for animals to stay warm and find food. When winter is coming, some animals change their behavior.

See Also

Seasons and Weather
pages 196–197

What Causes the Seasons?
pages 218–219

Some animals move to warmer places when it gets cold. Many birds fly south before winter comes. There, they can find lots of food. In the spring, they fly back north again. Other animals move to warmer places for the winter, too.

∧ Caribou move south for the winter.

When cold weather comes, many plants die. The animals that eat those plants could go hungry. To stay alive during the cold winter, some animals **hibernate** [HY bur nayt], or go into a deep sleep. Then they don't need food. Other animals save food during warm weather to eat when it gets cold.

∧ In the fall, squirrels bury nuts to eat during the winter.

Sending Messages

Some behaviors help animals "talk" to each other. Animals can't really talk, but they can make sounds. They also can move their bodies to send messages.

Animals send different kinds of messages. They tell an enemy to go away. They warn each other of danger. They help each other find food. Or they signal to a mate so they can reproduce.

Animals use sounds to send messages. A baby sea lion calls its mother when it is scared or hungry. Wolves howl to let other wolves know where they are. A rattlesnake shakes its tail to make a noise. The noise tells an enemy that the snake could bite. A beaver slaps the water with its flat tail. The sound tells other beavers that danger is near.

Moving can also send a message. A male peacock raises his large, colorful tail to show a female. This tells the female that he likes her.

Nature Changes Habitats

Organisms have adaptations that help them survive in their habitats. Sometimes habitats change. Some changes are natural. Floods, droughts, and fires happen naturally. These things can change habitats.

Some changes are good for the habitat. Other changes are harmful.

During a storm, there can be lightning. Lightning can strike something and cause a fire. The fire can spread. It can kill many plants and animals. After the fire, the ground and trees will be black and burned.

Fire can help a forest, too. After the fire, ashes are left on the ground. The ashes have nutrients that plants need. Burned areas are good places for new plants to grow. Fire also opens new spaces for animals to live.

∧ New plants grow again after a forest fire.

Heavy rain can cause a flood. Plants can't move out of the way. Many plants die when they are under water. The flood also can kill animals or destroy their homes. Animals have to move away from the flooded place.

See Also

Weather
pages 189–195

When the flood is over, new plants can grow. A flood brings new soil with nutrients for plants. Animals move back when the flood water is gone.

Sometimes a habitat does not get enough rain. Too little rain for a long time is called a **drought** (DROUT). Many plants and animals die. When rain comes again, new plants grow. Animals have water to drink again.

Animals change habitats, too. If there are too many deer, they might eat all of the young trees. There won't be adult trees to supply food for other animals.

Animals change habitats when they make their homes. Beavers build dams on streams. A dam blocks the stream so a pond forms.

∧ A beaver dam floods the area behind it.

The water gets higher behind the dam. The water drowns plants that grew there. Below the dam, there is less water. Animals that lived there might have to move. Beavers cut down trees to make a dam. Animals that lived in the trees have to find other homes.

People Change Habitats

See Also

Technology Helps All People
pages 72–73

Pollution
pages 325–331

Fighting Pollution
page 333

Using Less
pages 334–337

People cause changes to habitats. Sometimes the changes help a habitat. People plant bushes on hillsides to keep the soil from washing away.

People also cause harmful changes to habitats. One harmful change is pollution (puh LOO shun). **Pollution** is anything people add to the environment that can hurt living things.

Pollution can kill plants and animals. It can make animals sick and destroy their homes. It can hurt plants. It can make it hard for animals to get enough food. Pollution can hurt people, too. When pollution gets into water, it can make people sick. Air pollution can make it hard for people to breathe.

∧ Air pollution

∧ Water pollution

∧ Land pollution

People change habitats in other ways besides pollution. People destroy resources in habitats. They add new things that cause problems.

People build new houses and roads. They cut down forests. They use machines to change the shape of the land. They fill in wetlands with dirt and rocks. They build dams. These and other changes kill many plants and animals. The animals that aren't killed have to find new homes.

∧ Cutting down trees destroys a forest habitat.

People also add new organisms to habitats. They add their pets and farm animals. They add new plants that are food for people. They add flowers and trees that were not in the habitat before.

The new plants and animals change the habitat. The new animals may eat too many plants or animals in the habitat. The new plants may take up too much space. They may take too many nutrients out of the soil. The new plants and animals might cause the other plants and animals to die off. The new organisms might even take over the habitat.

∧ People brought kudzu to the United States. They thought the plant would help hold soil in place along highways. Then the kudzu plants spread! Now kudzu grows out of control in many places.

Energy in Ecosystems

See Also

What Do Plants Need?
pages 86–87

All organisms need energy to live and grow. They need energy to reproduce. Organisms get energy from food. Different living things get food in different ways.

Producers

Plants make their own food. They use sunlight to make food from carbon dioxide and water. The food that plants make is a kind of sugar. The sugar is their food. It gives them energy.

A **producer** (pruh DOO sur) is an organism that makes its own food. Plants are producers. Some very small ocean organisms are producers, too. Some kinds of bacteria are also producers. Bacteria are tiny organisms made of only one cell.

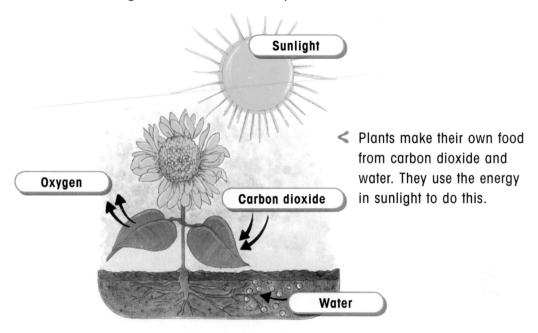

Sunlight

Oxygen

Carbon dioxide

Water

< Plants make their own food from carbon dioxide and water. They use the energy in sunlight to do this.

Consumers

Animals cannot make their own food. They get food by eating plants or other animals. An animal that gets food by eating plants or other animals is called a **consumer** (kun SOO mur).

Some animals eat only plants. A zebra eats only grasses. Other animals eat only animals. Lions eat many different kinds of animals. They do not eat plants. Other animals eat both plants and animals. A brown bear eats berries growing on bushes. It also eats fish that it catches in rivers.

A **predator** (PRED uh tur) is an animal that hunts and eats other animals for food. The animal that a predator eats is called its **prey** (PRAY). Lions hunt and eat zebras. The lion is a predator. The zebra is its prey.

See Also

What Do Animals Need?
page 99

Food Chains
pages 152–153

Food Webs
pages 154–155

∧ Some animals get food by eating plants.

∧ Some animals get food by eating other animals.

Decomposers

Some organisms get their food from dead plants and animals. They break down the dead things into tiny pieces. This is how they get energy. An organism that gets energy from breaking down dead things is called a **decomposer** (dee kum POH zur). *Decompose* means to break down into smaller pieces.

Have you ever seen a mushroom growing outside? A mushroom is part of a fungus (FUHNG gus). A **fungus** is a decomposer. It grows in the ground where a dead thing is buried. It grows on dead trees. The fungus breaks down the dead thing into tiny pieces. It uses the pieces for food to get energy.

∧ This fungus is getting food by breaking down a dead tree.

Maybe you have seen mold growing on bread or a piece of fruit. Mold is a decomposer. Many kinds of bacteria are decomposers, too.

See Also

Soil
pages 182–185

Decomposers are very important in ecosystems. They recycle dead things. They add nutrients to the soil. Plants use these nutrients to grow. When animals eat the plants, they get nutrients.

Living Things Need Each Other

Different kinds of organisms need each other. Animals need plants for food, homes, and shelter. Plants also need animals. They need the nutrients that animals leave in their wastes. Decomposers need dead plants and animals to break down for food. Plants need the nutrients that decomposers add to the soil.

Some plants have flowers. Flowers have pollen in them. To make seeds, pollen has to move from one part of a flower to another part. Animals help plants by moving pollen. Bees, butterflies, and other insects visit flowers to drink nectar. As they visit flowers, they spread pollen. Bats and birds also spread pollen.

Plants also need to spread their seeds. This way, the young plants will have room to grow. Animals help plants spread seeds.

When an animal eats a fruit, it also eats the seeds inside the fruit. When the animal moves somewhere else, the seeds drop out in the animal's waste.

Some seeds have little hooks on them. These seeds stick to animals that pass by. When the seeds fall off the animal, new plants may grow there.

See Also

Flowers and Cones
page 91

Food Chains

Animals get energy from eating other organisms. In this way, energy flows through an ecosystem. A **food chain** is the path of energy from one organism to another organism in an ecosystem.

All food chains start with energy from the sun. A plant gets energy from the sun. It uses this energy to make its own food. Plants are producers. A producer is always the first organism in a food chain.

Some animals eat plants. Mice eat plants. When a mouse eats wheat, it gets energy from the wheat. An animal that eats plants is next in the food chain.

Some animals eat other animals. Owls eat mice. When an owl eats a mouse, it gets energy from the mouse. An animal that eats other animals is at the end of the food chain.

∧ A mouse gets energy by eating a plant.

∧ An owl gets energy by eating a mouse.

See Also

Producers
page 148

Consumers
page 149

Energy flows from the wheat plant to the mouse and then to the owl. The picture on this page shows the food chain. The arrows show how energy flows.

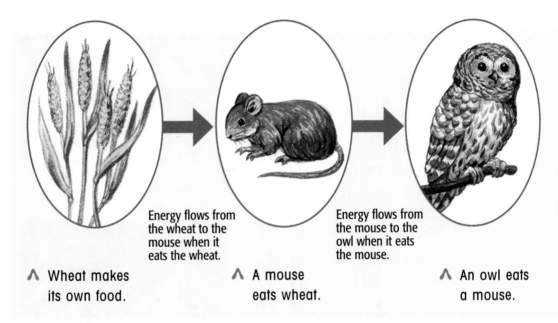

Energy flows from the wheat to the mouse when it eats the wheat.

Energy flows from the mouse to the owl when it eats the mouse.

∧ Wheat makes its own food.

∧ A mouse eats wheat.

∧ An owl eats a mouse.

A food chain is like a real chain. A chain will not be strong if one link is broken. The same is true of a food chain. When one organism in a food chain dies out, the organisms that eat it can die out, too.

Food Webs

See Also

Food Chains
pages 152–153

Keyword: Food Webs
www.scilinks.org
Code: GSS23055

Most animals eat many different kinds of food. A mouse eats wheat. It also eats grass, corn, and other plants. Mice eat small insects, too. An owl eats mice. It also eats squirrels, rabbits, snakes, and other small animals.

Mice aren't the only animals that eat plants. Rabbits and insects eat plants, too. Owls aren't the only animals that eat mice. Snakes and coyotes also eat mice. Coyotes even eat snakes! They eat fruit and berries, too.

Energy flows in many pathways in an ecosystem. A food chain can't show many pathways and many organisms. It shows only one line of organisms.

∧ Grasshoppers eat plants.

∧ Rabbits eat plants.

∧ Coyotes eat mice, rabbits, and insects.

A **food web** is made up of many different food chains. It shows that energy flows in many different pathways in an ecosystem.

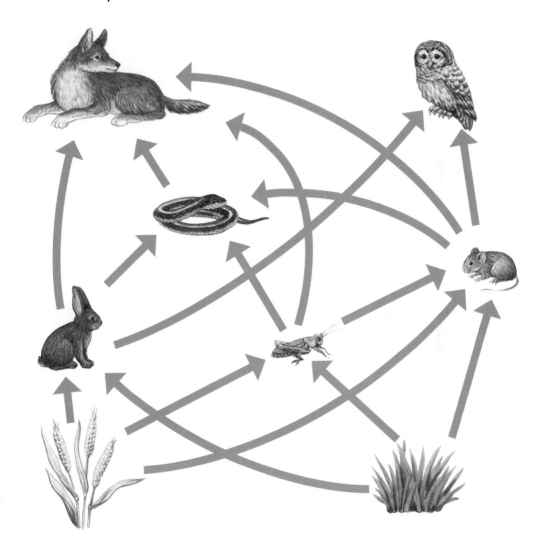

A food web lets you see what would happen if the ecosystem changed. Look at this food web. Suppose all the mice and rabbits died out. What would happen to the other animals in the food web?

Earth Science

Mountains are tall and rocky. Beaches are low and sandy. Why do different parts of Earth look so different? A person who studies Earth science might answer this question. **Earth science** is the study of planet Earth and other objects in the sky.

Can't we explore sand at the beach instead?

The Earth

Most of Earth is covered with water. The rest is covered with land. From space, the water part looks blue. The land part looks brown or green.

See Also

Water on Earth
page 160

Living things make their home on Earth. Many kinds of plants and animals live in the oceans, rivers, and lakes that are water. Many other kinds of living things live on land, including you!

Earth is shaped like a round ball, but it is not perfectly round. It bulges a little around the middle.

∧ Earth is covered by water and land.

Structure of Earth

Earth has three layers. They are the crust, the mantle, and the core.

Imagine Earth as a peach. The peach's skin is like Earth's crust. Earth's **crust** is the thin layer on the outside of Earth.

The juicy part of the peach is like Earth's mantle. Earth's **mantle** is the middle layer of Earth. The mantle is much thicker than the crust.

The center of a peach, its hard pit, is like Earth's core. Earth's **core** is at the center of Earth.

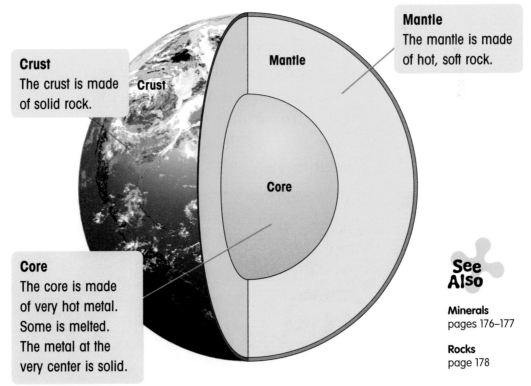

Mantle
The mantle is made of hot, soft rock.

Mantle

Crust
The crust is made of solid rock.

Crust

Core

Core
The core is made of very hot metal. Some is melted. The metal at the very center is solid.

See Also

Minerals
pages 176–177

Rocks
page 178

Water on Earth

Most of the water on Earth is in the oceans. An **ocean** is a very large body of salt water. Salt water is water that has salt in it.

The rest of the water on Earth is fresh water. Fresh water is water that does not have salt in it. Most rivers, lakes, and streams are made up of fresh water. Fresh water is also found underground.

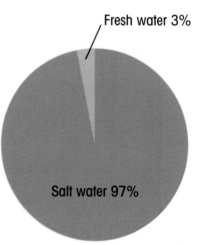

Fresh water 3%

Salt water 97%

∧ Only a very small amount of water on Earth is fresh water.

See Also

Glaciers
page 170

Most of Earth's fresh water is frozen as ice. The areas around the North and South Poles are covered with glaciers. A **glacier** (GLAY shur) is a thick layer of ice that stays frozen all year. Glaciers in mountains look like rivers made of thick ice. Glaciers near the poles are thick sheets.

> A glacier stays frozen all year round.

Living Things Need Water

Can you imagine life without water? It would not be possible. All living things need water to live. Both plants and animals use water to get energy from food. They also need water to grow.

People use water for all sorts of things. Farmers need water to make their crops grow. Factories use a lot of water to make things. Power plants use moving water to make electricity.

There is only a certain amount of water on Earth. People cannot make more water. So they must take care of Earth's water. If they waste clean water, there might not be enough for everyone.

See Also

What Do Plants Need? pages 86–87

What Do Animals Need? page 99

∧ People use water for drinking, cooking, and cleaning.

∧ People who take care of pets must give them water.

∧ People must water the plants they grow for food.

Water Moves Around Earth

See Also

States of Matter
page 245

Heat Energy
pages 276–279

Water has three forms—liquid, solid, and gas. Scientists call these forms states. The liquid state is water. The solid state is ice. **Water vapor** is the gas state. There is water vapor in the air.

Water can change from one state to another. This happens when water either warms up or cools down.

Liquid water can change into water vapor when it is warmed up. This change from a liquid to a gas is called **evaporation** (ih vap uh RAY shun). It can happen when heat energy is added to water. Water evaporates from lakes and oceans when the sun heats it. The water vapor rises up into the air.

∧ Water vapor enters the air when lake water evaporates on a hot day.

Water vapor cools when it loses heat energy. With enough cooling, it can turn into a liquid. The change from a gas to a liquid is called **condensation** (kahn dun SAY shun).

When water vapor condenses on land, it forms dew. Dew is drops of water that form on grass.

When water vapor condenses in the sky, it becomes clouds. A **cloud** is a clump of tiny water drops that hangs in the air.

> Dew forms when water vapor in the air condenses on cool mornings.

Did you know?

Water is the only substance on Earth that is found in all three states in nature.

Keyword: Clouds
www.scilinks.org
Code: GSS23075

See Also

Water Cycle
pages 164–165

Clouds
pages 194–195

Changing States
pages 246–247

Water Cycle

See Also

Changing States
pages 246–247

Water can change state again and again. As it changes from state to state, it moves between Earth and the air. This movement of water between the air and Earth is called the **water cycle.**

Imagine water in a lake. The sun shines on the lake. Water near the top of the lake evaporates. Water vapor rises up into the air. As it rises, it cools. The water vapor condenses. It forms tiny water drops that make up clouds. The tiny drops join together into larger drops. The drops fall to Earth as precipitation. **Precipitation** (prih sip ih TAY shun) is water or ice that falls to Earth. Rain and snow are precipitation.

> Snow is frozen precipitation.

Some of the water goes into the ground. Water found in the ground is called **groundwater.** What does not go into the ground flows downhill. Water that flows along Earth's surface is called **runoff.** Runoff flows into streams. Streams flow into rivers. Rivers flow into lakes and oceans. Water in lakes and oceans can evaporate again. This starts the water cycle all over again.

SCI LINKS
N S T A
Keyword:
Water Cycle
www.scilinks.org
Code: GSS23060

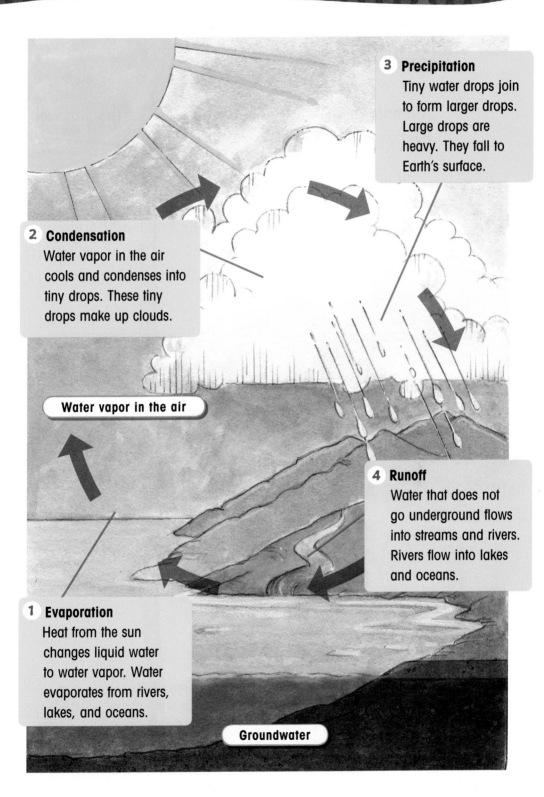

3 Precipitation
Tiny water drops join to form larger drops. Large drops are heavy. They fall to Earth's surface.

2 Condensation
Water vapor in the air cools and condenses into tiny drops. These tiny drops make up clouds.

Water vapor in the air

4 Runoff
Water that does not go underground flows into streams and rivers. Rivers flow into lakes and oceans.

1 Evaporation
Heat from the sun changes liquid water to water vapor. Water evaporates from rivers, lakes, and oceans.

Groundwater

Landforms

A **landform** is a natural land shape on Earth's surface. Earth has many kinds of landforms.

A **mountain** (MOUN tun) is a landform that pokes way up into the sky. Mountain ranges are groups of mountains in the same place. The low land between mountains is called a **valley** (VAL ee). Some valleys are wide and flat. Other valleys are deep and narrow.

∧ A mountain range

∧ A valley

See Also

Slow Changes to Earth's Surface
pages 168–171

Fast Changes to Earth's Surface
pages 172–175

A **canyon** (KAN yun) is a deep and narrow valley. The Grand Canyon in Arizona is one of the largest canyons in the world.

Some of Earth's landforms are flat. A **plateau** (pla TOH) is a large, flat area that is higher than the land around it. It is high above the ground like a mountain, but it is flat on top. Plateaus often have steep sides. *Mesa, butte*, and *tableland* are words that mean small, flat-topped landform. These landforms look like small plateaus.

A **plain** is a flat landform that is not higher than the land around it. Plains often have rich soil and are good for growing crops.

See Also

Soil
pages 182–185

∧ A mesa

∧ A plain

Did you know?

A large area called the Great Plains covers most of the middle of the United States. There are many farms on the Great Plains. Much of the food you eat grows on these farms.

Slow Changes to Earth's Surface

Earth's surface is always changing. Some changes happen very slowly. It takes millions of years for some landforms to form.

The Grand Canyon formed very slowly from weathering and erosion. **Weathering** (WETH ur ing) is the breaking down of rock into tiny pieces. **Erosion** (ih ROH zhun) is the carrying away of weathered material from one place to another. Weathering and erosion together change Earth's surface.

Water caused the weathering and erosion of the Grand Canyon. Other forces cause weathering and erosion, too.

∧ The Grand Canyon in Arizona

Wind and Water

Wind and water cause weathering. They pick up tiny pieces of sand and move them across rock. The pieces of sand rub the rock and wear it away.

∧ Over many years, wind and water wore away the soft rock in Bryce Canyon National Park in Utah. Strange rock shapes formed.

∧ If water wears away rock underground, a cave may form. Water moving through the ground caused this cave to form.

Wind and water also cause erosion. Over millions of years, a river takes away a lot of rock and soil. It can take away so much that a canyon forms.

Wind and water carry away rock and soil. When they slow down, they drop the rock and soil. New land forms where this weathered material falls.

SCI LINKS.
N S T A
Keyword:
Changes to
Earth's Surface
www.scilinks.org
Code: GSS23065

Glaciers

See Also

Water on Earth
page 160

Friction and Motion
page 285

Glaciers can cause weathering and erosion. Some glaciers are large frozen rivers of ice. They move downhill very slowly. As they move, they scrape the land they pass over. They carry away soil and small pieces of rock. The small pieces of rock under the glacier grind against larger pieces of rock. After a while the larger pieces of rock wear away. A large glacier can make a valley wider as it moves between mountains.

Glaciers carry rocks and soil until they stop moving or melt. Then they drop whatever they are carrying.

> A glacier made this valley wider over thousands of years.

> A glacier picked up this huge rock and moved it far away. The rock fell to this place when the glacier melted.

Plant Roots

Plants can cause weathering. Plant roots grow as a plant grows. Imagine that a seed lands in a rock crack. The seed sprouts and starts to grow roots. The growing roots spread out inside the crack. They push against the rock and make the crack larger. The rock breaks into small pieces. This is a kind of weathering.

∧ Tree roots grew into a crack in the rock. The rock will break as the roots spread out in the crack.

Freezing and Thawing

Freezing and thawing can cause weathering. Liquid water often collects in cracks in a rock. The water expands in the cracks when it freezes. *Expand* means to take up more space, or get bigger. The ice pushes against the rock and makes the cracks larger. The rock starts to break into small pieces. This is another kind of weathering.

∧ Water freezes in a rock crack. The rock breaks as the ice expands.

See Also

Roots
page 89

Changing States
pages 246–247

Fast Changes to Earth's Surface

Some changes to Earth's surface happen quickly. What causes fast changes?

Earthquakes

See Also

Structure of Earth
page 159

Earth's crust is made up of large moving pieces. The pieces move very slowly in different directions. They bump against each other. They can even get stuck. Sometimes they become unstuck with a sudden snap. This sudden movement of Earth's crust is called an **earthquake** (URTH kwayk).

Earthquakes shake the ground and everything on it. Strong earthquakes can damage buildings. They also make new landforms. Mountains form where the crust bends up. The land drops in other places.

Keyword:
Changes to
Earth's Surface
www.scilinks.org
Code: GSS23065

> An earthquake damaged this building.

Word Watch

The word *quake* means *to shake.*
During an earthquake people can often feel the ground shake.

Volcanoes

Hot, liquid rock lies deep below Earth's surface. Sometimes the liquid rock explodes out of a crack or hole. A **volcano** (vahl KAY noh) is a mountain with an opening that lets out material from deep inside Earth.

Melted rock at Earth's surface is called **lava** (LAH vuh). Hot lava flows down the sides of a volcano. When lava cools and hardens, it forms new landforms.

See Also

Landforms
pages 166–167

Kinds of Rocks
pages 179–181

Some volcanoes erupt suddenly. Ash and rock fly out in an explosion. Others erupt slowly. Lava flows down the sides of the volcano like a river of fire.

∧ A volcano called Mount St. Helens in Washington State erupted in 1980. One side of the mountain was blown away.

See Also

Water Cycle
pages 164–165

Slow Changes to Earth's Surface
pages 168–171

Floods

A **flood** (fluhd) happens when a body of water overflows onto dry land. Heavy rain or melting snow can cause a flood. The ground does not soak up all the water fast enough. The water runs off into rivers and streams. The rivers and streams overflow.

Floods change Earth's crust. They wash away soil in one place and drop it somewhere else. Water flows to places where it is usually dry. The flood water can cause damage. Many floods destroy homes and other buildings when they fill with water.

∧ The city of New Orleans flooded in 2005 when Hurricane Katrina dropped lots of rain. The levees could not hold all the water. They broke and caused a flood.

People sometimes build dams or levees (LEHV ees) along rivers to protect against floods. These structures help hold the water in.

Landslides

Heavy rain sometimes loosens the rocks and soil on a hillside. The soil turns into mud. The rocks and mud slide down the hill in a **landslide.** A large part of the hill is now gone.

Earthquakes also cause landslides. An earthquake shakes the rocks and soil on a hill. They can come loose and slide down the hill.

Landslides can destroy houses and other buildings. People try to prevent landslides by planting trees on hills. The tree roots help hold the soil in place. They keep the land from getting loose and sliding away.

∧ Heavy rains caused a landslide in Laguna Beach, California in 2005. The ground under these homes turned to mud. The mud and homes slid down the hillside.

Did you know ?

Wildfires can cause landslides, too. A fire burns all the plants in an area. There are no longer roots to hold the land in place and it slides away in heavy rain.

See Also

Roots
page 89

Minerals

See Also

Rocks
page 178

Physical Properties
pages 238–239

Earth's crust is made of rock. Rocks are made of minerals. A **mineral** (MIN ur ul) is a solid material found in nature that has never been alive. There are many different kinds of minerals.

Properties of Minerals

Properties are characteristics of a substance. You can use properties to tell one mineral from another. You can tell some minerals apart by looking at their color. Another property is how shiny they are. You can also test them to see how hard they are by scratching them. Graphite (GRAF yt) is a mineral that is soft and black. The mineral gold is harder than graphite. It is yellow and shiny. Diamond is the hardest mineral. Nothing can scratch a diamond except another diamond.

Keyword: Minerals and Rocks
www.scilinks.org
Code: GSS23070

∧ Graphite

> Diamond

∧ Gold

Uses of Minerals

Different minerals are used for different jobs. Graphite is used in pencils. Talc is ground up to make talcum powder, which keeps skin dry. People use the minerals gold, silver, and diamond to make jewelry. People also use diamonds to cut very hard metals.

See Also

What Do Plants Need? pages 86–87

What Do Animals Need? page 99

Soil pages 182–185

1 Aluminum bats are made from the mineral bauxite.

2 Window glass is made from the mineral quartz.

3 Some sunscreen has an ingredient made from the mineral sphalerite.

Animals need certain minerals to be healthy. They get minerals by eating plants. Plant roots take up minerals with water from soil.

Rocks

Rocks make up Earth's crust. A **rock** is a solid material made up of minerals. There are many kinds of rock. Some rock is made of only one kind of mineral. Other rock has several mixed together.

Keyword:
Minerals and
Rocks
www.scilinks.org
Code: GSS23070

Marble is a rock used for statues and buildings. White marble is made of the mineral calcite. Small amounts of other minerals can make marble different colors.

Black marble is mostly calcite.

The minerals serpentine and chlorite make marble green.

⋀ These chess pieces are made from black marble and green marble.

See Also

Physical
Properties
pages 238–239

Different kinds of rocks have different properties. People think about these properties when they use rocks. Softer rocks are used to carve statues. Harder rocks are used to make buildings.

Did you know?

The game of marbles got its name because early marbles were made of the rock marble. Today most marbles are made of glass.

Kinds of Rocks

There are three main kinds of rocks. Each kind of rock is formed a different way.

Igneous Rock

Melted rock lies deep inside Earth. **Igneous** (IG nee us) **rock** forms when melted rock cools and hardens.

∧ Granite

When the rock cools slowly, it can form large grains. Grains are crystals of mineral. Granite is an igneous rock that has large grains of several minerals. Granite cooled slowly inside Earth.

When a volcano erupts, melted rock comes to the surface. The rock cools and hardens quickly. The grains formed are very small, if they form at all. Obsidian (ahb SID ee un) is an igneous rock that looks like black glass. It has no mineral grains because it hardened so quickly.

∧ Obsidian

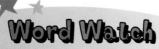

Word Watch

The word *igneous* comes from the Latin word for fire. Igneous rock forms from melted rock that is as hot as a fire.

See Also

Volcanoes page 173

Sedimentary Rock

See Also

Slow Changes to Earth's Surface
pages 168–171

Fossils
pages 186–187

Rivers carry tiny pieces of sand, rock, and shells. This material is called **sediment.** When river water comes to a lake or an ocean, sediment falls to the bottom. It forms layers. Over time, the layers press together. They get hard and form rock. Rock that forms from hardened layers of sediment is called **sedimentary** (sed uh MEN tuh ree) **rock.**

Most sedimentary rock has layers you can see. The layers are often different colors. The colors come from the minerals in the sediment. You can tell the age of rock by looking at the order of the layers. Layers at the bottom formed first. They are older than layers at the top. You can tell the age of fossils in sedimentary rock by looking at what layers they are in.

∧ Sandstone is a sedimentary rock. It forms from weathered rock and other sediments.

∧ Limestone is a sedimentary rock that formed from the old shells of animals. It is often white.

Metamorphic Rock

Igneous and sedimentary rocks can change. They can be squeezed and heated deep inside Earth's crust. This changes the rock from one kind to another. **Metamorphic** (met uh MOR fik) **rock** is rock that forms when other kinds of rock are heated and squeezed.

Marble is one kind of metamorphic rock. Marble formed from limestone, a sedimentary rock. Statues and buildings are sometimes made of marble.

Slate is another metamorphic rock. It formed from the sedimentary rock shale. School blackboards used to be made of slate. Slate is sometimes used for roofs and floors, too.

∧ This statue was carved from white marble.

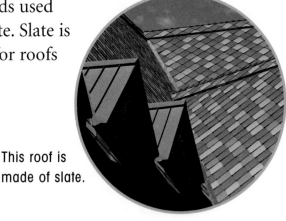

> This roof is made of slate.

See Also

Igneous Rock
page 179

Soil

See Also

Animal Life Cycles
pages 119–125

Decomposers
page 150

Soil is the loose material that covers Earth's surface. It is a mixture made of small pieces of rock, minerals, and bits of dead plants and animals. Soil also has air and water in it.

How Soil Forms

Weathering causes large rocks to break apart into smaller rocks. Small rocks become gravel and sand. Plants start to live in the sand. When they die, they break down and mix with the sand. **Humus** (HYOO mus) is the broken down parts of plants and animals in soil. After thousands of years, soil forms from broken down rocks and humus.

< Soil contains bits of rock, minerals, humus, air, and water.

Air

Humus

Minerals

Rock

Water

Layers of Soil

If you could dig a very deep hole, you would see that soil is made of layers. Plants grow out of the top layer.

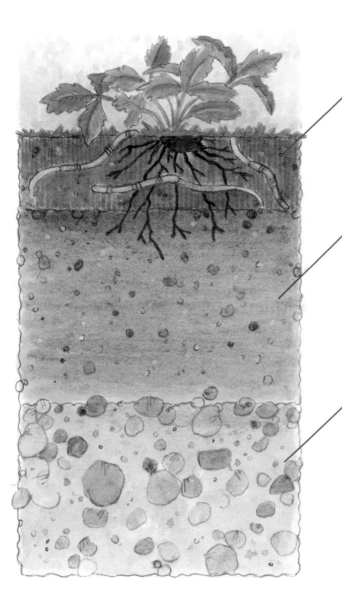

Topsoil
The top layer of soil is called topsoil. Topsoil is dark and crumbly. It has a lot of humus. Plants grow well here because they get nutrients from the humus.

Subsoil
Below the topsoil layer is a layer of subsoil. Subsoil has little humus. It is lighter in color than topsoil. There are small pieces of rock in it.

Rock
Below the subsoil is a layer of rock. The rock at the top of this layer weathers slowly. The weathered rock becomes part of the subsoil layer.

See Also

Slow Changes to Earth's Surface pages 168–171

Kinds of Soil

See Also

What Do Plants Need? pages 86–87

Layers of Soil page 183

There are many kinds of soil. Each kind has weathered rock, minerals, humus, air, and water in it. Different kinds of soil have different amounts of these things.

Clay is the smallest rock particle. Soil that has a lot of clay is sticky because clay holds a lot of water. Plant roots have trouble pushing through heavy clay soil. It also does not have much humus, which plants need.

∧ Plants have trouble growing in heavy clay soil.

Sand particles are larger than clay. Sand does not hold water as well as clay does. Water drains away quickly from sandy soil. It also does not have much humus. Few plants can grow in very sandy soil because they need more water and nutrients.

∧ Plants also have trouble growing in very sandy soil.

The best soil for growing most plants has some clay, some sand, and lots of humus. It holds water, but not too much. It also has lots of air.

∧ Plants grow best in soil that has a lot of humus and holds some water.

Soil Is Important

Imagine Earth without soil. Plants could not grow.
They could not get the water and nutrients that soil
has. Animals that eat plants could not get energy either.
There would be no plants for them to eat. Animals that
eat other animals also could not get energy. All living
things on land depend on soil.

Keyword: Plants
www.scilinks.org
Code: GSS23030

∧ Plants need soil to grow.

Soil is home to many animals. Earthworms, spiders,
and many insects live in soil. These animals live on
materials they find in soil. Without soil, they would die.

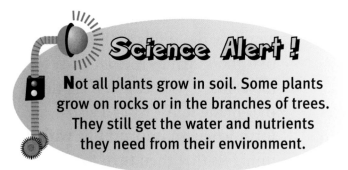

Science Alert!

Not all plants grow in soil. Some plants
grow on rocks or in the branches of trees.
They still get the water and nutrients
they need from their environment.

See Also

Decomposers
page 150

Living Things Need Each Other
page 151

Food Chains
pages 152–153

Fossils

A **fossil** is the remains of an animal or plant that lived long ago. There are different kinds of fossils.

Imprint fossil of dinosaur footprint

An **imprint** is a fossil that shows the shape of part of an animal or plant. Your foot leaves its shape when you step in mud. A fossil of your footprint might stay after the mud hardens into rock.

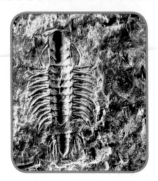

Mold fossil of a trilobite

A **mold** is a fossil that forms after a living thing dies and is buried in sand or mud. The sand or mud turns into rock. The dead thing breaks down and leaves a hollow shape of itself in the rock.

Cast fossil of an ammonite

A **cast** is a fossil that forms when a hollow mold fills with minerals that then turn to rock. A cast fossil looks like a rock copy of the thing that made it. A cast can also form when an imprint fills with minerals that then turn to rock.

What Fossils Tell Us

Fossils can tell you about plants and animals that lived long ago. Scientists learned everything they know about dinosaurs by studying fossils. They have also learned about plants the dinosaurs ate by studying fossils. They have even learned about insects that lived then.

A fossil fish in a mountain rock tells you that the mountain rock must have been underwater back when the fish lived.

Fossils can also tell you what the environment was like in the past. Scientists have learned from fossils that some places are very different than they were in the past. There are fossils of palm trees near the North Pole. Palm trees live only in warm places. The fossils show that the North Pole was once warm.

Weather and Climate

You look out of the window and you notice that snow is falling. If it is snowing, it must be cold outside. What should you wear today? What you wear depends on the weather and climate where you live.

The weather is usually cooler in winter and warmer in summer. You need different clothes for each season. Long pants keep you warm in winter. Shorts keep you cool in summer.

> Winter clothes

> Summer clothes

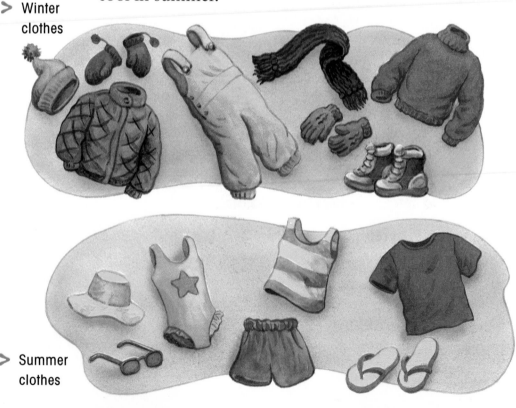

Weather

Air is all around you. It covers Earth like a blanket. **Weather** is a description of the outside air in a certain place at a certain time.

Air is always moving. You feel it as wind. Moving air brings different kinds of weather. It may be sunny when you wake up. Then, moving air brings rain clouds and it starts to rain. Weather is always changing.

Weather changes often happen in patterns. It is usually cooler at night than in the daytime. There is more rain in the rainy season than in the dry season.

∧ A sunny day

> A rainy day

See Also

Water Cycle
pages 164–165

Temperature

An important part of weather is the temperature of the air. **Temperature** (TEM pur uh chur) is a measure of how hot or cold something is. The tool used to measure temperature is a **thermometer** (thur MAHM ih tur).

See Also

Using a Thermometer pages 52–53

What Causes Day and Night pages 216–217

Heat Energy pages 276–279

A thermometer may measure temperature in degrees Fahrenheit (FAR un hyt) or in degrees Celsius (SEL see us). Some thermometers measure both.

< A thermometer is used to measure the temperature of the air.

The sun heats the air, land, and water. Air is usually warmer in the afternoon than it is in the morning. This is because the sun has been warming the air all day. At night, the air gets cooler because the sun does not shine on Earth where it is night. The air starts to warm up again in the morning.

Keyword: Thermometers
www.scilinks.org
Code: GSS23015

Humidity

Another important part of weather is humidity. **Humidity** (hyoo MID ih tee) is the amount of water vapor in the air. You cannot see water vapor, but you may feel it. A lot of water vapor in the air makes your skin feel wet. Too little makes your skin feel dry.

Water gets into the air by evaporation. Water can evaporate from a lake or the ocean. It can also evaporate from wet ground. If a lot of water evaporates, the humidity in the air gets higher.

See Also

Water Moves Around Earth pages 162–165

Humidity is measured with a hygrometer (hy GRAHM ih tur). A hygrometer looks a little like a thermometer.

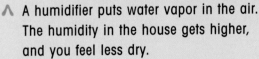

∧ A humidifier puts water vapor in the air. The humidity in the house gets higher, and you feel less dry.

See Also

Water Cycle
pages 164–165

States of Matter
page 245

Changing States
pages 246–247

Precipitation

Water condenses in air to form clouds. It falls to Earth as **precipitation.** Rain, snow, sleet, and hail are kinds of precipitation. The kind of precipitation that falls has to do with temperature. When the air is warm, rain falls. **Rain** is liquid water that falls from clouds.

∧ A rain gauge (gayj) measures the amount of precipitation that has fallen.

Water in the air freezes in cold air. It falls to Earth as snow. **Snow** is solid water that falls from clouds. Falling snow may turn to sleet. **Sleet** happens when falling snow melts and then freezes again.

Another kind of frozen precipitation is hail. **Hail** happens when falling rain bounces around in cold air and turns to balls of ice. Hail forms during thunderstorms.

∧ Large balls of hail can cause damage when they fall on cars and homes.

Wind

Wind is another important part of weather. **Wind** is moving air. It can be measured by its speed and direction. Wind can be strong or gentle. A very strong wind might blow during a storm. It can cause damage. Gentle winds might feel good against your skin.

See Also

Measuring Motion
pages 286–289

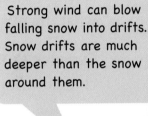

Strong wind can blow falling snow into drifts. Snow drifts are much deeper than the snow around them.

∧ This tool measures wind speed. Wind pushes against the cups and makes them spin.

< A wind vane shows wind direction. The arrow points to the direction the wind is coming from. Here, the wind is blowing from north to south.

Clouds

Look up into the sky. Do you see any clouds? A **cloud** is a clump of tiny water drops that hangs in the air. Clouds form when water vapor condenses in the air.

There are many kinds of clouds. Some are puffy and white. Others are light and feathery. Some clouds form high up in the sky. Others form near the middle of the sky. The kind of cloud you see gives you a clue about what the weather is going to be.

Cumulus (KYOOM yuh lus) **clouds** are thick white clouds with puffy tops and flat bottoms. Small cumulus clouds mean good weather.

See Also

Water Moves Around Earth
pages 162–163

Water Cycle
pages 164–165

Precipitation
page 192

> Cumulus clouds are white and puffy.

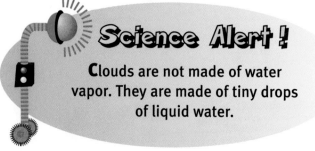

Science Alert !

Clouds are not made of water vapor. They are made of tiny drops of liquid water.

SCI LINKS.
N S T A
Keyword: Clouds
www.scilinks.org
Code: GSS23075

Stratus (STRAT us) **clouds** are flat and layered. They can cover the whole sky. Thin stratus clouds up high in the sky mean cloudy, dry weather. Heavy stratus clouds down low in the sky mean light rain.

∧ Stratus clouds are flat, gray, and layered.

Cirrus (SEER us) **clouds** are high, thin, wispy clouds. They mean dry, clear weather. Cirrus clouds are so high in the sky that they are made of ice, not liquid water.

∧ Cirrus clouds are high and feathery.

Many clouds are like two or more different kinds of clouds. Cumulonimbus (KYOOM yuh loh NIM bus) clouds are large, heavy, and dark gray. They mean stormy weather is coming.

∧ Cumulonimbus clouds are called thunderheads. They bring thunderstorms.

Seasons and Weather

See Also

Adaptations Help Organisms Survive
pages 134–135

What Causes the Seasons
pages 218–219

Weather is always changing. But, changes in weather follow the same patterns every year. These patterns follow the seasons. A **season** is a time of year. Each season has a weather pattern. There are four seasons—winter, spring, summer, and fall. The seasons always follow this order.

The temperature of the air changes with the season. Winter is the coldest season. Then the air begins to warm up as spring comes. Summer is the warmest season. In fall, the air temperature falls.

Winter

Spring

Summer

Fall

Animals can also change as seasons change. Some animals grow thick fur to keep them warm in cold winters.

∧ Some trees change in different seasons.

Seasons are not the same everywhere. In some places, the seasons are very different from one another. Winter in New York is much colder than summer in New York. It snows a lot there in winter. In other places the seasons are more alike. Winter in Florida is only a little cooler than summer in Florida. You can still swim there in winter, and there is no snow.

∧ Winter in New York is cold.   ∧ Winter in Florida is warm.

Some places have a season when it rains a lot. This is called the rainy season. In another season it is very dry. Other places have about the same amount of rain in all four seasons.

The number of daylight hours also changes with the seasons. Winter has the fewest hours of daylight. It gets dark early. Nighttime lasts longer than daytime in winter. In spring, there are more hours of daylight. Summer has the longest days.

See Also

What Causes Day and Night pages 216–217

Climate

See Also

Weather
pages 189–195

Imagine you wanted to visit a warm place during winter. You probably would not want to visit Alaska. Alaska has a cold climate. **Climate** (KLY mit) is the general weather conditions in an area over a long period of time.

Climate is different from weather. If you say "Tomorrow it will snow in Alaska," you are talking about weather. If you say "It snows a lot in winter in Alaska," you are talking about the climate.

Climate has to do with the temperature and precipitation over many months. It is cold for many months each year in Alaska. It snows or rains on many days during the year. Alaska has a cold, wet climate.

The Hawaiian Islands have a warm, wet climate. It rains often. The temperature is hardly ever cold.

∧ Alaska has a cold, wet climate. A lot of snow falls.

∧ Plants grow quickly in Hawaii's warm, wet climate.

Climate mostly depends on how far a place is from Earth's equator. The **equator** (ih KWAY tur) is an imaginary line around Earth halfway between the North Pole and the South Pole. Places close to the equator have warm climates. Places far from the equator are cool. Because Alaska is far from the equator, it has a cold climate.

See Also

Kinds of Ecosystems
pages 130–131

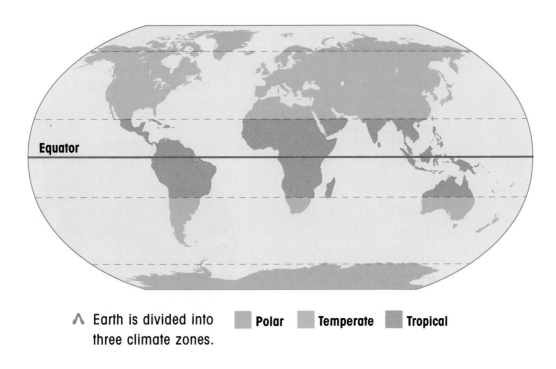

∧ Earth is divided into three climate zones.

Polar   Temperate   Tropical

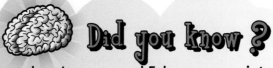

Did you know ?

December, January, and February are winter months north of the equator. These months are summer months south of the equator.

See Also

Kinds of Ecosystems
pages 130–131

Polar Climate

The areas around the North Pole and South Pole have a polar climate. A **polar climate** has cold winters and cool summers. Much of the area around the poles is tundra. In the tundra, the ground stays frozen all year. Very few plants grow there.

∧ Areas around the poles have a long cold winter and a short cool summer.

Tropical Climate

Places that are near the equator have a tropical (TRAHP ih kul) climate. A **tropical climate** is very warm and wet for most of the year. Many rainforests are in tropical climates. Lots of different kinds of plants and animals live there.

∧ A tropical rainforest is wet and hot almost all year.

Word Watch

The North and South Poles were named for imaginary poles. These poles are the ends of the imaginary line that passes from top to bottom of Earth.

Temperate Climate

Areas between the tropical zone and the polar zone have a temperate climate. A **temperate climate** has cold or cool winters and hot or warm summers. Most of the United States has a temperate climate. A temperate climate can have very different seasons. You can easily tell the difference between winter and summer in many places.

Places with temperate climates may be dry or wet. A desert has a dry temperate climate. It rains very little in a desert. The Mojave Desert in California is warm and dry. Wetlands have wet temperate climates. The Everglades in Florida are wetlands. The ground is wet almost all year long there.

Climate also depends on how high the land is. High areas are colder than low areas. Mountains have colder climates at the top than at the bottom.

∧ Forest trees in some temperate climates lose their leaves for winter.

∧ The same trees have leaves during the summer.

Space

You live on Earth. Earth might seem like the biggest and most important object there is. In fact, Earth is only a tiny place in space. **Space** is the area in all directions beyond Earth.

You might think that the word *space* means something empty. A parking space is empty until a car parks there. Empty spaces separate words in a book to make the words easier to read.

Space is not completely empty. Planets, moons, the sun, and stars are some of the objects found in space. Pieces of rock and ice are in space, too.

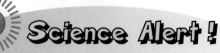

Science Alert!

There are many objects in space, but the area between them is mostly empty. There is no air in space.

You cannot always see the objects in space. During the day, the sun is too bright for you to see stars and planets. At night, clouds sometimes cover the sky and block the stars and planets. Even if you cannot see them, they are always there.

People have always watched the night skies. Some people just like to look at stars. Other people study space as a job. A scientist who studies space is called an astronomer (uh STRAHN uh mur). Astronomers study objects in space using tools such as telescopes.

Astronomers sometimes send rockets into space. These rockets carry tools that help them learn more about space.

See Also

Studying Space
pages 230–233

Studying Space
pages 230–233

SC**i**LINKS.
N S T A

Keyword: Space
www.scilinks.org
Code: GSS23080

< Since ancient times, people have been interested in the night sky.

Planets Around the Sun

See Also

The Moon
pages 220–221

Stars
pages 224–225

The Sun
pages 226–227

Earth is a planet. A **planet** is a large object in space that moves around the sun. The **sun** is the closest star to Earth. Each planet moves in its own path around the sun. A planet's path is called its **orbit** (OR bit). *Orbit* also means to move around something else. Planets orbit the sun.

There are eight planets that orbit the sun. The sun, the planets, and their moons make up our **solar system.** A **moon** is a small round body that orbits around a planet. Earth has one moon.

The planets are not really lined up on one side of the solar system. It is easier to show them that way in a picture.

∨ Eight planets move around the sun in our solar system. The solar system also has dwarf planets, moons, asteroids, and comets. Some dwarf planets are also plutoids.

Sun

Mercury

Venus

Earth

Mars

One very distant object in our solar system is Pluto (PLOO toh). Astronomers used to call Pluto a planet. Then astronomers decided that Pluto is too small to be called a planet. They now call small, round objects that orbit the sun dwarf planets. Two other dwarf planets are Ceres and Eris. Pluto and Eris are also called plutoids. A **plutoid** is a dwarf planet with an orbit beyond Neptune. Scientists expect to discover many more plutoids.

Science Alert !

The objects in this picture are not the right distances apart. They are also not the right size. The sun is really over 100 times wider than Earth. A picture with the right sizes and distances would have objects that are too small to see.

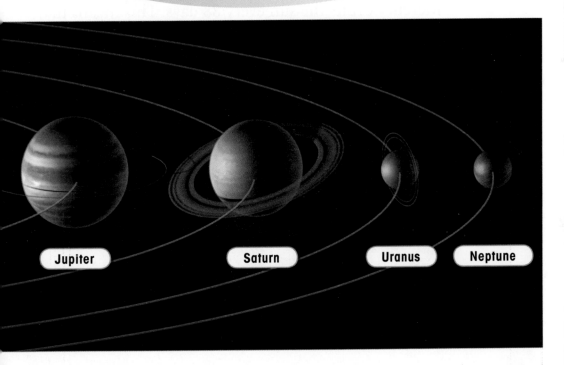

Jupiter   Saturn   Uranus   Neptune

Mercury

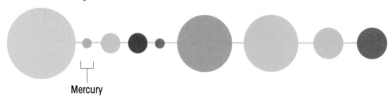

Mercury

See Also

Structure of Earth
page 159

The Moon
pages 220–221

Mercury (MUR kyuh ree) is the closest planet to the sun. It is also the smallest planet in our solar system. It has no moons. Mercury is made of rock. Like Earth, it has a crust, a mantle, and a core. Its outside looks like our moon. It has dents, flat areas, and hills.

People cannot live on Mercury. Neither can plants or animals. It is very hot during the day because it is close to the sun. At night, it gets very cold. Mercury has no air. There is no water to drink.

Mercury orbits the sun every 88 days. This means that it takes 88 days for Mercury to go completely around the sun and come back to the same place again.

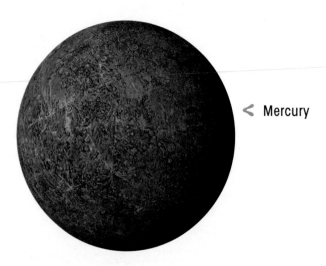

< Mercury

Venus

Venus

Venus (VEE nus) is the second planet from the sun. It is about the same size as Earth, but it has no moon. Venus is the brightest object in the sky except for the sun and our moon. It looks like a very bright star in the sky. Ancient people noticed Venus because it was so bright. They saw it in the sky just after sunset.

Venus is covered by thick clouds. The clouds trap heat and make Venus very hot. Venus is the hottest planet. You could not live on Venus. There is no air or water. There are many volcanoes and plains. It is covered with rocks and ash.

See Also

Landforms
pages 166–167

Volcanoes
page 173

∧ Venus would look like this without its clouds.

It takes Venus about 225 days to orbit the sun.

Keyword: Space
www.scilinks.org
Code: GSS23080

Earth

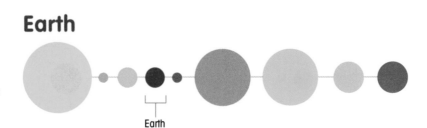

Earth

Earth is the third closest planet to the sun. You live on Earth. It is the only planet in our solar system where scientists have found living things. Plants and animals need air, water, and the right temperature to live. The blanket of air around Earth keeps the temperature from getting too hot or too cold for living things. There is air and liquid water for living things to use.

∧ Earth has air, water, and food for living things.

Earth has a thin crust, a thick mantle, and a core. The crust is made of solid rock. The mantle is made of hot soft rock. The core is very hot metal. Some of the metal is melted. The metal at the very center is solid.

Earth has one moon. The moon orbits Earth while Earth orbits the sun. It takes Earth about 365 days to orbit the sun. One complete trip around the sun equals one year on Earth.

About three-fourths of Earth's surface is covered by water. Mountains, valleys, plateaus, deserts, and forests cover the rest of Earth's surface. The areas near the two poles are frozen and look white from space. White wispy clouds swirl around Earth.

See Also

Water on Earth
page 160

Landforms
pages 166–167

How Earth Moves in Space
page 215

What Causes the Seasons
pages 218–219

∧ Earth

When astronauts looked at Earth from space, they thought it looked like a big blue marble.

Mars

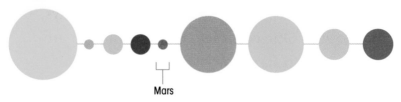

Mars

See Also

Landforms
pages 166–167

Volcanoes
page 173

How Earth
Moves in Space
page 215

Mars (mahrz) is the fourth planet from the sun. It is much smaller than Earth. The surface of Mars is covered with red rocks and rusty red soil. This is why Mars is called the Red Planet. It has canyons, high mountains, valleys, and volcanoes. Ice covers the North and South Poles.

Mars has two tiny moons. It takes Mars and its moons about 687 days to orbit the sun. This means that a year on Mars is almost twice as long as a year on Earth.

> Mars

Did you know?

Some scientists think that liquid water and life may exist on Mars. Scientists have not found these things yet, but they are still looking.

Jupiter

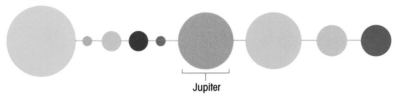

Jupiter

Jupiter (JOO pih tur) is the fifth planet from the sun. It is cold and dark because it is far away from the sun. One trip around the sun takes almost 12 years.

Jupiter is much larger than the other planets. It does not have solid ground because it is made of gas. If you look at Jupiter through a telescope, you can see a very large red area called the Great Red Spot. Astronomers think the Great Red Spot is a giant storm. Jupiter has very pale rings. The rings are made of dust. Most telescopes cannot show Jupiter's rings.

Jupiter has more than 60 moons. Four are large, but most are very small.

Great Red Spot

∧ Jupiter

Saturn

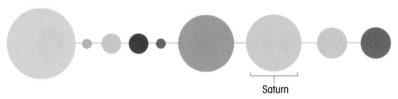

Saturn

Saturn (SAT urn) is the sixth planet from the sun. It is a large planet, but it is not as large as Jupiter. Saturn is cold and dark. It takes almost 30 years for Saturn to orbit the sun. Saturn has more than 50 moons.

When you look at Saturn through a telescope, the first thing you see is its beautiful bright rings. Other planets have rings, but Saturn's rings are the largest and brightest. The rings are made of ice, dust, and rocks. You may also see that Saturn has pale stripes.

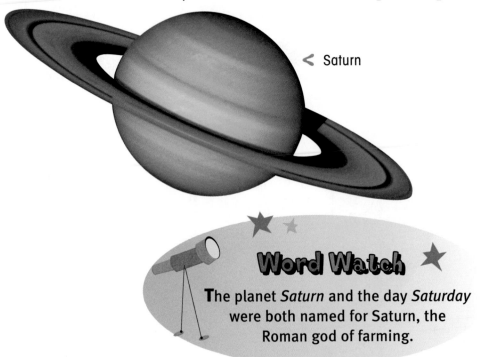

< Saturn

Word Watch

The planet *Saturn* and the day *Saturday* were both named for Saturn, the Roman god of farming.

Uranus

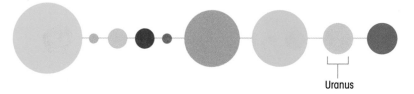

Uranus

Uranus (YUR uh nus) is the seventh planet from the sun. Because it is so far away from the sun, it is dark and very cold. Uranus takes 84 years to orbit the sun.

Uranus is a large planet made of frozen gases. It has pale stripes and pale rings that are hard to see even with a telescope. Uranus has a blue-green color.

All planets spin, or rotate. Most planets spin with their North Pole on top and their South Pole at the bottom. Uranus is different from all other planets. It spins on its side.

∧ Uranus

Did you know?

Scientists have discovered 27 moons of Uranus. Five are large. The rest are very small.

Keyword: Space
www.scilinks.org
Code: GSS23080

Neptune

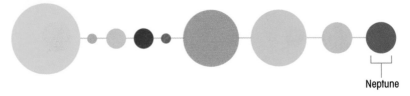

Neptune

Neptune (NEP toon) is the eighth planet from the sun. It is made of frozen gases. Neptune is cold and dark because it is so far from the sun. Its orbit around the sun takes almost 165 years. Neptune has 13 moons.

Astronomers do not know very much about Neptune because it is so far away. It looks blue when you look at it with a powerful telescope. Even with a telescope, it is hard to see what the planet looks like.

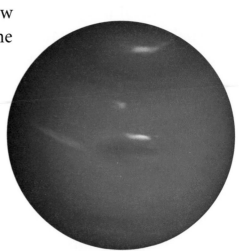

∧ Neptune

Did you know?

Astronomers used to see a Great Dark Spot on Neptune's surface. In 1994, it disappeared. Scientists do not know what it was or where it went.

How Earth Moves in Space

Earth moves two different ways in space. Like other planets, Earth revolves. To **revolve** means to move in a path around the sun. The path an object takes around another object in space is its **orbit.** It takes one year for Earth to revolve around the sun. One year is 365 days.

See Also

What Causes Day and Night pages 216–217

What Causes the Seasons pages 218–219

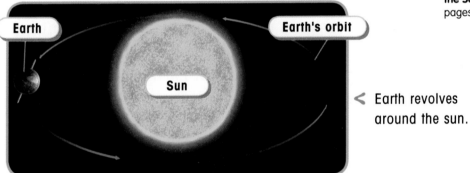

Earth

Earth's orbit

Sun

< Earth revolves around the sun.

While Earth orbits the sun, it also rotates. To **rotate** (ROH tayt) means to spin. Imagine that someone poked a rod through Earth from the North Pole to the South Pole. This rod is called an **axis** (AK sis). Earth rotates on its axis. One rotation takes Earth 24 hours.

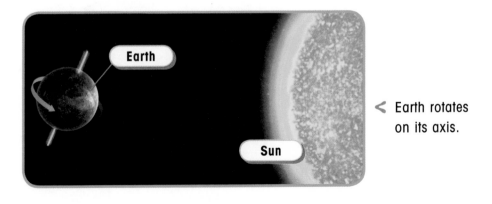

Earth

Sun

< Earth rotates on its axis.

What Causes Day and Night

See Also

How Earth Moves in Space
page 215

Imagine that it is morning. You are on the playground at school. The side of Earth where you live faces the sun. The sun lights this part of Earth. The other side of Earth faces away from the sun. It is dark there because the sun is not lighting that part of Earth now.

The sun seems to move across the sky as the day goes on. In fact, the sun does not really move. Different parts of Earth begin to face the sun as Earth rotates. Night begins when the part of Earth where you live has rotated away from the sun.

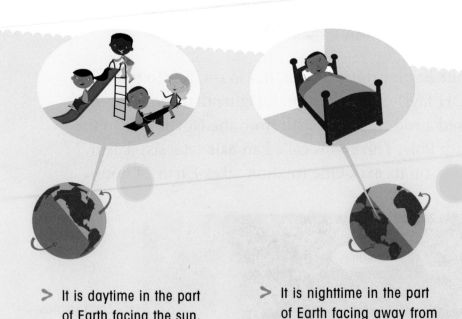

> It is daytime in the part of Earth facing the sun.

> It is nighttime in the part of Earth facing away from the sun.

Earth makes one complete rotation, or turn, every 24 hours. During a turn, the sun appears to rise in the east and set in the west. One turn is called a day.

∧ The sun appears to move across the sky during the day.

The length of daytime changes through the year. In summer, there are more hours of sunlight per day. In winter, there are fewer. No matter how many hours of sunlight, there are always 24 hours in a day.

See Also

Seasons and Weather
pages 196–197

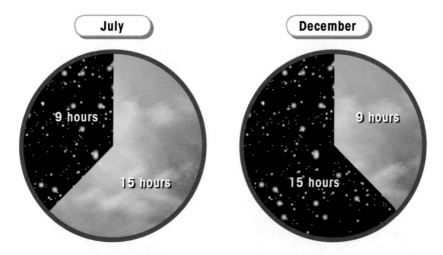

∧ Numbers of hours of daylight and nighttime in Minnesota in July and December

What Causes the Seasons

See Also

Climate
pages 198–199

How Earth Moves in Space
page 215

Earth's imaginary axis does not point straight up and down. The axis is tilted. The tilt of the axis is important. It explains why we have seasons.

As Earth moves around the sun, the axis at the North Pole sometimes points more toward the sun. The north end of Earth leans toward the sun. It gets more direct light from the sun. There are more hours of daylight and fewer hours of darkness. The land and water warm up. It is summer north of the equator.

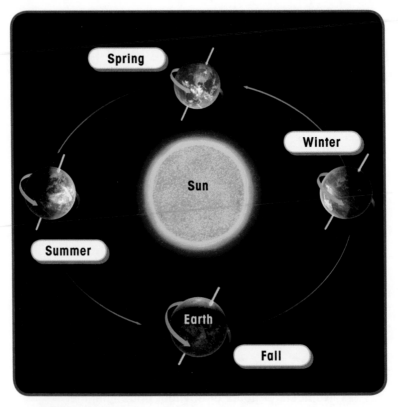

∧ Seasons north of the equator.

During another part of the year, the axis at the North Pole points more away from the sun. The north end of Earth leans away from the sun. It gets less direct light from the sun. There are more hours of darkness and fewer hours of daylight. The land and water cool down. It is winter north of the equator.

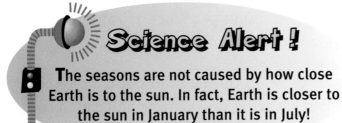

Science Alert !

The seasons are not caused by how close Earth is to the sun. In fact, Earth is closer to the sun in January than it is in July!

In spring and fall, Earth's axis is not tilted toward the sun or away from the sun. Day and night are about the same length during those seasons. It is not as hot as summer. It is not as cold as winter.

Did you know ?

Seasons are opposite north and south of the equator. We are used to winter starting in December and summer starting in June. Australia is south of the equator. In Australia, winter starts in June and summer starts in December.

Keyword: Space
www.scilinks.org
Code: GSS23080

The Moon

See Also

Landforms
pages 166–167

Slow Changes to Earth's Surface
pages 168–171

Earth's moon is a large ball of rock. It is only one-fourth the size of Earth. The moon's surface has tall mountains and flat plains. It is covered with rocks and craters. A **crater** (KRAY tur) is a round dent with high sides. A crater is formed when an object from space hits the surface of a moon or planet. If you drop a ball into a sandbox, a crater forms in the sand.

There is no air or water on the moon. It is much hotter than Earth during the daytime and much colder than Earth at night. Nothing can live there.

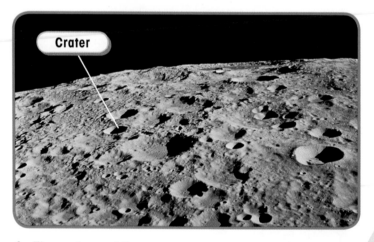

Crater

∧ The surface of the moon is covered with rocks, craters, and dust.

Astronauts first walked on the moon in 1969. They left footprints in the dust on the moon's surface. The footprints will not wear away because there is no water or wind on the moon. Those footprints are still there!

The moon is the closest object in space to Earth. It is a satellite of Earth. A **satellite** (SAT l yt) is any object that orbits a planet. It takes one month for the moon to make one complete orbit around Earth.

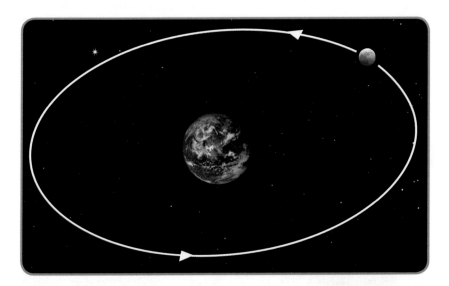

See Also

How Earth Moves in Space
page 215

Bouncing Light
page 268

The moon is very bright in the sky, but the moon does not make its own light. In fact, the light you see comes from the sun. Sunlight reflects off the moon. To **reflect** means to bounce off. The moon looks bright on the side of the moon facing the sun. The reflected light makes it bright. The moon looks dark on the side facing away from the sun.

The moon seems to move across the sky, just as the sun does. Like the sun, it rises in the east and sets in the west.

The Moon Seems to Change Shape

See Also

The Moon
pages 220–221

The moon's shape looks different from night to night. The shape you see looks different every night of a month. The different shapes are called the moon's **phases** (FAYZ iz). It takes about 28 days to see all of the moon's phases. After 28 days they start over again.

Why does the moon seem to change shape? Remember that the sun shines on only half the moon. We do not see the half that is not lit.

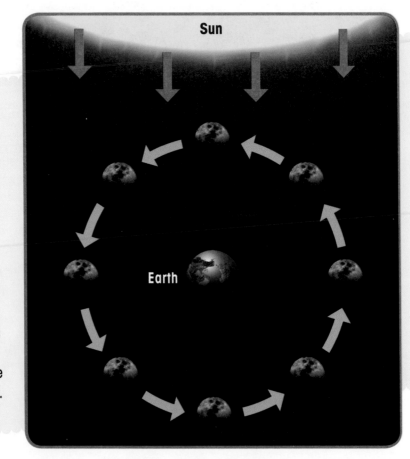

> Only one side of the moon is lit up. The lit side is the side facing the sun.

As the moon moves around Earth, we see different amounts of its sunlit side. The moon's phases are the parts we can see.

New Moon
The moon is between Earth and the sun. You cannot see any of the moon's sunlit side.

Growing Crescent
You can see only a thin sliver of the moon. The part that you can see is growing larger.

Shrinking Crescent
You can see only a thin sliver of the moon. The part that you can see is getting smaller.

First Quarter
You can see about half of the moon's sunlit side.

Last Quarter
You can still see about half of the moon's sunlit side.

The part of the moon that you can see keeps growing larger.

The part of the moon that you can see is getting smaller.

Full Moon
Earth is between the moon and the sun. All of the moon's sunlit side is facing Earth.

∧ The photos show how each moon phase looks from Earth.

Stars

See Also

What Causes Day and Night
pages 216–217

The Sun
pages 226–227

You can see millions of tiny lights in the sky on a clear night. Each dot of light is a star. A **star** is a big ball of hot gases that gives off light. Stars look tiny because they are very far away. The sun is a star. It is the closest star to Earth, so it looks bigger than other stars.

Stars are different sizes. White dwarf stars are about the same size as Earth. The sun is a medium-sized star. Supergiant stars may be millions of kilometers wide.

Stars are not spread evenly through space. They often appear in groups.

⋀ There are more stars in the sky than anyone can count.

Stars are always in the sky but you do not see them in daytime. Light from the sun is so bright it blocks out other stars. It is dark at night, so you can see the other stars. They seem to move across the sky during the night. However, it is really Earth that is moving.

Some stars are very bright. Stars may appear bright because they are closer to Earth. They also may appear bright because they are bigger or hotter than other stars.

Stars are different colors. Blue stars and white stars are hottest. Red stars are coolest, but even red stars are very hot.

Earth's atmosphere makes stars seem to twinkle. Stars do not twinkle for astronauts who see them through a spaceship window.

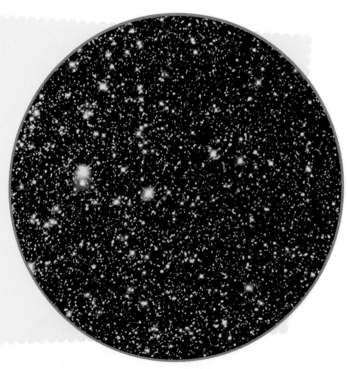

Science Alert !

Stars do not usually look different colors to your eyes. You have to look at them with a special tool to see the colors.

See Also

Constellations
pages 228–229

The Sun

See Also

Planets Around the Sun
pages 204–214

What Causes Day and Night
pages 216–217

The **sun** is the star at the center of our solar system. It is the largest and brightest object in the day sky. The sun looks small because it is so far away. The sun is about 150 million kilometers (about 93 million miles) away from Earth. Even though it is far away, it is the closest star to Earth. All the other stars are much farther away than the sun is.

As Earth rotates, the sun seems to move across the sky. However, it is really Earth that is moving.

The sun is only a medium-sized star, but it is much larger than Earth. If the sun were hollow, it would take more than one million Earths to fill it up!

∧ The sun is a yellow star that is the center of our solar system.

Like all stars, the sun is made of hot gases. The gases give off energy as heat and light. Energy from the sun warms Earth. It keeps living things warm. Light from the sun helps people and animals to see. Plants need light to make their food.

Not all of the sun's energy is good for people. You can get a bad sunburn if you stay in the sun too long. Too much sun can make you get sick.

See Also

What Do Plants Need?
pages 86–87

What Do Animals Need?
page 99

Producers
page 148

You should always wear a hat and sunscreen when you are outside in the hot sun. A hat will keep you cool. Sunscreen will keep you from getting sunburned.

∧ Plants could not make food if the sun did not shine on Earth.

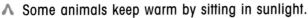
∧ Some animals keep warm by sitting in sunlight.

Constellations

See Also

Stars
pages 224–225

Long ago, people looked at the stars and thought they made pictures. A **constellation** (kahn stuh LAY shun) is a group of stars that looks like it forms a picture in the sky. People named the groups of stars. They named them for their heroes. They named them for animals and other things. A bear, a lion, and a dog all are constellations.

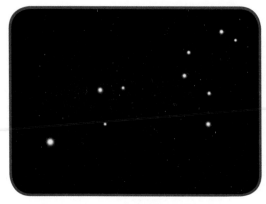

∧ These stars form the constellation Leo, the lion. Can you find a lion in these stars?

∧ Leo is a constellation that looks like a lion. The star in its chest is one of the brightest stars in the sky.

Different people see different pictures in the same group of stars. For example, some people think one group of stars forms a picture of a scoop, or a dipper. They call this constellation the Big Dipper. Other people call the same constellation the Big Bear. They think it looks like a bear.

Some constellations can be seen only at certain times of the year. That's because Earth is orbiting the sun. As Earth moves to different sides of the sun, different constellations are in the night sky.

Constellations also look as if they move across the sky through the night. That's because Earth rotates, or spins. The position of a constellation in the night sky can change. The stars that make it up stay the same.

Constellations can help you find other stars in the sky. Find the two stars that form the front of the Big Dipper. They point to a star in the Little Dipper. This star is Polaris, or the North Star. Polaris is always seen above the North Pole. Ancient sailors used Polaris to find north. They used the star to steer their ships.

See Also

What Causes Day and Night pages 216–217

What Causes the Seasons pages 218–219

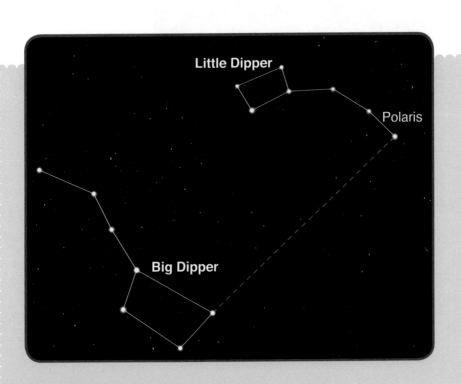

Little Dipper

Polaris

Big Dipper

Studying Space

Objects in space are so far away that they are hard to see. Scientists can use tools to study them from Earth. They can also go a short distance into space and study them while in orbit.

Telescopes

See Also

Light Energy
pages 266–270

One of the most helpful tools that astronomers use is a **telescope.** A telescope is a tool that makes far-away objects look larger and clearer. When you make an object look larger, you **magnify** it. You can see many more stars with a telescope than you can without one.

< A telescope can help you see things that are very far away.

Some telescopes use lenses. Lenses are curved pieces of glass that catch light and magnify objects. These kinds of telescopes work like a pair of eyeglasses. Other telescopes use a curved mirror and lenses. The mirror catches light. The lenses magnify.

Some telescopes stay on Earth. Others go into space where they have a better view. The **Hubble Space Telescope** is in space. It orbits Earth and takes pictures of things in space.

See Also

Bouncing Light
page 268

Bending Light
page 269

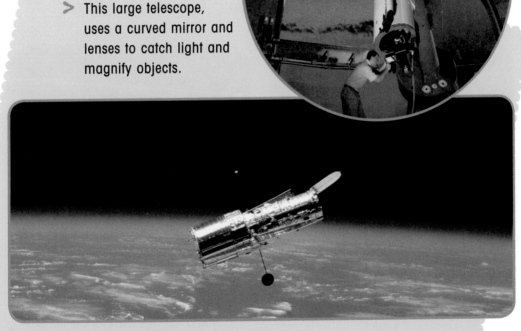

> This large telescope, uses a curved mirror and lenses to catch light and magnify objects.

∧ The Hubble Space Telescope stays above the clouds, so they never block its view.

See Also

Mars
page 210

Jupiter
page 211

Saturn
page 212

Space Probes

Scientists cannot visit other planets. They are too far away. Instead, scientists send space probes to study planets. A **space probe** is a craft that carries tools but not people. Space probes do not return to Earth. They send back information about the places they visit.

Some space probes fly past a planet. They take pictures of the planet for scientists to study.

Other probes go into orbit around a planet. They collect data about the planet's weather. They measure the temperature of the planet. They take pictures of the planet's surface.

Space probes called rovers actually land on a planet. They collect rocks and soil. They look for water.

∧ The *Voyager* space probes flew by Saturn and Jupiter. They sent data back to scientists on Earth. The data told scientists about the rings of Saturn and Jupiter.

∧ Two rovers landed on Mars in 2004. They found clues that there was once liquid water on Mars.

Space Shuttle

The **space shuttle** carries astronauts into orbit around Earth. It also brings them back. There is air, water, and food in the space shuttle. If an astronaut goes outside of the shuttle, he or she must wear a space suit. It carries air so he or she can breathe. It keeps the astronaut warm.

While in orbit, astronauts do experiments. They fix satellites that have broken parts. They launch new satellites into orbit. When the astronauts are ready to come home, the space shuttle leaves its orbit. It glides back to Earth.

∧ The Space Shuttle is launched into space.

 Did you know?

Sixteen countries are working together to build an International Space Station that will orbit Earth. It should be finished in 2010. Scientists will be able to live and work in the station for long periods of time.

See Also

What Do Animals Need? page 99

Physical Science

I hope I win!

Why do you go faster down a hill? How do brakes help you slow down? A person who studies physical science can answer these questions. **Physical** (FIZ ih kul) **science** is the study of matter, forces, motion, and energy.

Matter

Take a look around you. Everything you see is made of matter. **Matter** (MAT ur) is anything that takes up space. You are made of matter. Your chair is made of matter. So is your desk and your pencil.

∧ Objects like your desk and pencil are made of matter.

Even very small things are made of matter. Sand grains are very small but they take up space. So do tiny dust particles. Dust particles are so small that they can float in air. They are still made of matter.

See Also

Measuring Matter
pages 242–243

Word Watch

The word *matter* has other meanings. Something that is important *matters*. Have you ever asked a friend what's wrong? You might have said "What's the *matter*?"

Keyword: Matter
www.scilinks.org
Code: GSS23085

Is water matter? Well, it takes up space. So yes it is! The water in the ocean takes up space on Earth. Water also takes up space inside a drinking glass. Water even takes up space inside your body. Most of the matter in your body is water.

Even things too small to see are made of matter. You can't see air, but air is matter too. Breathe in deeply. Feel the air going into your lungs. You can use the air in your lungs to blow up a balloon. The air takes up space inside the balloon. So, the balloon gets bigger.

∧ Water is matter, too.

< Air is matter. It takes up space inside a balloon.

See Also

Wind
page 193

Physical Properties

How would you describe an apple? You might say that an apple is red, or that it is round. "Red" and "round" are physical properties of the apple. **Physical properties** (FIZ ih kul PRAH pur teez) are characteristics that you can observe. Color and shape are two physical properties of matter.

You use your senses to observe physical properties. You can see the shape and color of a leaf. You can feel the texture of a rock. You can taste the flavor of an apple. You can sniff a flower to see how it smells.

See Also

Bouncing Light page 268

You can also see how matter acts. Some objects float in water. Other objects sink. Some objects are shiny. Others are dull.

∧ A metal spoon and a wooden block have different properties. A metal spoon is shiny. A wooden block is dull.

Matter can be sorted by its properties. Have you ever sorted your dirty clothes? You sort the clothes by their color. Light colors go in one pile, dark colors in another.

The properties of an object or material make it useful for certain tasks. Suppose you cannot reach something in a tall cupboard. You can use a wooden step stool. Wood is strong. But it would not be safe to step on an empty box. Cardboard is not strong enough to hold you up.

∧ You sort clothes by their properties.

Even sounds can help you sort matter. Tap a plastic pen on your desk. Then, tap a wooden pencil. They make different sounds.

∧ The properties of a wooden stool make it good for standing on.

See Also

Sound Energy
page 260

Observing Matter

One way you observe matter is with your eyes. When you look at a T-shirt, you can see its color and shape. You can see how big it is.

All matter is made up of smaller parts. T-shirts are made of cotton cloth. The cloth is made of cotton thread. The thread is made of very small pieces of cotton. These pieces of cotton are made of even smaller parts. These parts are too small to see without tools.

All matter is made of tiny particles called **atoms** (AT umz). There are more than 100 types of atoms! Atoms are very tiny. You can see them only with very powerful microscopes.

T-shirt

Cotton cloth

Cotton thread

Cotton fibers

You can use tools to magnify objects. To **magnify** (MAG nuh fy) means to make look bigger. A **hand lens** is a tool used to make objects look bigger. Fleas are very small animals that sometimes live on pets. You can see what a flea looks like through a hand lens.

See Also

Using a Hand Lens
page 51

∧ Using a hand lens

Some things are too small to see even with a hand lens. A **microscope** (MY kruh skohp) is a tool used to make objects look even bigger. A flea looks bigger through a microscope than through a hand lens.

Keyword: Matter
www.scilinks.org
Code: GSS23085

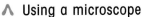

∧ Using a microscope

Measuring Matter

You can use tools to measure many physical properties of matter. Do you know how tall you are? **Height** is a measure of how tall something is. You can measure height with a ruler or meter stick.

See Also

Measuring Length
page 54

Measuring Liquids
page 58

You can also use a ruler or meter stick to measure the length and width of an object. **Length** is a measure of how long the object is. **Width** is a measure of how wide the object is.

You use a ruler to find the volume of a box.

Volume (VAHL yoom) is the amount of space matter takes up. You multiply an object's length, width, and height to find its volume.

You cannot find the volume of liquids with a ruler. You must use a measuring cup.

∧ You use a measuring cup to find the volume of a liquid.

Mass is the amount of matter in an object. You have less mass than your teacher. Your teacher has much less mass than an elephant. An elephant has a lot of mass. Mass is measured using a balance.

See Also

Using a Balance
page 62

Gravity and Motion
page 284

∧ You use a balance to measure mass.

Weight (WAYT) is a measure of how hard gravity pulls on an object. Weight depends on how much mass an object has. Your teacher has more mass than you do. So, your teacher weighs more than you do. Weight is measured with a scale.

∧ You use a scale to measure weight.

Weight and mass are not the same. Weight depends on gravity. Mass does not. There is less gravity on the moon than on Earth. You would weigh less there. But your mass is the same on Earth and on the moon.

Physical Changes

See Also

Physical Properties
pages 238–239

A **physical change** (FIZ ih kul CHANYJ) is a change in a physical property of matter.

You break food into smaller pieces when you chew. Breaking something into smaller pieces is a physical change. Chewing changes the size and shape of the food. Chewing does not change the food into a different kind of matter.

Cutting and tearing are physical changes. They change the size and shape of objects. When you cut paper, you change the size and shape of the paper. It's still paper when you are done.

Sanding is also a physical change. You change the smoothness of wood when you sand it. Sanding does not change the wood into a different material. You still have wood.

∧ Chewing, cutting, and sanding all cause physical changes in matter.

States of Matter

Matter can be in three different states, or forms. The three **states of matter** are solid, liquid, and gas. Water is a liquid. Ice is a solid. Water vapor is a gas. Water, ice, and water vapor are all the same kind of matter.

A **solid** keeps its shape and volume. An ice cube does not change shape when you put it into a glass. It is still shaped like an ice cube. Its volume does not change either. It takes up the same space.

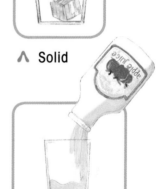

∧ Solid

A **liquid** (LIK wid) can change shape, but it always keeps the same volume. Pour a bottle of juice into a glass. The juice takes the shape of the glass. It does not take up more room than it did in the bottle.

A **gas** changes its shape and its volume. The tiny particles of gas spread out and fill any space. Water vapor is part of the air around you, but you cannot see it.

∧ Liquid

∧ Gas

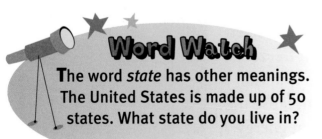

Word Watch

The word *state* has other meanings. The United States is made up of 50 states. What state do you live in?

Changing States

See Also

Heat Energy page 276

Matter can change state when heat energy is either added to it or taken away from it.

When matter **melts,** it changes from a solid to a liquid. Solids can melt when heat energy is added. A fruit pop will melt when you take it out of the freezer. That's because heat energy from the room is added to the frozen pop.

∧ Melting

 Science Alert !

A plastic ice cube tray would not melt if you took it out of the freezer. It is a solid at room temperature. It *would* melt if you added enough heat energy to it.

When matter **freezes,** it changes from a liquid to a solid. Liquids can freeze when heat energy is taken away. Water will freeze when you leave it in the freezer. That's because the freezer takes heat energy away from the water.

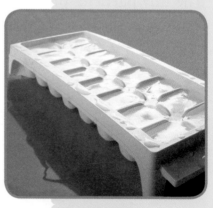

∧ Freezing

When matter **evaporates** (ih VAP uh raytz), it changes from a liquid to a gas. Liquids can evaporate when heat energy is added. Water left in a cup on the table will evaporate in a few days. Water will also **boil** when you put it on the stove burner. Boiling is evaporating that happens very fast.

∧ Boiling

When matter **condenses** (kahn DENTS iz), it changes from a gas to a liquid. Gases can condense when heat energy is taken away. You might notice that your car windows fog up when you ride on a chilly morning. That's because your breath is full of water vapor. The cold window glass takes heat energy away from the water vapor. So, tiny drops of liquid water form on your window.

See Also

Water Cycle
pages 164–165

∧ Condensing

Chemical Properties

See Also

Heat Energy
page 276

Have you ever seen rust on a bicycle or a metal gate? Only some kinds of metals rust. Wood cannot rust. Neither can plastic. The ability to rust is a chemical property of some kinds of metals. **Chemical properties** (KEM ih kul PRAH pur teez) describe how matter can react with other kinds of matter.

> The ability to rust is a chemical property.

The ability to burn is a chemical property of wood. Have you ever sat by a campfire? The wood logs burn bright. Most metals cannot burn.

Chemical properties are harder to observe than physical properties. How do you know if a metal gate will rust? You have to wait to see if the metal gets rusty.

∧ The ability to burn is a chemical property.

Chemical Changes

A **chemical change** (KEM ih kul CHANYJ) happens when one kind of matter changes into another kind of matter. The new kind of matter has different chemical properties.

See Also

Forms of Energy
pages 256–257

Burning is a chemical change. When wood burns, it reacts with gases in the air. New kinds of matter are made. Ash is one kind of matter that is made. The properties of ash are not the same as the properties of wood. Wood has the ability to burn. Ash cannot burn.

∧ Burning is a chemical change.

Some chemical changes are useful. We use chemical changes to cook our food. When an egg is cooked, the clear part becomes white. The yellow part gets harder. The egg is ready to eat!

Burning is another useful chemical change. Some people use wood-burning stoves to heat their homes. Cars burn gasoline to get the energy they need to move.

∧ Cooking is a chemical change.

Mixtures

A **substance** (SUB stunts) is a single kind of matter. Water is a substance. It is made of one kind of matter.

Most of the matter around you is made of a mixture of substances. A **mixture** (MIKS chur) is a combination of two or more substances. The substances in a mixture each keep their own properties.

See Also

Physical Properties pages 238–239

Chemical Properties page 248

This table shows some kinds of common mixtures.

∧ A salad is a mixture of vegetables. The lettuce in the salad has the same properties it had before it was mixed into the salad. So do the carrots and the radishes.

Common Mixtures	
Granola	solids and solids
Mud	solids and liquid
Soapy water	solid and liquid
Orange juice	solids and liquids
Clouds	liquid and gases

Keyword: Matter
www.scilinks.org
Code: GSS23085

Solutions

A **solution** (suh LOO shun) is a kind of mixture. The substances in a solution are spread out evenly in every part of the mixture. You cannot see the separate substances.

Word Watch

The word *solution* has other meanings. When you solve a problem, you find the answer, or the *solution*.

Salt water is a solution. Salt dissolves when you add it to water. To **dissolve** (dih ZAHLV) means to mix evenly into a mixture. The salt seems to disappear when it dissolves. The salt particles are still there. They are just too small to see. Salt water tastes salty. So, you know the salt particles are there.

∧ Salt water is a solution.

This table shows some kinds of common solutions.

Common Solutions	
Salt water	solid in liquid
Sugar water	solid in liquid
Soft drinks	gas in liquid
Air	gases in gases
Vinegar	liquids in liquids

Not all substances dissolve in water. Sand will not dissolve in water.

Separating Mixtures

See Also

Physical Properties
pages 238–239

You can use physical properties to separate the parts of a mixture. You know what olives look like. If you do not like the taste of olives, you can pick them off of your pizza.

You can use a strainer to separate some mixtures. Strainers have small holes. Small particles and liquids go through the holes in the strainer. Bigger pieces stay in the strainer. Straining can separate mixtures of solids like pebbles and sand. It can also separate mixtures of solids and liquids.

< A strainer separates a mixture of cooked pasta and hot water.

See Also

Magnets
pages 298–299

Magnetic Objects
pages 300–301

You can use magnets to separate mixtures that contain iron. The iron parts stick to the magnet.

> A magnet separates a mixture of iron nails and sawdust.

You can also use water to separate some mixtures. Suppose you have a mixture of salt and sand. How do you separate the sand from the salt?

See Also

Solutions
page 251

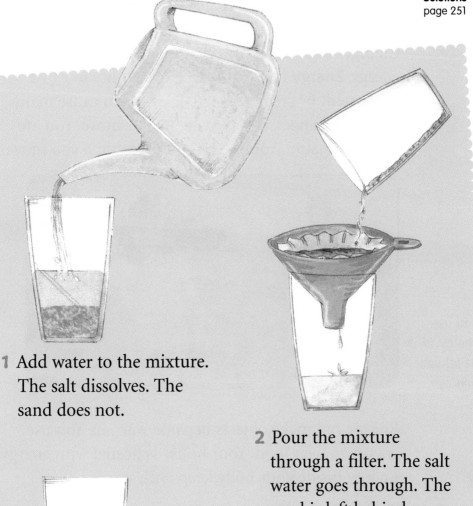

1 Add water to the mixture. The salt dissolves. The sand does not.

2 Pour the mixture through a filter. The salt water goes through. The sand is left behind.

3 Let the water evaporate. The salt is left behind.

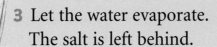

∧ How to separate a mixture of sand and salt

Energy

Changes happen all the time. All changes involve energy. **Energy** (EHN ur jee) is the ability to cause movement or create change. Energy can cause many kinds of changes. It can make matter move. You are made of matter. You use energy every time you move.

> You use energy to pedal your bike.

Energy can make objects become warmer. You use energy to heat food. Your house is heated with energy. Energy inside your body keeps you warm.

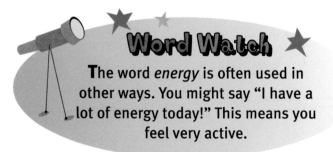

Word Watch

The word *energy* is often used in other ways. You might say "I have a lot of energy today!" This means you feel very active.

Energy can cause matter to change states. You add heat energy to make solids change to liquids. Adding heat energy to ice can make it melt. Melting ice changes from a solid to a liquid.

∧ An ice cube melts when you add heat energy to it.

See Also

Matter
pages 236–237

Changing States
pages 246–247

Chemical Changes
page 249

Heat Energy
pages 276–279

Energy can also cause chemical changes. You add energy to food when you cook it. Cooked food looks and tastes different than raw food. Matter in the food changes into new kinds of matter when you cook it.

< The matter in bread changes when you toast it.

Forms of Energy

There are many forms of energy.

Form	Examples
Chemical energy	The energy stored in food, fuel, and batteries
Energy of motion	A car moving, a person walking, a ball bouncing
Electrical energy	Electricity used by microwave ovens, computers, and music players
Heat energy	Heat from sunlight, a campfire, the stove
Light energy	Light from the sun and light bulbs
Sound energy	The sound of a radio, a honking horn, a dog's bark

Keyword: Energy
www.scilinks.org
Code: GSS23090

Energy Changes

Energy can change from one form to another. Your body changes the chemical energy in food into the energy of motion. Cars change chemical energy into the energy of motion, too.

Keyword: Energy
www.scilinks.org
Code: GSS23090

∧ Cars change the chemical energy in gasoline into the energy of motion.

Lamps change electrical energy into light energy. So do flashlights. Solar-powered calculators change light energy into electrical energy.

Energy is never made or lost. It just changes from one form to another.

∧ Batteries store chemical energy. Energy leaves a battery as electrical energy. Flashlights change the electrical energy into light energy.

Electrical energy changes into sound energy when you ring a doorbell. Sound energy changes into electrical energy when you talk on the phone. The energy of motion changes into sound energy when you clap your hands.

Objects can have stored energy because of where they are. A skateboarder at the top of a ramp has stored energy. As the skateboarder goes down the ramp, the stored energy changes into the energy of motion.

∧ Stored energy

∧ Energy of motion

Did you know?

The energy of motion can change back into stored energy. Suppose the skateboarder goes back up the ramp. As she goes up, her energy of motion changes back to stored energy.

Sound Energy

Have you ever heard the sound of a cat purring? **Sound energy** is energy you can hear. Sound energy is made when matter vibrates. To **vibrate** (VY brayt) means to move back and forth quickly. You can feel a cat vibrate when it purrs loudly.

All sound is made by matter that is vibrating. The vibrations move the air around the vibrating object. This makes waves in the air. **Sound waves** carry sound energy through the air. The sound waves travel to your ears and you hear the sound.

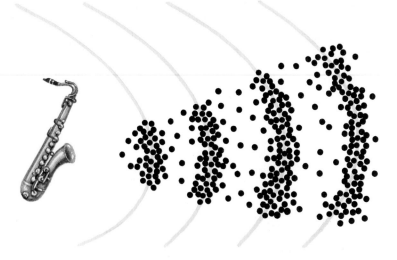

∧ As sound waves move through the air, particles of air bunch together and then spread apart.

Sound Moves through Matter

Sound waves travel through air. A radio makes sound waves that travel through the air to your ears. You hear the music.

∧ Sound travels through gases.

Sound can also travel through liquids. Have you ever tried to talk to a friend under water? It can be hard to understand the words, but you hear the sound. Sound moves through water in waves, just as it moves through air.

∧ Sound travels through liquids.

Sound also travels through solids. Have you ever heard noise coming from another room when you are trying to sleep? The sound waves travel through the walls of your room.

∧ Sound travels through solids.

Did you know?

Sound waves travel at different speeds in different materials. They travel fastest through solids. They travel slowest through gases.

High Sounds

Most birds make a high sound when they chirp. A chirp has a high pitch. **Pitch** is how high or low a sound is.

> Most birds make high-pitched sounds.

Sounds with a high pitch are made by objects that vibrate quickly. Smaller objects usually vibrate more quickly than larger objects. They make sound waves that are close together.

A guitar player can change the pitch by pressing down on the strings. This makes the strings shorter. Shorter strings vibrate faster and make sounds that have a higher pitch.

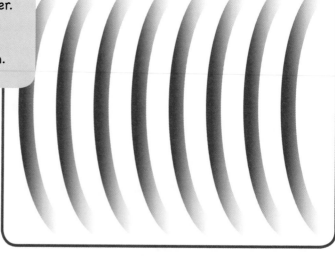

∧ High sounds have sound waves that are close together.

Low Sounds

Dogs make a low sound when they growl. A growl has a low pitch. So does the moo of a cow. Cows make low-pitched sounds.

Sounds with a low pitch are made by objects that vibrate slowly. Larger objects usually vibrate more slowly than smaller objects. They make sound waves that are far apart.

∧ Cows make low-pitched sounds.

Some sounds are too high or low for you to hear. Animals can hear them. Dogs can hear very high sounds. Elephants can hear very low sounds.

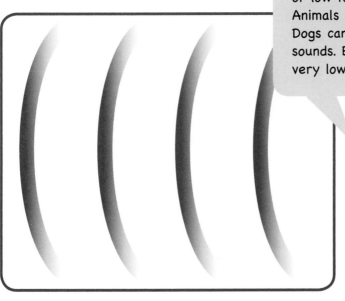

∧ Low sounds have sound waves that are far apart.

Soft Sounds

The **volume** (VAHL yoom) of a sound is how loud or soft it is. **Loudness** is another word for volume.

You make a soft sound when you whisper to a friend. A whisper has a low volume. It does not have enough energy to travel very far. That's why you have to be close to someone to hear a whisper.

∧ A whisper is a soft sound.

Soft sounds are made by objects that vibrate weakly. They make small sound waves. Soft sounds have less energy than loud sounds. Soft sounds don't usually hurt your ears.

> Soft sounds have weak vibrations.

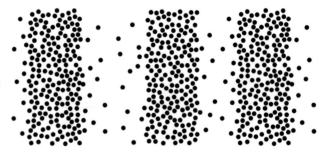

Word Watch

Volume has two meanings in science. It can describe the loudness of sound. It can also describe how much space matter takes up. You can figure out which meaning the word has by reading the sentence it is in.

Loud Sounds

You make a loud sound when you shout to a friend. A shout has a high volume. It has enough energy to travel far. That's why you can hear your friend shout from across the school yard. That's also why it hurts when someone yells in your ear!

∧ A shout is a loud sound.

Loud sounds are made by objects that vibrate strongly. They make big sound waves. Loud sounds have more energy than soft sounds. That's why they can hurt your ears.

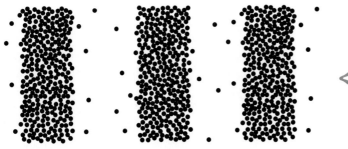

< Loud sounds have strong vibrations.

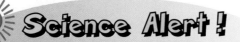

Science Alert !

Loudness is not the same as pitch. A high-pitched sound can have a low volume. A low-pitched sound can have a high volume.

Light Energy

At night, you turn on lamps so you can see in the dark. Lamps change electrical energy into light energy. **Light energy** is energy that you can see.

See Also

What Do Plants Need?
pages 86–87

The Sun
pages 226–227

The sun is another source of light energy. Light from the sun travels to Earth. You use this light to see. Light from the sun warms Earth, too. Plants use light energy to make food.

Light travels as waves. **Light waves** are waves that carry light energy. Light waves travel away from their source in all directions. They travel in straight lines. When they hit an object, you can see the object.

Light waves and sound waves are different kinds of waves. Sound waves must travel though matter. Light waves can travel through empty space.

Λ You could not see people on a stage without lights.

Shadows and Light

Light passes through a glass window. Light does not pass through most objects, though. Most objects block light. You see your shadow on a sunny day because you block light. A **shadow** is a dark spot that forms when an object blocks light.

As the sun changes position in the sky, the size and location of shadows change. Shadows are longer in the morning and evening. They are shortest at noon.

∧ Morning   ∧ Noon   ∧ Late Afternoon

Did you know?

Shadows change in a regular way. So, people can use shadows to tell time. Some of the first clocks ever made used shadows to tell time.

See Also

What Causes Day and Night pages 216–217

Bouncing Light

You can see yourself in a mirror. Mirrors reflect light waves in a certain way. To **reflect** (ree FLEKT) means to bounce off.

Mirrors have very smooth surfaces. So do shiny metal objects. Light waves bounce off of a smooth surface in the same pattern they hit it. So you can see yourself in the surface.

Most objects do not have a very smooth surface. Light waves bounce off of them in lots of directions. You can see the objects, but you cannot see yourself in them.

∧ A mirror has a very smooth surface. You can see yourself in a mirror.

∧ A wall does not have a very smooth surface. You can't see yourself in a wall.

Bending Light

Light waves pass through air and water. Sometimes the light waves bend, or **refract** (ree FRAKT), as they move from one material to another.

Objects can look different when light refracts. A straw in a glass of water seems broken, but it is not. Light bends when it passes from air to water. This makes the straw look broken.

< The straw looks broken because light refracts when it moves from air to water.

Eyeglasses bend light to help people see better. A hand lens bends light to make objects look bigger than they really are. Eyeglasses and hand lenses are made out of curved glass or plastic.

< A hand lens makes objects seem bigger.

See Also

Using a Hand Lens
page 51

Observing Matter
pages 240–241

Light and Color

Light is made up of every color in the rainbow. When light hits an object, some of the colors are absorbed. To **absorb** (ab ZORB) means to take in. Other colors are reflected, or bounced back. The reflected colors bounce back to your eyes. You see only the reflected colors.

See Also

Bouncing Light
page 268

∧ Yellow flowers reflect yellow light. Green leaves reflect green light.

Dark colors absorb more energy from sunlight than light colors do. That's why light-colored clothes are good for summer days. They will make you feel cooler in the sun.

∧ Dark colors absorb a lot of energy. That's why you feel hot when you wear a black T-shirt in the summer.

Electrical Energy

Matter is made up of very tiny parts. These parts are called **particles** (PAHR tih kulz). Some of these particles have a positive charge. Others have a negative charge. **Electrical** (ih LEK trih kul) **energy** is the energy of charged particles.

You may have heard that "opposites attract." This is true for charged particles. Negative particles move towards positive particles. **Electrical current** is the flow, or movement, of charged particles. The power in most homes comes from electrical current, or **electricity** (ih lek TRIS ih tee).

Remember, electrical energy is not heat energy. A toaster changes electrical energy into heat energy.

Keyword:
Electricity
www.scilinks.org
Code: GSS23095

∧ Toasters need electricity to work.

Electrical Circuits

Electrical current flows through metal wires. The path that electrical current takes is called an **electrical circuit** (SUR kit). Your house is full of electrical circuits. Each one is used to turn on something different.

You need three things to make an electrical circuit. You need metal wires, a source of electrical energy, and something to turn on.

Source of electrical energy

Metal wires

Something to turn on

∧ Things you need to make an electrical circuit

Electrical current will not flow through an open circuit. An **open circuit** is a circuit that has an opening in its path.

< An open circuit is not a complete loop. Electrical current cannot flow.

A **closed circuit** is a circuit that has a complete path. Electrical current will flow through a closed circuit.

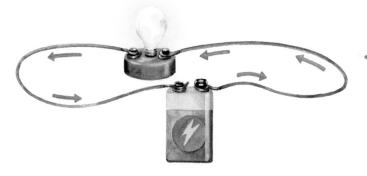

< A closed circuit is a complete loop. Electrical current can flow.

Word Watch

When a door is open, you can move through it. When a door is closed, you cannot move through it. Electricity is the opposite! Electrical current cannot go through an open circuit. But it can go through a closed circuit.

Keyword:
Electricity
www.scilinks.org
Code: GSS23095

Electricity at Home

See Also

Energy Changes
pages 258–259

Energy Resources
page 316

Electricity is produced at power plants. Power plants use other forms of energy to make electricity. The electricity is sent to your home over power lines.

Most appliances in your home plug into an electrical outlet in the wall. You use switches to turn them on and off. When you flip the switch on, you close the circuit. The appliance turns on. When you flip the switch off, you open the circuit. The appliance turns off.

> Wall switches open and close circuits.

In your home, electricity is changed into other kinds of energy. Televisions and computers change electricity into light and sound energy. Some clocks light up. They change electrical energy into light energy.

< Computers change electricity into light and sound energy.

Radios change electricity into sound energy. A microwave oven beeps when it is done heating food. It changes electricity into sound energy.

Some room heaters change electricity into heat energy. So do toasters, electric stove burners, and some ovens. Most clothes dryers change electricity into heat energy and the energy of motion.

∧ Clothes dryers change electricity into heat energy and the energy of motion.

Most appliances change electricity into more than one kind of energy.

Heat Energy

The particles in matter are always moving. Moving particles have energy. **Heat energy** is the energy of moving particles.

Particles with more heat energy move faster. So the particles in warmer objects move faster. Warm objects have more heat energy than cool objects.

> The particles in hot cocoa move faster than the particles in chocolate milk. Hot cocoa has more heat energy than chocolate milk.

Heat energy moves from warmer things to colder things. Heat energy moves until both things are equally warm.

Keyword: Energy
www.scilinks.org
Code: GSS23090

> Your mouth feels warm when you drink hot cocoa. The cocoa is warmer than your mouth. So heat energy moves from the cocoa to your mouth.

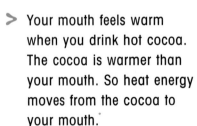

Measuring Temperature

Chilled juice is cold, but not as cold as a snowball. **Temperature** (TEM pur uh chur) describes how hot or cold something is. Warmer matter has more heat energy than colder matter. So it has a higher temperature.

You measure temperature with a **thermometer** (thur MAHM ih tur). Temperature is measured in degrees Celsius (SEL see us) or degrees Fahrenheit (FAR un hyt).

There are many kinds of thermometers. Some are used to measure the temperature of the air. Others are used to measure body temperature.

∧ Thermometers measure temperature in degrees Celsius (°C) or degrees Fahrenheit (°F).

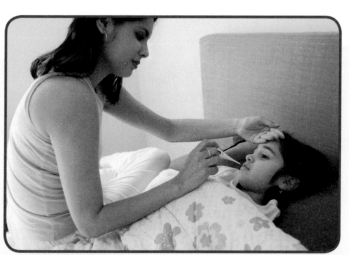

∧ Your body temperature is normally between 97 and 99°F (36–38°C). Your temperature goes up when you have a fever.

See Also

Matter
pages 236–237

Using a
Thermometer
pages 52–53

Producing Heat

Heat energy is produced from other kinds of energy. Most kinds of energy can change into heat energy.

∧ Chemical energy changes into heat energy when wood burns.

∧ Energy of motion changes into heat energy when you rub your hands together.

See Also

Energy Changes pages 258–259

Friction and Motion page 285

∧ Electrical stoves change electrical energy into heat energy.

∧ Light energy from the sun changes into heat energy when it hits Earth.

Using Heat

People use heat energy in many ways. Food is cooked with heat energy. Homes and cars are warmed with heat energy. Clothes dryers use heat energy to dry laundry. Hair dryers use heat energy to dry wet hair. The water in your home is heated so that you don't have to take a cold shower or bath!

∧ Heat energy is used to warm water.

Heat energy is used in many factories. It is used to melt metals in metal factories. The metal might be used to make car parts or cans. Heat energy is also used to melt glass and plastic. The glass or plastic can then be made into bottles.

∧ Heat energy is used to melt glass.

Word Watch

People often use the word *heat* as a verb. When you *heat* water, you make it warmer by adding heat energy to it.

See Also

Changing States
pages 246–247

Motion and Forces

Lay a pencil in the center of your desk. How can you get the pencil to move? You could push it. You could pick it up. You could blow on it. Any of these would move the pencil. To make something move, you have to use a force. A **force** (FAWRS) is a push or a pull.

SCi LINKS.
N S T A
Keyword: Forces
and Motion
www.scilinks.org
Code: GSS23100

You use force every time you move an object. A pull brings an object closer to you. You pull out your desk chair before you sit down. You pull on your bike when you pick it up off the ground.

A push moves an object away from you. You push a shopping cart. You can push with your feet, too. You push a ball when you kick it.

∧ You pull on objects when you pick them up.

∧ You push on objects when you kick them.

What Is Motion?

An object's **position** (pu ZI shun) is its location, or where it is. You can describe position by comparing one object's location with another. Your pillow is *on* your bed. Your clock is *next to* your bed.

This table shows words that describe position.

Position Words	
Above or **Over**	**Next to** or **Beside**
Below or **Under**	**Between** or **In between**
On or **On top of**	**To the right of** or **To the left of**

Motion (MOH shun) is a change in position. You are in motion when you walk across the street. You move from one side of the street to the other side. You change your position.

Objects can move in many ways. They can move forwards or backwards. They can move up or down. They can move in a straight line or in a circle.

< Your position changes as you cross the street. You are in motion.

Forces Cause Motion

See Also

Motion and Forces
page 280

Friction and Motion
page 285

Forces can make objects move in different ways. A force can make an object start moving. A ball starts moving when you throw it. Forces can also stop a moving object. A ball stops moving when you catch it.

Forces can make objects slow down. Brakes slow down your bike. They apply a force to the wheels.

Force can make objects go faster, too. Suppose you are riding a scooter. You push it and it goes faster.

∧ Forces can make objects go faster or slower.

Forces can make objects change paths. You kick a rolling soccer ball to change its path. How do you turn your bike? You use force on your handlebars.

Force is needed to change an object's motion. Without a force, moving objects keep moving in the same way.

∧ Forces can make objects change paths.

Suppose you want to throw a ball really far. You have to throw it hard. So you use more force. Large forces move objects farther than small forces. They also make objects move faster.

Larger forces are needed to move heavier objects. You use a large force to pick up a big stack of books. A small force will not move them.

< You must use a large force to lift a heavy stack of books.

∧ A ball goes farther when you use more force. It also moves faster.

Gravity and Motion

See Also

Measuring Matter
pages 242–243

Motion and Forces
page 280

Suppose you are holding an apple. Then you let go of it. The apple falls to the ground. You did not push or pull the apple. Gravity made the apple move.

Gravity (GRAV ih tee) is a force that pulls objects toward each other. The pull between objects and Earth is very strong. That's because Earth has a lot of mass.

All objects will fall to the ground unless another force holds them up. That's why an apple falls when you drop it.

∧ You push up on an apple when you hold it. So the apple does not fall.

∧ Gravity pulls the apple to the ground when you let go of it.

Friction and Motion

Friction (FRIK shun) is a force that slows objects down. It is produced when objects rub together. The rougher the objects are, the more friction there is between them.

The road rubs against your bike tires. This slows down your bike. You must pedal your bike to keep it moving. Friction can be helpful, too. Brakes use friction to stop your bike.

You can skate on ice. There is not much friction between your skates and the smooth ice. That's why you can glide easily across the ice. But ice skates won't work on pavement. Pavement is rough. There would be too much friction.

∧ There is very little friction between ice skates and smooth ice.

Friction produces heat energy. When you rub your hands together, they get warmer.

See Also

Forces Cause Motion
pages 282–283

Producing Heat
page 278

Measuring Motion

See Also

What Is
Motion?
page 281

You can describe motion in several ways. You can describe what direction an object is moving. You can measure how far an object goes. You can measure how long it takes to get from one place to another. You can also measure how fast an object goes.

Direction

The path a moving object follows is its **direction** (di REK shun). You can describe an object's direction by saying that it is turning right or left. You can say it is moving east or west, or north or south. You can say an object is moving up or down.

See Also

How to Read
a Map
pages 382–383

∧ This car is turning left. It is moving south.

Distance

How far can you run? **Distance** (DIS tuns) is a measure of how far an object moves. You compare where an object started with where it stopped. This tells you the distance it moved.

See Also

Measuring Length
page 54

< This person ran a distance of 100 meters.

Measuring distance is like measuring length. You can measure distance with a measuring tape or a meter stick. It is measured in centimeters or meters.

You can describe big distances as "long" or "far." You can describe small distances as "short" or "near."

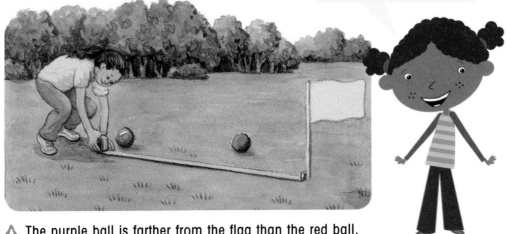

∧ The purple ball is farther from the flag than the red ball.

Time

How long does it take you to walk to the grocery store? **Time** is a measure of how long it takes an object to go a distance. To find the time, you need to know when an object started and stopped moving. You compare these two times.

4:15 PM   5:15 PM

∧ It took one hour to walk to the store.

Time is measured with a watch or a stopwatch. Usually, a stopwatch is used for races. Shorter times are measured in seconds and minutes. Longer times are measured in minutes and hours.

See Also

Using a Stopwatch
page 67

∧ People can run some races in just a few seconds.

Speed

Speed is a measure of how fast an object is moving. To find speed, you need to know how far an object went. You also need to know how much time it took to get there. Then you compare the distance with the time.

∧ A fast horse can run about 18 meters in 1 second.

Faster objects can go a certain distance in less time. The person who runs the fastest in a race finishes in the shortest amount of time. Slower objects take more time to go a certain distance.

< Biking is faster than walking.

 Did you know?

In the United States, car speeds are measured in miles per hour. Say a car has a speed of 30 miles per hour. That means the car travels 30 miles in one hour.

See Also

Distance
page 287

Time
page 288

Simple Machines

See Also

Motion and Forces
page 280

In science, **work** means using a force to move an object. You do work when you rake leaves. You use a force on the rake when you pull it. The rake moves. So you have done work.

You do work when you pick up an object. You pull the object up. The object moves.

Keyword: Simple Machines
www.scilinks.org
Code: GSS23105

You do work when you push a chair in. You do not do work if the chair does not move when you push on it.

∧ You do work when you rake leaves.

∧ You do work only when an object moves.

Word Watch

We use the word *work* in other ways, too. Adults go to work. This means they go to their jobs. Your chores are work. Chores are tasks you have to do.

A **simple machine** is a tool that makes work easier. A hammer and a screwdriver are simple machines. So is a door knob. You use a force on a simple machine. The tool pushes or pulls an object. The object moves.

Some simple machines let you use less force to do the same work. Other simple machines change the direction of a force. You push down and the machine pushes up.

∧ You use force to turn a door knob. The door knob moves the door latch.

< A hammer helps you do work. It would be hard to push a nail into wood with your thumb. You need less force to move the nail when you use a hammer.

See
Also

Motion and
Forces
page 280

Lever

You can probably bat a ball farther than you can throw it. The bat makes it easier to move the ball. A bat is a simple machine called a lever. A **lever** (LEV ur) is a bar that moves around a fixed point. *Fixed* means stays in one place.

A crowbar is a lever. It is used to pull out nails. You use a small force to push the handle. The claw uses a large force to pull the nail. So the nail comes out more easily.

∧ You use a small force on the bat. The bat uses a large force on the ball.

Crowbars also change the direction of a force. You push down on the crowbar. The crowbar pulls up on the nail.

Fixed point

< A crowbar is a lever.

Wheel and Axle

A door knob is a wheel and axle. A **wheel and axle** (AK suhl) is a wheel stuck to a rod. The rod is the axle.

Turning the wheel makes the axle turn. A screwdriver is a wheel and axle. The handle is the wheel part. You turn the handle. The axle turns the screw.

∧ You use a small force on the handle. The axle uses a large force on the screw.

A pencil sharpener is a wheel and axle. The part you turn is the wheel. You use a small force to turn it. This makes a large force at the axle.

∧ A pencil sharpener is a wheel and axle.

Pulley

Some simple machines help you lift objects. A **pulley** (PUL ee) is a rope that goes around a wheel. You attach an object to one end of the rope. You pull on the other end. The pulley lifts the object into the air.

Pulleys do not reduce the force you use. They change the direction of the force. You pull down on the rope. The pulley lifts the object up. This can be useful if you are raising a flag up a tall pole.

See Also

Motion and Forces
page 280

SC**LINKS**
N S T A

Keyword: Simple Machines
www.scilinks.org
Code: GSS23105

∧ This man uses a pulley to lift a bucket of water out of a deep well.

∧ You pull down on the rope. The flag goes up the pole.

Ramp

You might not be able to lift a heavy box, but you could probably push it up a ramp. A **ramp** is a slanted surface. Ramps are used to move heavy objects to a higher or lower place. A ramp is also sometimes called an **inclined plane** (IN klynd PLAYN).

See Also

Forces Cause Motion
pages 282–283

∧ Ramps are used to move heavy objects up into buildings.

You need to use a large force to lift a heavy object. You use less force when you push the object up a ramp, but you have to push it a longer distance.

Remember, simple machines make work easier. But you still do the same amount of work.

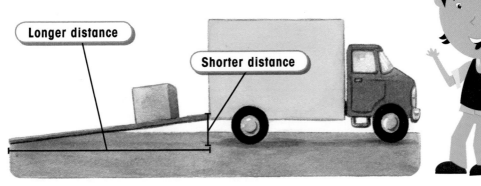

Longer distance

Shorter distance

∧ Ramps are longer than they are high.

Wedge

See Also

Motion and Forces
page 280

Ramp
page 295

Splitting wood without an ax would be hard. An ax is a simple machine called a wedge. A **wedge** is made of two inclined planes. The planes are stuck together. A wedge has a pointed end and a wide end.

A wedge lets you use less force to do work. You apply a small force to the wide end of the wedge. This makes a large force at the pointed end. The large force pushes outward. This is how an ax splits wood.

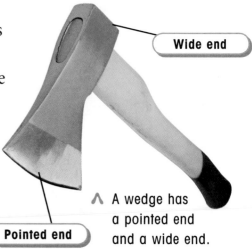

Wide end

Pointed end

∧ A wedge has a pointed end and a wide end.

∧ An ax is used to split wood.

Screw

Screws are used to hold boards together. A **screw** is a rod with an inclined plane wrapped around it. The inclined plane makes the threads of the screw. A screw uses an inclined plane to make work easier.

See Also

Ramp
page 295

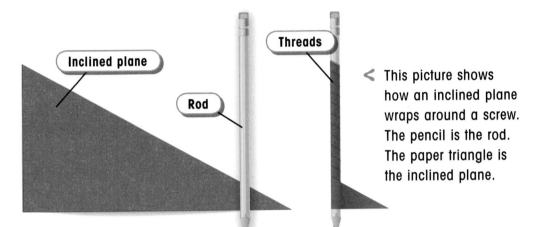

< This picture shows how an inclined plane wraps around a screw. The pencil is the rod. The paper triangle is the inclined plane.

You use a screwdriver to drive a screw into wood. It takes a small force to turn the screw. This makes a strong force at the screw tip. A screw moves into wood easily, but you have to turn the screw many times.

> A screw is easy to drive into wood.

Magnets

Your refrigerator door probably has magnets stuck to the front. Magnets hold pictures and artwork to the metal door. A **magnet** is an object that pulls on some metal objects. The magnet sticks to these objects.

∧ Magnets stick to a refrigerator door. The door is made of metal.

There are many kinds of magnets. Some magnets are shaped like bars. Others are shaped like rings or horseshoes. Magnets come in many sizes.

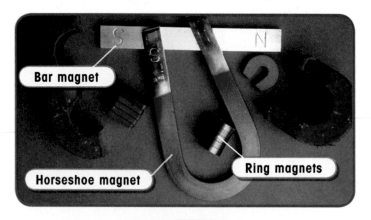

Bar magnet

Horseshoe magnet

Ring magnets

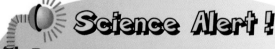

Science Alert !

Big magnets are not always stronger than small magnets. Some small magnets are very strong.

The pull between an object and a magnet is a force. This force is called **magnetism** (MAG ni tiz um).

Magnets can pull on objects even if they are not touching. The magnets have to be close to the objects for this to happen. Magnetism is weaker when objects are farther away from the magnet.

Magnets can work through materials such as paper, plastic, and glass. They can even work through water.

∧ The magnet is too far from the metal door. The pull is weak, so the magnet will not stick.

< Magnets can pull on the metal door through paper.

A magnet might work through a few pieces of paper, but it won't work through a whole book. A book is thick. The magnet is too far away from the metal.

See Also

Motion and Forces page 280

Magnetic Objects

Magnets pull on **magnetic** (mag NET ik) objects. Nails and paper clips are magnetic objects. So are safety pins and scissors.

Most magnetic objects have iron in them. Iron is a kind of metal. Magnets pull on iron. They also pull on nickel, another kind of metal.

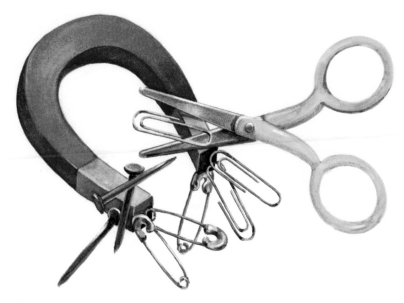

∧ Magnetic objects will stick to magnets.

Did you know?

Earth's core is made of iron and nickel. That helps Earth act like a giant magnet!

Magnets do not pull on all metal objects. Some metal objects are nonmagnetic. **Nonmagnetic** (NON mag net ik) objects are not pulled by magnets.

Paper and plastic are nonmagnetic. So are wood and glass. Magnets will not stick to a wooden table or a glass window.

∧ Nonmagnetic objects will not stick to magnets.

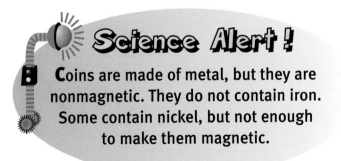

Science Alert !

Coins are made of metal, but they are nonmagnetic. They do not contain iron. Some contain nickel, but not enough to make them magnetic.

Poles of a Magnet

All magnets have two poles. A **pole** is a place on a magnet where magnetism is the strongest.

∧ The poles of a bar magnet are at the ends. The force of magnetism is strongest there. That's why paper clips stick to the ends of a bar magnet.

The poles are usually on opposite sides of a magnet. One pole is called the north pole. The **north pole** is labeled *N.* The other pole is called the south pole. The **south pole** is labeled *S.*

South pole

North pole

∧ Magnets have a north pole and a south pole. The north pole of a bar magnet is at one end. The south pole is at the other end.

The poles of a ring magnet are on the flat sides. One side is the north pole. The other side is the south pole.

Magnets can push or pull on other magnets. One magnet pushes on another magnet if the two north poles face each other. They do the same if the two south poles face each other. North poles repel other north poles. **Repel** (ri PEL) means to push away. South poles repel other south poles.

See Also

Motion and Forces
page 280

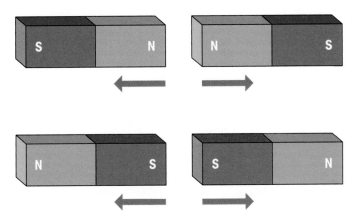

∧ Poles that are alike push away from each other.

A magnet pulls on another magnet if a north pole faces a south pole. North poles and south poles attract each other. **Attract** (uh TRAKT) means to pull together.

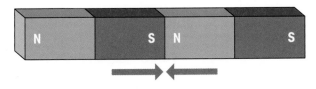

∧ Unlike poles pull together.

Keyword:
Magnets
www.scilinks.org
Code: GSS23110

Magnetic Fields

A magnet can pull or push objects that are in its magnetic field. A **magnetic field** is the space around a magnet where the force of magnetism acts. You cannot see a magnetic field.

The magnetic field is strongest near a magnet's poles. It is weaker farther away from the poles. It is also weaker farther away from the magnet.

See Also

Polar Climate
page 200

Poles of a Magnet
pages 302–303

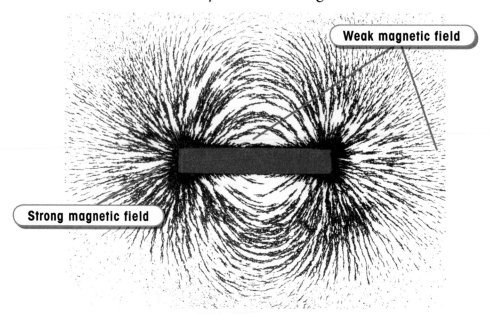

Weak magnetic field

Strong magnetic field

∧ This picture shows the magnetic field of a bar magnet. The tiny bits of iron line up to show the field.

Did you know?

Earth is a giant magnet. It has a magnetic north pole and a magnetic south pole. It also has a magnetic field. Earth's north pole pulls a magnetic compass needle. The needle points to Earth's magnetic pole.

SC LINKS.
NSTA

Keyword: Magnets
www.scilinks.org
Code: GSS23110

How People Use Magnets

Many objects you use every day contain magnets. Can openers use magnets to hold the lids of cans. Refrigerator doors have magnets in them. The magnets help the doors stay shut.

Bank cards have magnetic strips on the back. The magnetic strips store information. Computers have magnets inside, too.

You can use a compass to help find your way. A compass needle is a magnet. The needle points toward Earth's magnetic north pole. So you know which way is north! You also know which way is south, east, and west.

See Also

Poles of a Magnet
pages 302–303

Natural Resources and the Environment

I know we have to protect our natural resources... but this is crazy!

Materials in nature that people can use
are called **natural resources.** Air, water, soil,
and trees are some of Earth's natural resources.
These resources are found in the **environment.**
We must protect natural resources so they
are not damaged, wasted, or used up.

Earth's Natural Resources

See Also

What Do Plants Need?
pages 86–87

What Do Animals Need?
page 99

Wood
page 320

Water on Earth
page 160

All organisms need air, water, shelter, and food to live. They get these things from natural resources in their environment.

People use many kinds of natural resources. They use soil to grow food. They use water to cook food and wash clothes. They use wood from trees to build furniture and houses.

Nature can replace many of the natural resources that people use. New trees can grow where trees were cut down. Rain water can replace water that people use. A natural resource that nature can replace is called a **renewable resource.**

∧ Trees are a renewable resource.

Keyword: Natural Resources
www.scilinks.org
Code: GSS23115

Word Watch
Renewable means "able to be made new again." Trees are renewable because new ones can grow.

Not all of Earth's natural resources are renewable. Cars, ships, and tall buildings are made of iron. Iron is a metal from Earth's crust. Iron will be gone forever once people use it up. People can reuse iron, but they cannot get more. What about coal and oil? It takes millions of years for coal and oil to form. People use coal and oil much faster than that. Coal and oil cannot be reused.

See Also

Structure of Earth
page 159

Rocks and Minerals
pages 312–313

Oil
page 318

Coal
page 319

Reuse
page 336

People change their environment when they use natural resources.

∧ People dig coal out of Earth's crust. Coal is a nonrenewable resource.

Iron, coal, and oil are nonrenewable (nahn rih NOO uh bul) resources. A **nonrenewable resource** is a natural resource that nature cannot replace fast enough for people to use again.

Material Resources

See Also

Plants
page 85

Material resources are materials in nature that people use to make things. Plants and animals are material resources. So are rocks and minerals. Land, soil, and water are material resources, too.

Plants and Animals

Plants provide much of your food. The bread in a peanut butter and jelly sandwich comes from wheat plants. Peanut butter comes from peanuts that grow on plants. Jelly comes from the fruit that grows on trees, bushes, or vines.

The jeans and T-shirt you wear come from cotton plants. The medicine you take when you are sick might come from plants. Your pencil, paper, and books come from trees.

∧ People use plant resources to make many useful things.

Animals provide many resources for people. Milk, cheese, meat, and fish come from animals. Eggs come from chickens. Your leather shoes and belt come from the skin of cows. Wool is the hair of sheep. A wool sweater keeps you warm just as the wool kept the sheep warm.

See Also

Animals
page 98

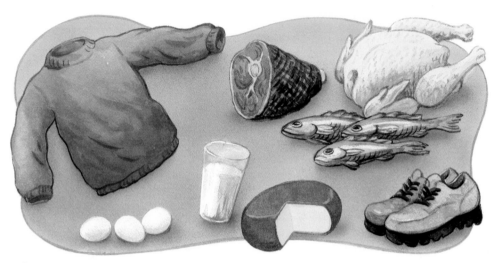

∧ People use animal resources to make food and clothes.

Plant and animal resources are renewable if people use them wisely. People can plant new trees to replace trees they cut down. Farmers can raise young animals to replace the animals that people use.

Did you know ?

People borrow ideas from animals to make useful things. Scientists studied animal eyes to make cameras that can take pictures close up or far away.

Rocks and Minerals

See Also

Minerals
page 176

Uses of Minerals
page 177

Rocks
page 178

Kinds of Rocks
pages 179–181

Rocks and minerals are material resources. People use them to make things. Concrete sidewalks are made of small pieces of rock cemented together. Clay contains ground-up rocks and minerals. People use clay to make bricks. Minerals are also used to make glass.

∧ Streets and buildings are made from rocks and minerals.

Diamonds and other gems are minerals. Rubies are red, and emeralds are green. Many diamonds have no color at all.

∧ Diamond   ∧ Ruby   ∧ Emerald

Marble and granite are rocks that people use for buildings and statues. These rocks can be carved into shapes that look like people or objects.

< The Lincoln Memorial is made of white marble.

Some rocks have valuable metals in them. Iron, silver, and copper are metals that come from rocks. People use iron in bridges and buildings. They use silver for electric switches and jewelry.

See Also

Electricity at Home
pages 274–275

> Rock with silver

∨ Silver jewelry

Rocks and minerals take millions of years to form. They are nonrenewable resources.

Land and Soil

See Also

Wind and Water
page 169

How Soil Forms
page 182

Plants and Animals
pages 310–311

People need land to live. Farmers work fields that cover large areas of land. Farms provide us with food. People build houses and other buildings on land.

Soil is another important material resource. Soil has nutrients that plants need to live and grow. People use soil to grow crops and other plants. They use these plants for food, clothing, and other things.

It is important to protect soil. One way to protect soil is to make sure it is covered. Wind can blow bare soil away. Plants cover the soil. Plant roots hold soil in place. That's why farmers often leave old plants in a field until they plant new crops.

∧ Bare soil washes away easily.

Water

Living things need fresh water to live. Most of Earth's surface is covered with ocean water. Ocean water is too salty to drink. It is too salty to use for cooking and watering plants.

See Also

Water on Earth
page 160

Water Moves Around Earth
pages 162–163

< All living things need water.

Fresh water comes from lakes, rivers, and under the ground. Water is a renewable resource because it is recycled in nature. But people sometimes use water faster than nature can recycle it. People can save water by using only what they need.

∧ You can save water by turning it off when you are not using it.

Energy Resources

See Also

Forms of Energy
pages 256–257

Electrical Energy
page 271

Producing Heat
page 278

Some natural resources provide energy. An **energy resource** is anything in nature that people can use for energy.

People use energy to keep their homes warm in winter and cool in summer. Cars and trucks use energy to move people and things from place to place. Factories use energy to run machines. The machines make things people use. People use energy to make electricity. Electricity makes the lights work in school and at home. It makes your TV, radio, and computer work.

∧ Cars and trucks use energy.

∧ Homes and offices use energy.

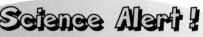

Science Alert!

All of the electricity we use is made from other energy resources. Nature does not give us electricity we can use.

Fossil Fuels

Oil, coal, and natural gas are fossil (FAHS ul) fuels.
A **fossil fuel** is an energy resource formed from dead
plants and animals. Here's how fossil fuels form.

Plants and animals die. Soil covers the dead plants and
animals. The soil pushes down and squeezes the plant
and animal remains. Fossil fuels form from the remains
after millions of years.

∧ Plants like this moss
can form fossil fuels.

∧ Moss plants die and form thick
layers of peat.

< Peat turns into coal after
millions of years if it is
left in the ground.

People use fossil fuels much faster than nature can make
them. This means that fossil fuels are nonrenewable.
Fossil fuels also give off harmful chemicals when they
burn. People use fossil fuels because they are cheaper
than many other sources of energy. They are also easy
to take out of Earth's crust.

Oil

Oil is a liquid fossil fuel. It is turned into other kinds of fuel, like **gasoline.** When a car engine burns gasoline, the car has power to move.

The gas used in gas grills comes from oil, too. So does the black material used to pave roads. Even plastic comes from oil.

Gasoline is called gas, but it is not a gas. Natural gas is a gas. So is the gas in gas grills.

∧ The heat from gas cooks your hamburgers.

< People use many things made of plastic.

Keyword: Natural Resources
www.scilinks.org
Code: GSS23115

Oil is pumped out of Earth's crust. It flows through pipes to places where it will be used. Sometimes, the oil is pumped into large ships. The ships take the oil to places that have no oil.

Natural Gas

Many stoves use natural gas. **Natural gas** is a gas found underground that is used for fuel. The gas company pumps the gas out of Earth's crust. It sends it through pipes to your home. Natural gas gives off heat and light when it burns. The heat warms your house and cooks your food.

∧ Natural gas is used in many stoves.

Coal

Coal is a black, solid fossil fuel that is burned to produce electricity. Most electricity made in the United States comes from burning coal. Miners dig the coal out of Earth's crust. Trains carry the coal to power plants all around the country. Power plants burn coal to produce electricity.

∧ Coal is used to produce electricity.

See Also

Forms of Energy
pages 256–257

Energy Changes
pages 258–259

Electrical Energy
page 271

Wood

See Also

Stems
page 90

Plants and Animals
pages 310–311

Wood is the hard stem of a tree. Wood gives off heat and light when it is burned. People have used wood as a fuel for thousands of years. Wood is renewable if people plant trees to replace the ones they cut down and burn.

∧ Wood is burned to produce heat and light.

Ethanol

See Also

Oil
page 318

Ethanol (ETH uh nawl) is a fuel made from corn. It can be mixed with gasoline and used to run cars. Corn is renewable. Gasoline comes from oil, which is nonrenewable. Using ethanol makes Earth's supply of oil last longer.

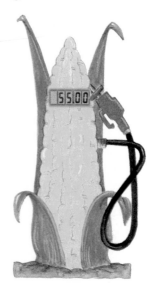

Heat from Earth

Heat that comes from inside Earth is called
geothermal (jee oh THUR mul) **energy.** In some
parts of the world the heat is very near Earth's surface.
People in these places use geothermal energy to heat
their homes and cook their food.

∧ Geothermal energy makes this water warm enough for swimming
Inside the buildings geothermal energy turns into electricity.

People also use geothermal energy to produce
electricity. Geothermal energy heats water
underground. It turns the water into steam. The
steam powers machines that produce electricity.

Geothermal energy will never run out. It is renewable.
But it is not available everywhere. Geothermal heat is
close to Earth's surface in only a few places.

See Also

Structure of Earth
page 159

Changing States
pages 246–247

Electrical Energy
page 271

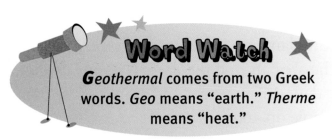

Word Watch

Geothermal comes from two Greek
words. *Geo* means "earth." *Therme*
means "heat."

See Also

Electrical Energy
page 271

Energy from Dams

Have you ever dropped a leaf into a river? The river sweeps the leaf away. The moving water in rivers has energy. This energy can be changed into electricity.

∧ Falling water has a lot of energy.

Many power plants are found near dams built across rivers. The water moves through special machines in the dams. The machines produce electricity.

∧ Dams use the energy of falling water to produce electricity.

See Also

Ecosystems
page 129

Energy from dams is renewable. But building a dam changes the area around the dam. It floods the land above the dam. Many plants and animals lose their homes. People do, too.

Energy from Wind

Moving air has energy, just as moving water does. A wind turbine (TUR byn) changes the energy of moving air into electricity. Wind blows on the blades of the turbine. The turbine changes the energy of moving air into electricity.

Wind energy is a renewable resource. It also does not pollute the environment. But some people think wind turbines are ugly and noisy. Birds can be hurt if they fly near the turbines.

See Also

Wind
page 193

**Electrical
Energy**
page 271

Pollution
page 325

Wind turbines work best in places with strong, steady winds.

∧ A group of wind turbines is called a wind farm. A wind farm may have thousands of turbines.

Energy from the Sun

See Also

Energy Changes
pages 258–259

Electrical Energy
page 271

Sunlight contains energy. Energy from the sun can never be used up. You can use it to warm a house. Solar collectors on a roof collect the sun's energy. This energy warms water in the house. The water stays warm during the day. It releases its warmth at night. The house stays warm even when the sun isn't shining.

You can also use energy from the sun to make electricity. Solar cells collect the energy from sunlight. They change the energy into electricity.

∧ Large solar collectors use the energy in sunlight to heat homes.

< Small solar cells power calculators.

Pollution

Pollution (puh LOO shun) is any harmful material that is added to the environment. Pollution can harm living things. It can also harm natural resources such as soil and water.

People often pollute the environment. Factories give off harmful gases. So do cars and planes. When people throw trash on the ground, they pollute the environment for all living things.

Nature can cause pollution, too. Ash and gases pollute the air when a volcano erupts. Living things can get sick from polluted air.

See Also

Environments and Ecosystems
page 128

Volcanoes
page 173

Fossil Fuels
page 317

Oil
page 318

∧ A volcano pollutes the air when it erupts.

Land Pollution

See Also

Environments and Ecosystems
page 128

Many things people do pollute the land. Sometimes people throw their trash on the ground. Trash that is not put in a trash can is called **litter.** Litter harms the environment.

∧ Litter

What happens to the trash you put in a trash can? It goes into a landfill. A landfill is a place to bury garbage. **Garbage** is any kind of solid waste.

Sometimes people dump poisons into the garbage. The poisons are in things like paint and batteries. The poisons leak out into the landfill. Sometimes, they leak into the environment and harm living things.

∧ Many landfills are filling up. Where will people put their garbage when the landfills are full?

Some chemicals are sprayed on crops to kill insects. The chemicals stay in the soil for a long time. They can be harmful to all kinds of living things.

See Also

Soil
page 182

∧ Planes spray chemicals that kill insects. The chemicals can pollute the environment.

Mining the ground for coal and metals can be very harmful to the environment. Mining can strip away all the plants and leave bare soil. Wind blows the bare soil away. Mining can also pollute the water near the mining area.

See Also

Coal
page 319

Rocks and Minerals
pages 312–313

Slow Changes to Earth's Surface
page 168

Did you know?

Each person in the United States makes about 4½ pounds of garbage a day.

Water Pollution

See Also

What Do Plants Need?
pages 86–87

What Do Animals Need?
page 99

Birds
pages 104–105

Slow Changes to Earth's Surface
page 168

Many plants and animals live in water. All living things need water to survive. That's why water pollution can be so harmful to living things.

Sometimes ships spill oil into the water. The oil harms fish and birds. Birds cannot fly or keep warm when their feathers have oil on them.

∧ This bird was in an oil spill.

Loose soil can pollute water in rivers and streams. It blocks sunlight from reaching plants that live in the water. Plants die because they need sunlight to make food. Fish that eat the plants for food die, too.

∧ Soil in this stream keeps sunlight from reaching water plants.

SCi LINKS.
N S T A

Keyword: The Environment
www.scilinks.org
Code: GSS23120

Plants that live in polluted water take in the chemicals. The chemicals then move through the food chain. In the 1950s, a chemical called DDT was used to kill insects that ate food crops. People did not know DDT could be harmful to other organisms. Rainwater washed the DDT into rivers and streams. Water plants took in the DDT. Fish ate the plants, and the DDT got into their bodies. Bald eagles ate the fish, and the DDT got into their bodies.

See Also

Extinct Animals
pages 116–117

Life Cycle of Birds
page 121

Food Chains
pages 152–153

∧ Chemicals move through food chains.

DDT made the eagles' eggshells very thin. The eggs broke easily. Few eagle babies hatched. Eagles almost became extinct. In 1972, a new law stopped people from using DDT. Healthy eagle chicks began to hatch again. There are many more eagles now. It is possible to clean up pollution.

Air Pollution

See Also

Fossil Fuels
page 317

Oil
page 318

Coal
page 319

Harmful materials released into the air cause air pollution. Plants do not grow well in polluted air. People have trouble breathing. Polluted air can make you cough. It can make your eyes hurt.

Most air pollution comes from burning fossil fuels. A car gives off harmful gases when it burns gasoline. Power plants give off harmful gases when they burn coal to make electricity. Tall smokestacks put the gases into the air.

∧ Cars pollute the air.

∧ Factories pollute the air.

One kind of air pollution is called smog. Smog forms when fossil fuels are burned. The harmful gases given off are trapped close to the ground.

∧ People may be warned to stay indoors when there is a lot of smog.

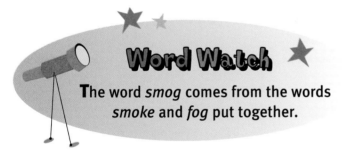

Word Watch

The word *smog* comes from the words *smoke* and *fog* put together.

Another kind of air pollution is called acid rain. Harmful gases from fossil fuels combine with water in the air to form acid rain. Acid rain harms trees and other plants. It also harms fish and other animals that live in water.

> Acid rain wears away the stone in buildings and statues.

Protecting Resources

See Also

Oil
page 318

Natural Gas
page 319

Nature gives us many natural resources. We must take care of them and protect them if we want them to last.

Conservation (kahn sur VAY shun) is the wise use of natural resources. When you conserve something, you use less of it so it lasts longer.

You can conserve energy. You can save oil by riding your bike to school instead of having someone drive you. You can wear warm clothes at home in winter. This way you need less energy to heat the house.

∧ Ride your bike to school.

∧ Turn down the heat in your house.

Fighting Pollution

We all must fight pollution if we want to conserve our natural resources. The best way to fight pollution is to prevent it. To *prevent* means to stop something from happening. You prevent litter by throwing your trash away in a trash can. You prevent water pollution by not using soap and other chemicals near a stream.

See Also

Land Pollution
pages 326–327

Water Pollution
pages 328–329

Air Pollution
pages 330–331

YES

∧ Throw trash in the trash can.

NO

∧ Don't put soapy water into streams.

Laws help prevent pollution, too. Some towns do not allow fireplaces. Smoke from the fires pollutes the air. Other laws prevent factories from dumping chemicals in rivers.

Using Less

Keyword:
Pollution
www.scilinks.org
Code: GSS23125

People need natural resources to lead comfortable, healthy lives. But sometimes people waste natural resources. We can prevent waste by using only what we need. The less we use, the more we'll have to use later.

Here are some tips for preventing waste.

1 Turn off the computer when you are done using it. This saves electricity.

2 Turn off the faucet when you brush your teeth. This saves water.

3 Turn off the lights when you leave a room. This saves electricity.

4 Close the refrigerator door as soon as you can. This saves electricity.

Reduce

When you **reduce** your use of resources, you use less of them. The fewer resources you use, the more there will be for everyone.

You can reduce how much water you use. Take shorter showers. Reduce your use of electricity. Dry clothes on a clothesline instead of using a clothes dryer. Solar energy is free!

A lot of things you buy are wrapped in paper or plastic. This wrapping ends up as trash. When you shop, look for items without extra wrapping.

See Also

Energy from the Sun
page 324

∧ Buying unwrapped fruits and vegetables reduces trash.

Reuse

When you **reuse** something, you use it again. Reusing saves resources and reduces trash.

You can reuse real dishes again and again. You just wash them, then use them again. Paper plates are not reusable. They are thrown away and end up as trash.

∧ Real dishes are reusable.

∧ Paper dishes are not reusable.

You can reuse grocery bags, too. Bring them to the store, and use them to take home more groceries. Pack your lunch in a lunchbox instead of a paper bag. You can use the lunchbox over and over again. This saves paper.

See Also

Plants and Animals
pages 310–311

Recycle

When you **recycle** something, you use it to make new things. Recycling saves natural resources.

^ This picnic table was made from recycled plastic milk bottles.

Old newspapers can be made into new, clean paper. Aluminum cans can be melted and used to make new cans. Plastic bottles can be recycled and made into new plastic objects.

The first step in recycling is sorting. Sort each material into a separate bin. Some towns pick up recycling bins at the curb. Or, you can take the materials to a recycling center.

^ Sorting materials for recycling.

See Also

Rocks and Minerals
pages 312–313

Oil
page 318

Protecting Forests

See Also

Plants and Animals
pages 310–311

Mammals
pages 102–103

Birds
pages 104–105

Arthropods
pages 114–115

People use a lot of trees. They use the wood to build houses and furniture. Paper and cardboard also come from trees. Trees are found in forests.

Many animals live in the forest. Insects live in tree bark. Birds and squirrels build nests in trees. These animals lose their homes when people cut down trees. They also lose their source of food. Squirrels and chipmunks get nuts and seeds from trees. Insects eat tree leaves.

∧ Owls nest in tree trunks.

∧ Squirrels need trees to give them food.

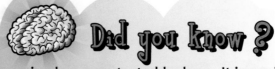
Did you know?

Many animals are protected by laws. It is against the law to hunt them. Golden eagles and whales are protected animals.

People need to protect forests so that the plants and animals that live there will be safe. A refuge (REH fyooj) is a protected area. People cannot hunt the animals that live in a refuge. People must have permission to pick flowers or plants.

Forest rangers help to protect the plants and animals that live in the refuge. Rangers look out for forest fires. They show people how to enjoy the refuge without polluting the environment.

See Also

Environments and Ecosystems
page 128

Pollution
page 325

Enjoy visiting parks and forests, but leave them exactly as you found them. Pick up your trash. Leave the plants for others to enjoy.

Audubon
National Wildlife Refuge
U.S. FISH AND WILDLIFE SERVICE
DEPARTMENT OF THE INTERIOR

Protecting Wetlands

See Also

Water on Earth
page 160

Land and Soil
page 314

A wetland is just what it sounds like. It is an area of land that has very wet soil. The soil is often covered with water.

> A swamp is a wetland with trees.

> A marsh is a wetland with grass.

People used to drain the water from wetlands. They did it to make dry land. They used the land for farming or building houses. Many plants and animals that lived in wetlands could not live on dry land. They died or moved away.

Now people know that wetlands are important natural resources. Wetlands help prevent floods. They help clean the water. The water in a wetland is rich in nutrients. Many fish, birds, snakes, and water plants live in wetlands.

See Also

Floods
page 174

> Mangrove trees live in wetlands near oceans. Fish raise their babies around mangrove roots. The babies are protected there.

< The roots of cattail plants clean the water. They remove harmful substances.

SC*LINKS*
N S T A
Keyword: The Environment
www.scilinks.org
Code: GSS23120

Today, there are strict rules about draining wetlands. There are many wetland refuges around the country.

Almanac

This Almanac has helpful information about numbers. Numbers are important in science. You use numbers whenever you collect data. **How to Look It Up** has hints for finding information about science. The **Study Habits** section tells you how to make the best use of your study time. The **Tests** section helps you get ready for taking tests. You can find useful sections about maps and units of measure at the end of the Almanac.

Numbers in Science

Imagine doing science without numbers. You use numbers every time you measure something. Suppose you want to see how much your puppy weighs. You need to use numbers.

You cannot measure the amount of rain that fell during a storm without using numbers. You cannot tell how hot or cold it is outside without the numbers on a thermometer. You cannot read a clock or a calendar. A ruler without numbers is not very useful!

See Also

Using a Thermometer
pages 52–53

Using a Ruler
page 55

Using a Balance
page 62

Using a Calendar
page 65

Using a Clock
page 66

SCI LINKS
N S T A

Keyword:
Thermometers
www.scilinks.org
Code: GSS23015

Keyword:
Balances
www.scilinks.org
Code: GSS23020

∧ You cannot measure a pencil using a ruler with no numbers.

Whole Numbers

Every number has digits. The numbers from 0 to 9 have only one digit. The number *5* is a one-digit number. You say this number as *five*.

The numbers from 10 to 99 have two digits. The number *55* is a two-digit number. You say this number as *fifty-five*.

The numbers from 100 to 999 have three digits. The number *555* is a three-digit number. You say this number as *five hundred fifty-five*.

Five	**Fifty-five**	**Five hundred fifty-five**
5	55	555
Ones	Tens Ones	Hundreds Tens Ones
The first digit from the right is the ones place.	The second digit from the right is the tens place.	The third digit from the right is the hundreds place.

Zero

Zero is a special number. Zero by itself means *nothing* or *none*. There are zero players on a soccer field when they have all gone home.

Zero is also a placeholder. Zero holds the place of the ones in the number *20*. There are zero groups of ones and two groups of tens in the number *20*. The number *20* is a different amount than the number *2*. The number *2* means the same as two groups of ones.

Sometimes zero is a placeholder in the middle of a number. If you take the zero out of the number *603*, you have the number *63*. The numbers *603* and *63* are very different. The zero is very important!

0 Players

20 Players

2 Players

Comparing Whole Numbers

See Also

Write Down Your Observations pages 18–19

Recycle page 337

Comparing numbers is a big part of looking at data. Suppose you count the number of plastic bottles your class recycles in April and May. You make a table to show your data.

Plastic Bottles Recycled	
Month	**Number of Plastic Bottles**
April	27
May	36

Did your class recycle more plastic bottles in April or May? Compare 27 and 36 to find the larger number. Look first at the tens place of both numbers. The digit 3 is larger than the digit 2. This means that *36* is larger than *27*. It doesn't matter that 7 ones are more than 6 ones because 30 is more than 20. Your class recycled more bottles in May than in April.

A whole number with more digits is always larger than a whole number with fewer digits. Sometimes, two numbers have the same number of digits. Compare the first digit of each number to find out which is larger. If the digits are the same, then compare the second digit of each number.

Roman Numerals

Long ago, people in ancient Rome used letters to write numbers. They used only three letters to write the numbers from 1 to 20.

I = 1   V = 5   X = 10

Roman Numerals	
Roman Numeral	**Number**
I	1
II	2
III	3
IV	4
V	5
VI	6
VII	7
VIII	8
IX	9
X	10
XI	11
XII	12
XIII	13
XIV	14
XV	15
XVI	16
XVII	17
XVIII	18
XIX	19
XX	20

When I comes before a V or X, you subtract it. When it comes after, you add it. For example, IX is 9. But XI is 11.

∧ Some clocks use Roman numerals. Almost all of them show the number 4 as IIII instead of IV! Why is this? There are many ideas, but no one knows for sure.

Fractions

A **fraction** is a number that stands for part of something. Suppose you have a kite with four equal parts. Three parts are yellow. One part is green. You can use a fraction to tell how much of the kite is green.

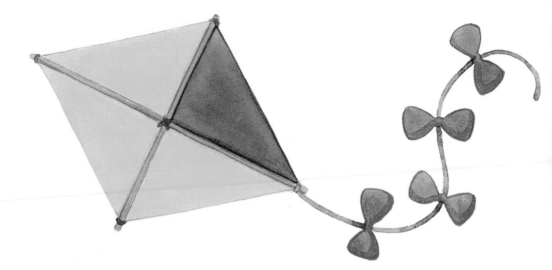

Every fraction has two numbers that are separated by a line. The numerator (NOO muh ray tur) is the number above the line. It tells how many of a part. The kite has one green part. The numerator in this example is 1.

The denominator (dih NAHM uh nay tur) is the number below the line. It tells the total number of parts in the whole. The kite has four parts. The denominator in this example is 4. So, $\frac{1}{4}$ of the kite is green.

Fractions of a Whole

You cut a sandwich into two equal parts. Each part is one-half. *One-half* means one out of two equal parts. Write this fraction $\frac{1}{2}$.

You can divide a pizza into four equal parts. Each of the parts is one-fourth. *One-fourth* means one out of four equal parts. Write this fraction $\frac{1}{4}$.

You can divide a pretzel stick into three equal parts. Each part is one-third. *One-third* means one out of three equal parts. Write this fraction $\frac{1}{3}$.

See Also

Look at the Data
pages 20–21

Fractions of a Group

Your class is raising mice. Eight babies are born. Five are brown. Three are white. Use a fraction to tell what part of the group is brown. The numerator 5 says that five mice are brown. The denominator 8 says that you have a total of eight mice. Five out of eight mice, or $\frac{5}{8}$, are brown. Three out of eight, or $\frac{3}{8}$, are white.

∧ $\frac{3}{8}$ of the mice are white. $\frac{5}{8}$ of the mice are brown.

You can use fractions to look at data from an experiment. Suppose you grew three plants. Two of the plants died. One plant lived. What fraction of the plants lived? One out of three, or $\frac{1}{3}$, lived. What fraction of the plants died? Two out of three, or $\frac{2}{3}$, died.

∧ $\frac{1}{3}$ of the plants lived. $\frac{2}{3}$ of the plants died.

Comparing Fractions

You have two ribbons. You divide one ribbon into four equal parts. Each part is one-fourth. You divide the second ribbon into three equal parts. Each part is one-third. Which is smaller—one-fourth or one-third?

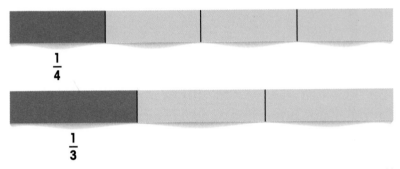

$\frac{1}{4}$

$\frac{1}{3}$

The more parts the ribbon is divided into, the smaller each part is. Each of the four parts is smaller than each of the three parts. This means that $\frac{1}{4}$ is less than $\frac{1}{3}$.

Some fractions are the same, or equal. Two out of four, or $\frac{2}{4}$, is the same as one out of two, or $\frac{1}{2}$.

$\frac{1}{2}$

$\frac{2}{4}$

Science Alert !

You must be sure that the two ribbons are the same length. You can't compare two fractions if the wholes or groups are different sizes.

Estimating

Scientists often make estimates instead of counting exact amounts. An **estimate** is a number close to an exact amount.

An estimate is a guess based on what you already know. Let's say you have a collection of baseball cards. You don't know exactly how many you have. But you do know about how many cards there are in a deck of playing cards. You can place your baseball cards in piles about the size of a deck of playing cards. You can use the number of piles to estimate how many baseball cards you have.

∧ There are about 50 cards in a deck of playing cards. You have 3 piles of baseball cards. So you have about 50 + 50 + 50 or 150 baseball cards.

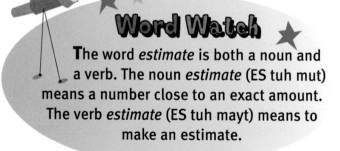

Word Watch

The word *estimate* is both a noun and a verb. The noun *estimate* (ES tuh mut) means a number close to an exact amount. The verb *estimate* (ES tuh mayt) means to make an estimate.

When to Estimate

Sometimes you can't find an exact number. There may be too many objects to count. You might not have the right tools to measure. In these cases, you can estimate.

You are looking at a flock of geese in the sky. There are too many geese to count each one. You can estimate how many geese there are.

∧ There are too many geese to count.

What if you want to know the distance between your desk and the chalkboard? The problem is you don't have a meter stick. You know that your foot is about 20 cm long. You can walk heel-to-toe from your desk to the chalkboard. Multiply the number of "feet" by 20 cm to estimate the distance.

See Also

Using a Meter Stick page 56

∧ Estimating distance without a meter stick

Ways to Estimate

See Also

Plants with Flowers
page 94

You want to know how many seeds a bean plant makes. Each bean pod contains four or five bean seeds. There are ten pods on the plant. You estimate that a bean plant makes 40 to 50 seeds. You don't know exactly how many seeds the plant makes, but you can estimate.

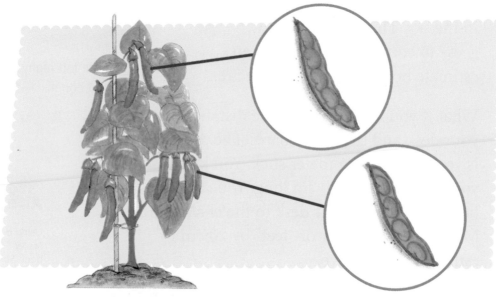

∧ The bean plant has 10 pods. Each pod has 4 or 5 seeds. About how many seeds did the bean plant make?

You want to estimate how many strawberries will fit on a plate. Picture a group of four strawberries. Now, estimate how many groups will fit on the plate. You estimate that three groups of four will fit. Your total estimate is 12 strawberries.

> How many strawberries are there on the plate?

You can estimate fractions, too. You need 20 rocks for an experiment. You have found six rocks. Is this closer to one-fourth or to one-half of what you need? One-half of twenty is ten. One-fourth of twenty is five. You can estimate that six rocks are closer to one-fourth than to one-half of what you need.

∨ 5 rocks = $\frac{1}{4}$ of 20

∧ 10 rocks = $\frac{1}{2}$ of 20

< Is 6 rocks closer to $\frac{1}{4}$ or $\frac{1}{2}$ of 20 rocks?

You can use time to estimate distance. It takes you 20 minutes to walk to school. You left home 10 minutes ago. You estimate that you are halfway to school.

Probability

Probability (prahb uh BIL ih tee) is the chance that something will happen. Probability is not just a guess. It is based on facts. You can use probability to predict some things that might happen in the future.

Certain and Impossible

Some events are certain. This means that you can be sure they will happen. You know for certain that the sun will rise every day. Spring always follows winter. Summer always follows spring.

See Also

What Causes Day and Night pages 216–217

What Causes the Seasons pages 218–219

Gravity and Motion page 284

You can be certain that a ball will come back down if you throw it into the air. Gravity will pull the ball back toward Earth.

∧ Some events are certain to happen.

Some events are impossible. This means that you can be sure they will *never* happen. It is impossible for the sun to rise at night. It is impossible for winter to come right after summer. It is impossible to see two dinosaurs playing in the school yard.

∧ Some events are impossible.

You can use your understanding of certain and impossible to make predictions. Suppose you have a bag of marbles. All the marbles are red. It is impossible to pick a green marble out of the bag. It is certain that you will pick a red marble.

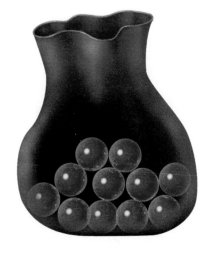

Likely and Unlikely

Some events are likely to happen. This means that they will probably happen. A volcano that has erupted many times in the past is likely to erupt again. But it is not certain.

See Also

Volcanoes
page 173

∧ Some events are likely to happen.

Other events are unlikely to happen. This means that they will probably not happen. Deserts are very dry areas. It hardly ever rains in the desert. It is unlikely that it will rain every day for a month in a desert. But it is not impossible.

∧ Some events are unlikely to happen.

Equally Likely

Suppose you reach into a bag that contains ten red marbles and ten blue marbles. You can pick a red marble. Or, you can pick a blue marble. Both events are equally likely because the numbers of red marbles and blue marbles are equal.

∧ Some events are equally likely.

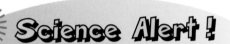

Science Alert!

You pick a red marble five times in a row. Each time, you replace the marble. You are still equally likely to pick a red or a blue marble the next time.

Not Equally Likely

Suppose you reach into a bag that contains five red marbles and ten blue marbles. The chance of pulling out a blue marble is greater than the chance of pulling out a red marble. That's because there are more blue marbles than red marbles in the bag.

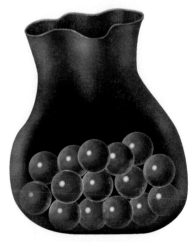

∧ Some events are not equally likely.

Making Predictions

You can use your understanding of probability to make predictions about what might happen in the future.

Suppose you are watching butterflies in a meadow. You count 10 butterflies in the morning. Eight are monarch butterflies. Two are swallowtail butterflies.

What kind of butterfly will you see next? It is likely that the next butterfly you see will be a monarch butterfly. You might see a swallowtail, but it is less likely.

Monarch butterfly

Swallowtail butterfly

How to Look It Up

Part of doing science is looking up information. Suppose you want to make a model of the solar system. You can look up the distance from each planet to the sun. What can you do if you want to grow tomato plants? You can look up how much fertilizer you need to use for healthy plants.

Keyword:
Reading and
Writing in
Science
www.scilinks.org
Code: GSS23140

You can find science information in many different places. You can look in library books. You can look in science magazines. Or you can search for the information on the Internet.

Make sure the information you find on the Internet comes from a place you can trust. Colleges and museums usually have trustworthy information.

Library

A library is a good place to find science books and magazines. Your school library will have materials at your grade level. So will the children's room of a public library. Ask the librarian for help if you cannot find what you need.

You can search for library materials by title, author, or subject. *Title* is the name of the book. *Author* is the person who wrote it. *Subject* describes what the book is about.

621.8
New

PULLEYS — Subject

Newton, Megan — Author

Fun with Pulleys — Title

HM Publishing/Boston, MA. 2001.
297 p.

< Some libraries list their books in a card catalog. Most libraries use computers.

Here is what you do when you find the listing for the book you want. Write down the title, the author, and the number given. The number tells you where to find the book on the library shelves.

Find the library shelf that holds books with the number you wrote down. Look at the spines of the books until you find the right number. Then look for the author name.

Nonfiction books in a library are on the shelves by subject. You may find other books on the same subject in the same place once you find the book you are looking for.

Internet

The **Internet** is a worldwide network of computers. It is also called the World Wide Web. When you use the Internet, your computer is connected to millions of others. The Internet will connect you to Web sites that have a lot of science information.

The tool you need to search the Internet is a search engine. A **search engine** is a Web site that lets you find other Web sites by typing in a subject. Some search engines are for students. Others are for scientists or for teachers.

You will find many links when you type in your subject. A **link** is a connection to a Web site that has information about the subject.

Suppose you have to write a report about ants. You open a search engine and type in the word *ants*. Hundreds of links appear.

Scroll down through the links. Click on the ones that seem to be for students your age.

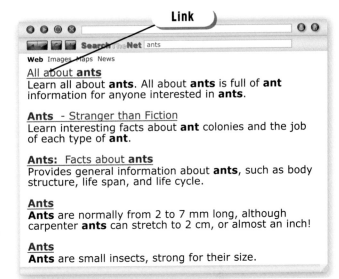

Link

Search ...Net ants

Web Images Maps News

All about ants
Learn all about **ants**. All about **ants** is full of **ant** information for anyone interested in **ants**.

Ants - Stranger than Fiction
Learn interesting facts about **ant** colonies and the job of each type of **ant**.

Ants: Facts about ants
Provides general information about **ants**, such as body structure, life span, and life cycle.

Ants
Ants are normally from 2 to 7 mm long, although carpenter **ants** can stretch to 2 cm, or almost an inch!

Ants
Ants are small insects, strong for their size.

In this book, you will see *sci*LINKs. Each *sci*LINK has a keyword and a code. The keyword is a science topic. The code takes you to Web sites about the topic. Go to the Web site www.scilinks.org. Set up a user name and password. Then, type in the *sci*LINK code for the keyword. You will see a screen with links. Each link takes you to a Web site that a science teacher has already picked out for you.

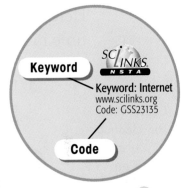

Keyword

SCi LINKS.
N S T A

Keyword: Internet
www.scilinks.org
Code: GSS23135

Code

See Also

How to Use
*Sci*LINKS
page xi

Staying Safe on the Internet

Follow these rules to stay safe on the Internet:

- Only visit sites approved by your school and your parents.
- Never give your name, address, or telephone number to anyone online.
- Do not give your password to anyone.
- Do not open any messages from people you don't know.

Study Habits

Do you have good study habits? Or does it seem like you never have time to do your homework? Good study habits at home and in school are very important.

In the Classroom

Here are some hints for how to make the most of your time in school.

1 **Listen carefully.** Pay attention when your teacher gives directions. Sit up straight, keep your feet on the floor, and look at your teacher. Write down what to do.

Leave time for cleanup if you are doing an investigation.

2 **Plan your time.** How much time in school do you have to do your work? Think about how long each part of your work should take. Use the time you have to get each part done.

3 **Keep track of time.** Check the clock while you work. If half the time is gone, you should be halfway finished.

4 **Check your work as you go.** This will save time later.

5 **Ask questions.** Write down questions as you think of them. Ask them as soon as you can. But don't interrupt anyone when you ask.

Keyword:
Reading and
Writing in
Science
www.scilinks.org
Code: GSS23140

6 **Ignore distractions.** A distraction (dih STRAK shun) is anything that takes your mind off your work. People talking in the hall are a distraction. So is a squeaky chair. Learn to ignore these things. They slow you down.

You can ignore unimportant sounds, but **do not ignore a fire alarm!**

At Home

Here are some hints for how to make the most of your study time at home.

1. **Find a quiet place to work.** Your room is a good place if it is quiet. A kitchen table is also a good place. Make sure you have a bright light shining on your work area.

2. **Gather the tools you need.** Make sure you have sharp pencils, erasers, scissors, and glue.

3. **Turn off the TV.** Television and loud music are distractions. They keep you from paying attention to your work.

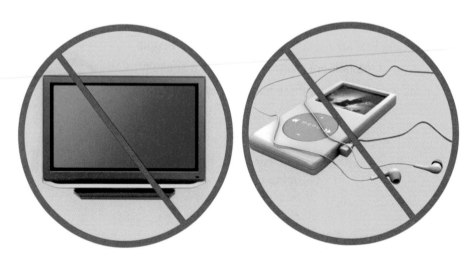

4 **Plan your time.** Think about how much time you need to do your work. Then, think about how long each part of your work should take.

5 **Keep track of time.** Check the clock while you work. If half the time is gone, you should be halfway finished.

6 **Check your work.** Look over your work when you finish. Make sure you have done everything you were supposed to do.

Remember to spend some time relaxing when you come home from school. Have a snack if you are hungry. Then, start your homework. Start your work early, before you become tired. It may help to break up your homework time. Do some now and some later.

Tests

Tests are part of school. Short quizzes, long tests, and standardized tests help to show what you know. No need to worry. There are things you can do to get ready.

Getting Ready

The first step is to keep up with your work. Ask questions about things you don't understand. Look for the answers as you read. Check your homework when you get it back. Learn from your mistakes.

Studying for the test is part of getting ready. Review your past work to be sure everything is clear. Study with other students. You can ask each other questions or explain things to each other.

Make a Venn diagram. A Venn diagram helps you sort objects or ideas into groups. Then, you can see how they are alike and different.

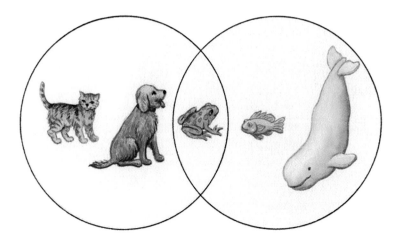

< Cats and dogs live on land. Fish and whales live in water. Frogs live on land and in water.

Make a concept map. A concept map helps you see how objects or ideas are connected.

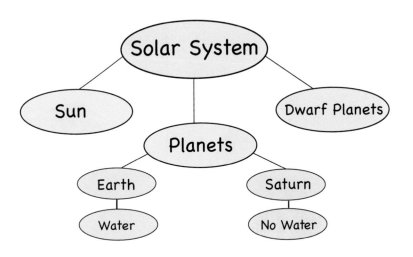

See Also

Venn Diagrams
pages 36–37

Amphibians
pages 108–109

Planets Around the Sun
pages 204–205

∧ The solar system is made up of the sun, the planets, and the dwarf planets. Earth is one planet. It has water. Saturn is another planet. It does not have water.

Taking a Test

Taking a test can be scary. It doesn't have to be. Here are some tips for taking a test.

- **Take** a deep breath. Being relaxed helps you remember what you studied.

- **Wait** until your teacher tells you what to do.

- **Write** your name on your test paper.

Be sure you have everything you need before you take a test. Do you have two sharp pencils? Do you have an eraser? Is your desk cleared off?

- **Listen** and follow along as your teacher reads the directions. Make sure you have everything you are supposed to have. Ask for anything that is missing.

- **Ask** questions if you do not understand something.

- **Work** each question in order. Answer all the questions you know. Skip any questions you are not sure of. Leave more time for questions that need longer answers.

- **Go back** and try to answer the questions you skipped.

- **Check** your work before you hand it in.

Science Alert !

Ask your teacher about questions you missed when you get your test back. Be sure you understand what the correct answers are.

Kinds of Tests

There are many different kinds of tests. You may have any kind in science class.

True-or-False Tests

True-or-false questions can be tricky. Read carefully. Watch for the words *not, all, none, never,* and *always.* These words can change the meaning of the question.

See Also

Birds
pages 104–105

Life Cycle of Birds
page 121

<u>false</u> 1. All birds can fly.

<u>true</u> 2. Birds always hatch from eggs.

<u>false</u> 3. Birds do not swim.

∧ True-or-false test

Try asking yourself questions to see if your answer is correct. Let's look at the first true-or-false question. To help you pick an answer, you might ask, "Are there some kinds of birds that can't fly?" The answer is yes. Penguins can't fly. So you know the answer to the statement "all birds can fly" is *false*.

Write the whole word *true* or *false* on the line, not just the letters *T* or *F*. That way, a *T* won't be confused with an *F*.

Fill-In-the-Blank Tests

Fill-in-the-blank tests have a blank line in a sentence. Write a word on the line to finish the sentence. Sometimes the line is in the middle of the sentence. Other times it is at the beginning or at the end of the sentence.

1. Water _melts_ when it changes from a solid to a liquid.
2. The planet in our solar system that is closest to the sun is _Mercury_ .
3. _Roots_ are plant parts that take in water and nutrients from the soil.

∧ Fill-in-the-blank test

Try asking yourself questions to help find the missing word. For the first question, you might ask, "What does water do when it changes from a solid to a liquid?" You know that water melts when it changes from a solid to a liquid. So you know that the missing word is _melts_.

Start your answer with a capital letter if the line is at the beginning of the sentence.

See Also

Roots
page 89

Planets Around the Sun
pages 204–205

Changing States
pages 246–247

Multiple-Choice Tests

Multiple-choice tests let you choose an answer. Only one choice is correct. Read all the answer choices. You may not know the correct answer. Your chances of choosing the right answer are better if you can rule out any of the choices.

See Also

Structure of Earth page 159

1. Which of Earth's layers is on Earth's surface?

   A. core

   B. mantle

   C. crust

   D. water

∧ Multiple-choice test

Look at the question. You can rule out choice D because water is not one of Earth's layers. You can rule out choice A, too. You remember that Earth's core is in the center, just like an apple's core. That leaves choices B and C. You know that bread crust is on the outside surface of bread. The best choice is C.

Be sure to read the directions. You may be asked to circle the correct answer. Or you may be asked to fill in the correct answer on a separate answer sheet.

Short-Answer Tests

Short-answer tests ask you to write down information. Your answer may be a word, a phrase, or a sentence. Be sure to write your answers in complete sentences if the directions tell you to.

1. What are four things that plants need?
   <u>Plants need air, water, light, and</u>
   <u>nutrients.</u>

2. What is pitch?
   <u>Pitch describes how high or low</u>
   <u>a sound is.</u>

3. Name three kinds of fossil fuels.
   <u>Three kinds of fossil fuels are coal,</u>
   <u>oil, and natural gas.</u>

∧ Short-answer test

See Also

What Do Plants Need? pages 86–87

High Sounds page 262

Low Sounds page 263

Fossil Fuels page 317

Think about your answer before you start writing. You might want to write down some notes before making a whole sentence. For the first question, you might make a list of all the things plants need first. Then you can make the list into a sentence and write it on the lines.

Use words from the question to write your answer. If the question asks you to name three kinds of fossil fuels, start your answer with **Three kinds of fossil fuels are … .**

Standardized Tests

Standardized tests are tests that are given to all students at one grade level. The tests show what students in different schools have learned.

See Also

Multiple-Choice Tests
page 376

Standardized tests usually have multiple-choice questions. Sometimes you have to mark your answer on a separate answer sheet. Usually you mark your answer by filling in a circle on the answer sheet.

Be sure to fill in the circle that has the same letter as the answer you have chosen. Fill in the circle completely. If you change an answer, erase your first answer completely.

Be careful to fill in the circle in the correct row. Hold your finger on the correct row, or cover the rows above if it helps.

Many standardized tests have questions with pictures. The picture may show something you can see, like parts of an insect. Or it may explain a process, like melting ice.

Study the question and picture below. The picture shows two pairs of magnets. What does the picture show that may help you answer the question?

1. Circle the pair of magnets that push away from each other.

N	S	S	N

N	S	N	S

See Also

Poles of a Magnet
pages 302–303

∧ Standardized test question with picture

Read the question first. Then, look at all the parts of the picture. Think about what the question is asking. Then, answer the question.

The poles of the magnets are labeled. You know that like poles push away from each other. Unlike poles pull toward each other. So you would circle the pair of magnets that have their south poles together.

Maps

See Also

Water on Earth
page 160

Landforms
pages 166–167

A map is a picture of all or part of Earth's surface. Some maps show landforms and bodies of water. Others show the borders of countries. Weather maps show weather patterns. A road map shows the roads in a city or state.

> You can find out how to get somewhere if you have a road map.

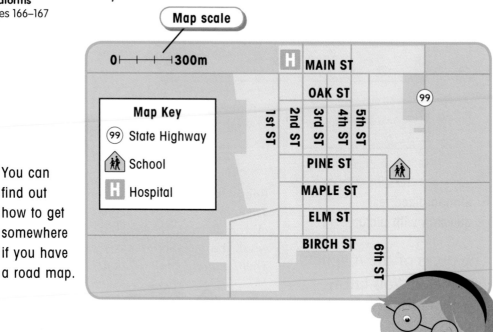

Map scale

0 |—|—|—| 300m

Map Key

(99) State Highway

School

H Hospital

H MAIN ST
OAK ST
1st ST 2nd ST 3rd ST 4th ST 5th ST
(99)
PINE ST
MAPLE ST
ELM ST
BIRCH ST
6th ST

A *map key* explains the symbols used on the map. Another name for map *key* is map *legend*. A *map scale* shows you how the distances on the map compare to the real distances.

The map on the right shows Florida. Look for the star on the map beside Tallahassee. The star tells you that Tallahassee is the state capital of Florida. The map also shows you what bodies of water surround Florida. It shows you what states border Florida.

Most shopping malls have maps. The maps help you find stores, bathrooms, and telephones. The maps are usually near the mall entrance. You can use this kind of map to find a toy store or a food court.

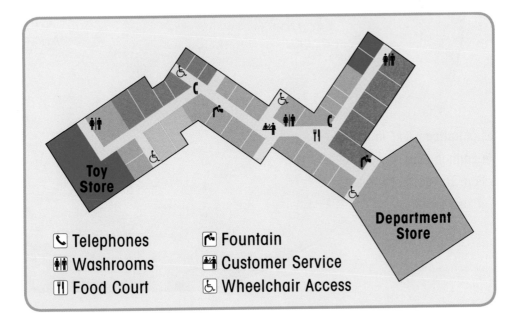

How to Read a Map

Use the words and symbols on a map to understand what it is showing.

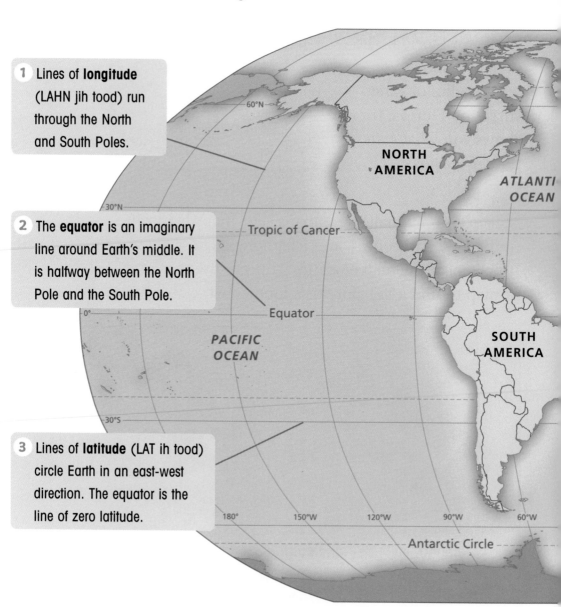

1 Lines of **longitude** (LAHN jih tood) run through the North and South Poles.

2 The **equator** is an imaginary line around Earth's middle. It is halfway between the North Pole and the South Pole.

3 Lines of **latitude** (LAT ih tood) circle Earth in an east-west direction. The equator is the line of zero latitude.

60°N

30°N

0°

30°S

NORTH AMERICA

ATLANTI OCEAN

Tropic of Cancer

Equator

PACIFIC OCEAN

SOUTH AMERICA

180°   150°W   120°W   90°W   60°W

Antarctic Circle

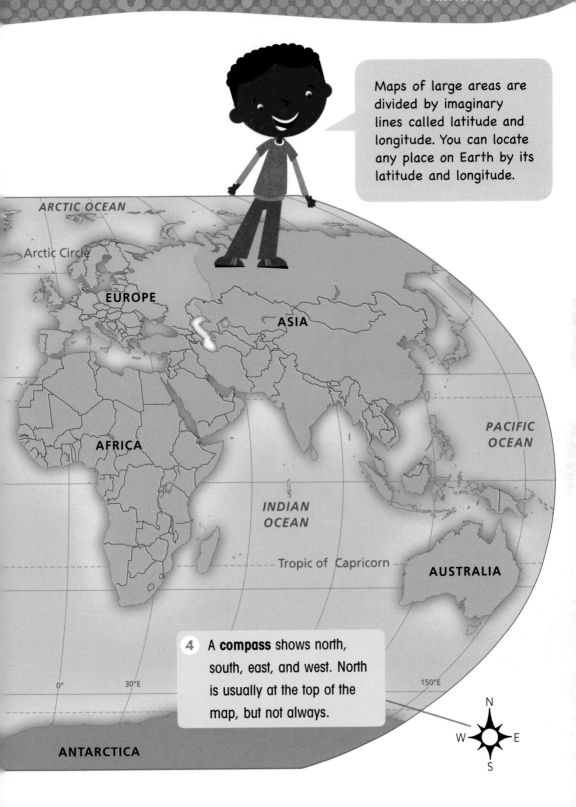

Maps of large areas are divided by imaginary lines called latitude and longitude. You can locate any place on Earth by its latitude and longitude.

ARCTIC OCEAN

Arctic Circle

EUROPE

ASIA

AFRICA

PACIFIC OCEAN

INDIAN OCEAN

Tropic of Capricorn

AUSTRALIA

4 A **compass** shows north, south, east, and west. North is usually at the top of the map, but not always.

0°   30°E   150°E

ANTARCTICA

N
W   E
S

Globes and World Maps

See Also

Water on Earth
page 160

Landforms
pages 166–167

Most maps are flat, even though Earth is ball-shaped. The shapes and sizes of landforms are not exact on flat maps. The best way to show the shapes of Earth's features is with a globe. A globe is a round model of Earth.

∧ This is a physical globe. It shows Earth's land masses and water. The surface is bumpy to show mountains.

∧ This is a political globe. It shows the outlines of countries and states.

A world map shows all of Earth, but it is flat. A world map may show the features on Earth's surface. It may show the outlines of countries and states. The colors on the map help you see where the countries and states are.

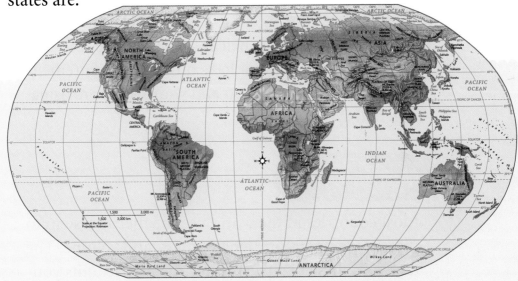

∧ A physical world map shows the features on Earth's surface.

∧ A political world map shows the countries of the world. Each country is a different color.

Units of Measure

You measure your pencil as 18 centimeters long. Your friend measures the pencil as 7 inches long. It is the same pencil! How can it have different measurements? This happens because you and your friend are using different systems of units.

Metric Units

Most countries in the world use the metric system to measure temperature, length, mass, and volume. The tables on these two pages show the metric units you use to measure things.

Temperature

°C

Ice melts at 0 degrees Celsius (0°C).

Water freezes at 0°C.

Water boils at 100°C.

50
40
30
20
10
0
-10
-20
-30
-40

Scientists use a metric system of units called SI. SI stands for International System of Units.

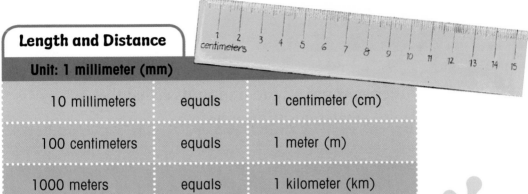

Length and Distance

Unit: 1 millimeter (mm)

10 millimeters	equals	1 centimeter (cm)
100 centimeters	equals	1 meter (m)
1000 meters	equals	1 kilometer (km)

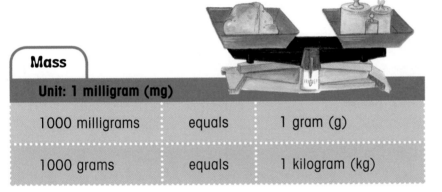

Mass

Unit: 1 milligram (mg)

1000 milligrams	equals	1 gram (g)
1000 grams	equals	1 kilogram (kg)

Volume

Unit: 1 milliliter (mL)

1000 milliliters	equals	1 liter (L)

See Also

Using a Thermometer
pages 52–53

Measuring Length
pages 54–57

Using a Balance
page 62–63

Measuring Liquids
pages 58–61

Did you know?

One metric unit can be changed to another metric unit by multiplying or dividing by 10.

Keyword: Ways to Measure
www.scilinks.org
Code: GSS23130

Customary Units

Americans use a system of units called the
United States customary system.

Temperature

Ice melts at 32 degrees Fahrenheit (32°F).

Water freezes at 32°F.

Water boils at 212°F.

Length and Distance

Unit: 1 inch (in.)		
12 inches	equals	1 foot (ft)
3 feet	equals	1 yard (yd)
5280 feet	equals	1 mile (mi)

Weight

Unit: 1 ounce (oz)		
16 ounces	equals	1 pound (lb)
2000 pounds	equals	1 ton (T)

Volume

Unit: 1 teaspoon (tsp)		
3 teaspoons	equals	1 tablespoon (tbsp)
16 tablespoons or 8 fluid ounces (fl oz)	equals	1 cup (c)
2 cups	equals	1 pint (pt)
2 pints	equals	1 quart (qt)
4 quarts	equals	1 gallon (gal)

Yellow Pages

History of Science

What is the history of science? The history of something is its story. History tells what happened to a person, place, or thing over time. The history of science is the story of science. It started many years ago. It is still happening today.

The story of science is the story of people. **Scientists** are people who study the natural world. They want to know how and why things happen. **Inventors** are people who use what they learn to make useful things or solve problems.

People have been studying the natural world for thousands of years. They are still studying it today. Each new piece of information that is discovered helps scientists make even more discoveries. There is always more to learn in science.

The next few pages show a time line of some big events in science. A **time line** is a list of important events in the order they took place. The time line also shows some big events in American History. These events will help you understand when the science events happened.

Keyword:
Inventors
www.scilinks.org
Code: GSS23150

After the time line, there are short biographies of some interesting scientists and inventors. A **biography** is the story of a person's life. Many different kinds of people become scientists and inventors. Both men and women study science. People from many different countries contribute to science.

Science Time Line 1490–1799

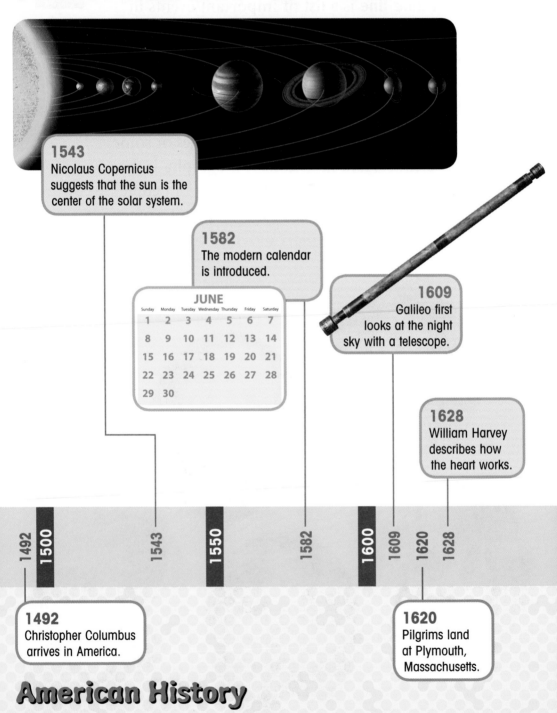

1543
Nicolaus Copernicus suggests that the sun is the center of the solar system.

1582
The modern calendar is introduced.

JUNE

Sunday	Monday	Tuesday	Wednesday	Thursday	Friday	Saturday
1	2	3	4	5	6	7
8	9	10	11	12	13	14
15	16	17	18	19	20	21
22	23	24	25	26	27	28
29	30					

1609
Galileo first looks at the night sky with a telescope.

1628
William Harvey describes how the heart works.

1492 1500   1543   1550   1582   1600 1609 1620 1628

1492
Christopher Columbus arrives in America.

1620
Pilgrims land at Plymouth, Massachusetts.

American History

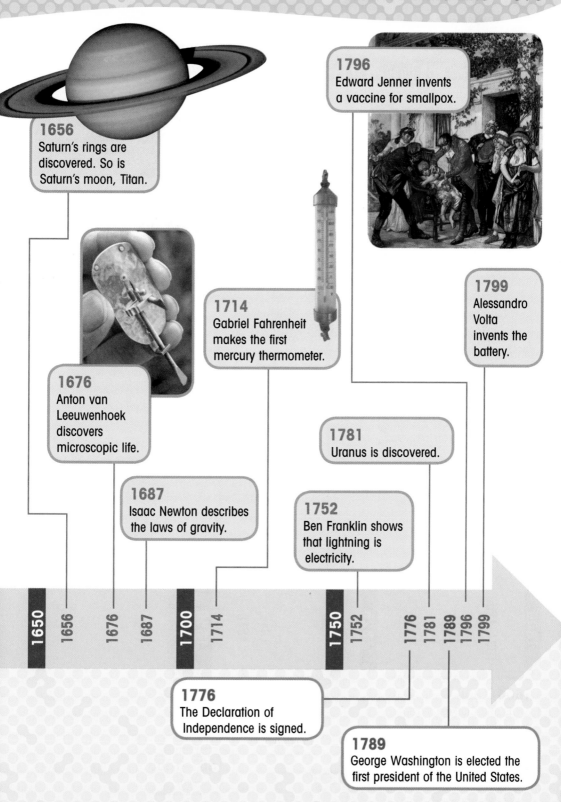

1796
Edward Jenner invents a vaccine for smallpox.

1656
Saturn's rings are discovered. So is Saturn's moon, Titan.

1799
Alessandro Volta invents the battery.

1714
Gabriel Fahrenheit makes the first mercury thermometer.

1676
Anton van Leeuwenhoek discovers microscopic life.

1781
Uranus is discovered.

1687
Isaac Newton describes the laws of gravity.

1752
Ben Franklin shows that lightning is electricity.

1650 1656 1676 1687 1700 1714 1750 1752 1776 1781 1789 1796 1799

1776
The Declaration of Independence is signed.

1789
George Washington is elected the first president of the United States.

Science Time Line 1800–1949

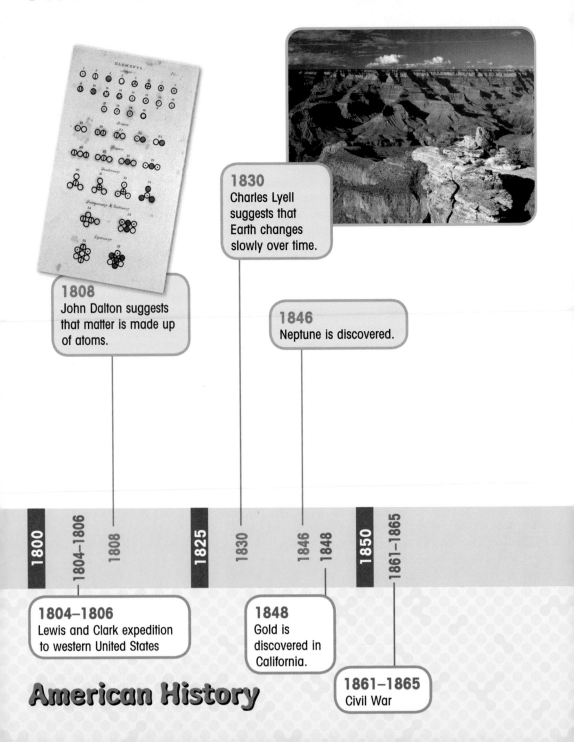

1830
Charles Lyell suggests that Earth changes slowly over time.

1808
John Dalton suggests that matter is made up of atoms.

1846
Neptune is discovered.

1800 | 1804–1806 | 1808 | 1825 | 1830 | 1846 | 1848 | 1850 | 1861–1865

1804–1806
Lewis and Clark expedition to western United States

1848
Gold is discovered in California.

1861–1865
Civil War

American History

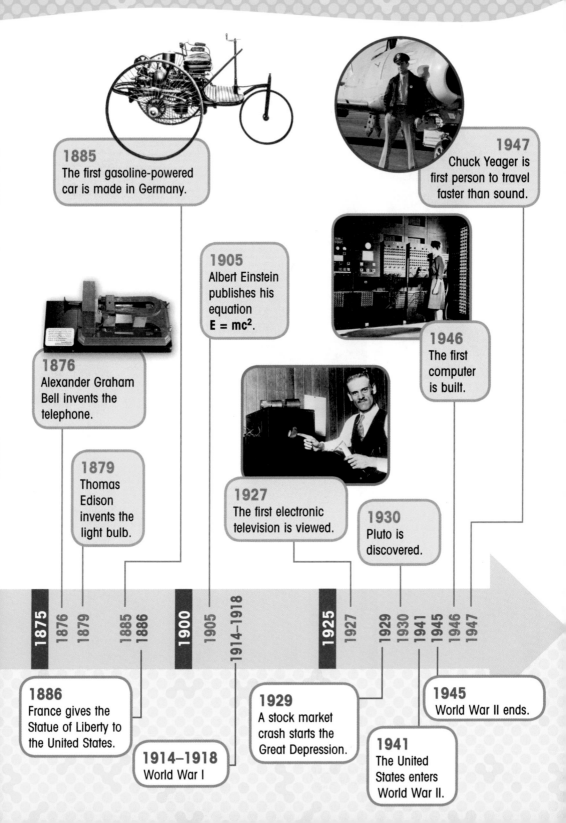

1885
The first gasoline-powered car is made in Germany.

1947
Chuck Yeager is first person to travel faster than sound.

1905
Albert Einstein publishes his equation $E = mc^2$.

1946
The first computer is built.

1876
Alexander Graham Bell invents the telephone.

1879
Thomas Edison invents the light bulb.

1927
The first electronic television is viewed.

1930
Pluto is discovered.

1875 | 1876 | 1879 | 1885 | 1886 | 1900 | 1905 | 1914–1918 | 1925 | 1927 | 1929 | 1930 | 1941 | 1945 | 1946 | 1947

1886
France gives the Statue of Liberty to the United States.

1929
A stock market crash starts the Great Depression.

1945
World War II ends.

1914–1918
World War I

1941
The United States enters World War II.

Science Time Line 1950–2009

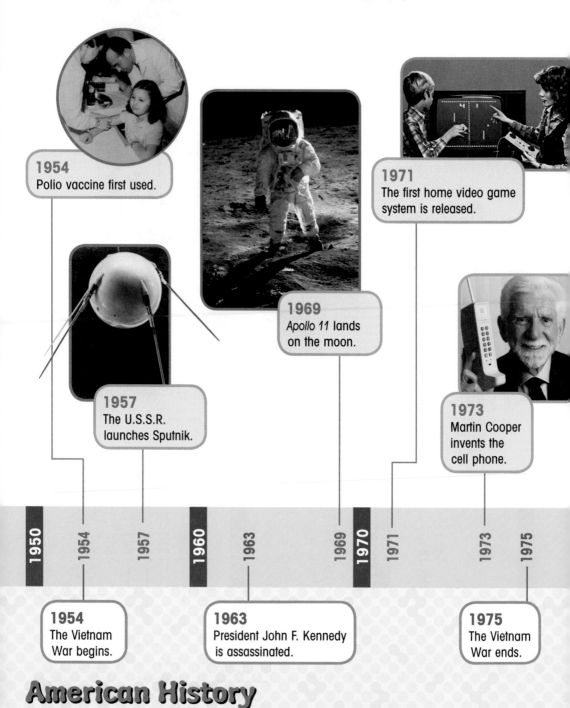

1954
Polio vaccine first used.

1957
The U.S.S.R.
launches Sputnik.

1969
Apollo 11 lands
on the moon.

1971
The first home video game
system is released.

1973
Martin Cooper
invents the
cell phone.

1950 | 1954 | 1957 | 1960 | 1963 | 1969 | 1970 | 1971 | 1973 | 1975

1954
The Vietnam
War begins.

1963
President John F. Kennedy
is assassinated.

1975
The Vietnam
War ends.

American History

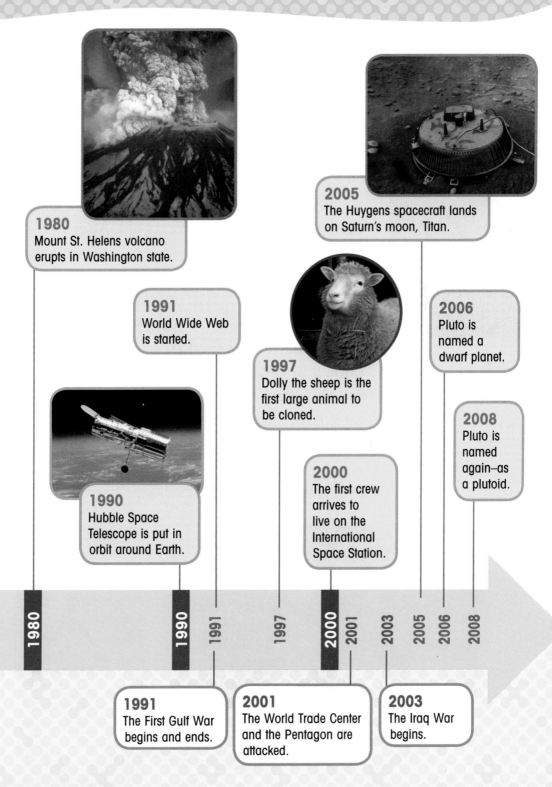

1980
Mount St. Helens volcano erupts in Washington state.

2005
The Huygens spacecraft lands on Saturn's moon, Titan.

1991
World Wide Web is started.

2006
Pluto is named a dwarf planet.

1997
Dolly the sheep is the first large animal to be cloned.

2008
Pluto is named again—as a plutoid.

1990
Hubble Space Telescope is put in orbit around Earth.

2000
The first crew arrives to live on the International Space Station.

1980   1990   1991   1997   2000 2001   2003   2005   2006   2008

1991
The First Gulf War begins and ends.

2001
The World Trade Center and the Pentagon are attacked.

2003
The Iraq War begins.

Famous Scientists and Inventors

See Also

Fossils
pages 186–187

Mary Anning (1799–1847)

Mary Anning lived on the coast of England. Her father taught her how to hunt for fossils when she was young. Sadly, her father died when she was about 11 years old. After his death, Anning's family was very poor. But the family made money by finding and selling fossils. Anning made her first big discovery when she was about 11 years old. She and her brother found the first *Ichthyosaur* fossil known in England. Later, Anning found the first *Plesiosaur* fossil. (Ichthyosaurs and plesiosaurs are reptiles that lived in the ocean millions of years ago.) Many consider Anning to be the greatest fossil-hunter who ever lived.

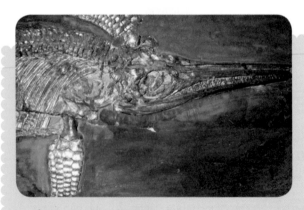

∧ *Ichthyosaur* fossil

> *Plesiosaur* fossil

Benjamin Bannaker (1731–1806)

Benjamin Bannaker was born in Maryland. Much of what Bannaker knew he learned on his own. Bannaker was given a watch when he was 21 years old. Bannaker took the watch apart and put it back together many times. Then, he used what he learned to build a clock. The clock was made of wood and kept time for 40 years. When Bannaker was older, he studied space on his own. Bannaker also published a popular almanac. An almanac is a book full of information about science and other things. Bannaker spoke out against slavery and supported equal rights for all people.

See Also

Using a Clock
page 66

Space
pages 202–233

< Bannaker's almanacs

See Also

What Do Plants Need?
pages 86–87

Land and Soil
page 314

George Washington Carver
(1864?–1943)

George Washington Carver was born into slavery in Missouri. As a child, he studied plants around his home. Carver learned to read on his own. He went to school when he could. In college, he studied agriculture—the science of farming. Carver was the first African-American student at Iowa State Agricultural College. He later became the first African-American teacher at that college. Carver then moved to Alabama. There, he taught farmers how to grow better crops. Carver told farmers that growing peanuts would make their soil better. (Growing peanuts in soil adds important nutrients to the soil.) He then found many different uses for the peanuts that were grown. One of those uses was peanut butter!

⌃ Peanut butter

< Peanut plants

Leonardo da Vinci (1452–1519)

Leonardo da Vinci was a famous Italian painter. He painted the *Mona Lisa* and *The Last Supper*. But da Vinci did more than paint. He studied architecture (the design of buildings) and science, too. Da Vinci dissected (cut open) animal and human bodies to study them. He then made detailed drawings of different body parts. He used these drawings to understand how the parts worked. Da Vinci also designed a lot of machines. Most of these machines were not built while he was alive. But some of the machines are similar to ones used today. For example, da Vinci designed and drew different flying machines. Some of them looked like helicopters and hang gliders we use today.

See Also

Simple
Machines
pages 290–297

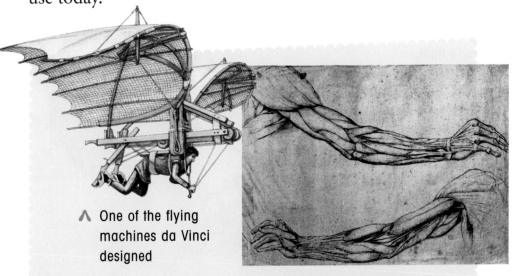

∧ One of the flying
machines da Vinci
designed

∧ Da Vinci's drawings of the
human body

Thomas Edison (1847–1931)

Thomas Edison was born in Ohio. He wasn't a very good student, but he became a great inventor. Edison's first important work was making the telephone and the telegraph better. A telegraph is a machine that sends information through wires. Edison then invented the phonograph. A phonograph is a machine that can record sounds and play them back. Edison even created tiny phonograph pieces to go inside dolls to make them talk! Edison's next big invention was the light bulb. Once he had the light bulb, he created a light system. Edison then started one of the nation's first electric companies. He needed something to power his light bulbs!

∧ Edison's light bulb

See Also

Technology Helps All People pages 72–73

Designing Technology pages 74–77

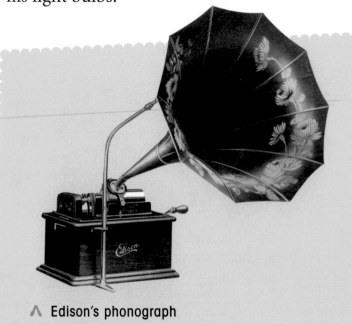

∧ Edison's phonograph

Albert Einstein (1879–1955)

Albert Einstein was born in Germany. When he was a teenager he moved to Switzerland, where he studied physics. (Eventually Einstein would move to the United States.) When Einstein was 26 years old he published several papers. These papers changed the way scientists saw the world. Einstein's theory of special relativity was part of the papers. Special relativity describes how things act when they are moving close to the speed of light. Einstein's famous equation $E = mc^2$ was also in the papers. This equation shows that a small amount of matter can be changed into a lot of energy! Einstein also explained that light acts like it is made of tiny particles. He called these tiny particles *photons*.

See Also

Matter
pages 236–237

Energy
pages 254–255

Light Energy
page 266

∧ Einstein at work

∧ The Hubble Space
Telescope

Sandra Faber (1944–present)

Sandra Faber is a space scientist at the University of California, Santa Cruz. Faber studies galaxies. A galaxy is a very large group of stars. Faber wants to find out how galaxies form. She uses powerful telescopes like the Hubble Space Telescope. Hubble is a telescope that orbits Earth. It can take pictures of things in space that telescopes on Earth cannot see. Soon after Hubble was put into space, Faber saw that something was wrong. Hubble's camera was taking fuzzy photos. Faber led a team of scientists who found out what was wrong. Then, they found a way to fix it. Astronauts fixed Hubble using Faber's instructions. Since then, Hubble has been taking amazing photos of far-off galaxies for Faber and other scientists.

See Also

Space
pages 202–203

Telescopes
pages 230–231

∧ Picture taken by the Hubble Space Telescope

Benjamin Franklin (1706–1790)

Benjamin Franklin was one of the founders of the United States. He was also a writer, an inventor, and a scientist. One of Franklin's science experiments was flying a kite in a thunderstorm. The experiment showed that lightning was a kind of electricity. Franklin used what he learned to invent the lightning rod. Lightning rods protect buildings from being damaged by lightning. Franklin's other inventions include swim fins, bifocal glasses, and a kind of wood stove. His stove put out more heat and less smoke than regular fireplaces. Franklin was also a firefighter and a librarian. He started one of the first volunteer fire departments in the United States. He also started the nation's first public library.

See Also

Bending Light
page 269

Electrical Energy
page 271

Library
pages 362–363

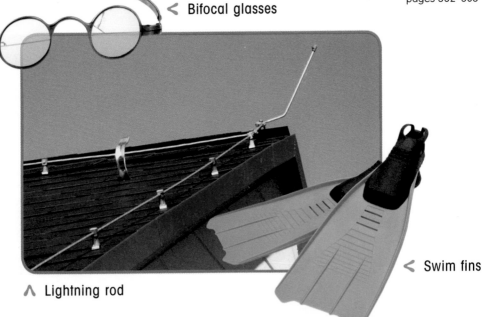

< Bifocal glasses

⋀ Lightning rod

< Swim fins

See Also

Planets Around the Sun
pages 204–214

How Earth Moves in Space
page 215

Stars
pages 224–225

Gravity and Motion
page 284

Galileo Galilei (1564-1642)

Galileo was an Italian scientist. He studied space and the way things moved. Galileo was the first to say that big objects and small objects fall to Earth at the same rate. According to legend, Galileo proved this idea by dropping two balls of different sizes from the top of the Leaning Tower of Pisa. This story may not be true, but Galileo's idea is correct. Galileo was one of the first people to use a telescope to look at the stars and the planets. He used the telescope to discover four of Jupiter's moons. He also saw Saturn's rings, but did not know what they were. Galileo also proved that the planets travel around the sun. Most people at the time thought that everything orbited Earth. Galileo's ideas were not well accepted in his lifetime.

∧ Galileo's telescope

Jane Goodall (1934–present)

Jane Goodall is a British scientist. She dreamed of studying animals when she was a little girl. So, when she was 26 years old, she went to Africa to study chimpanzees. At first, the chimps that Goodall wanted to study were afraid of her. They ran away, but Goodall kept watching them from a distance. Soon the chimps got used to her and she was able to watch their behavior. Goodall's most important discovery was finding that chimpanzees made tools. Before this discovery, it was thought that only humans made tools. Today, Goodall still studies animals in Africa. She also teaches people about conserving resources and protecting the environment.

See Also

Mammals
pages 102-103

Plants and
Animals Look
Like Their
Parents
pages 126–127

Adaptations
Help
Organisms
Survive
pages 134–135

Protecting
Resources
page 332

∧ Jane Goodall at work

See Also

Studying Space
pages 230–233

Forces Cause Motion
pages 282–283

Protecting Resources
page 332

Lonnie Johnson (1949–present)

Lonnie Johnson is an American inventor. When he was in high school, Johnson made a remote-controlled robot using junkyard scraps! After college, Johnson worked for NASA building different spacecrafts. He also kept inventing things at home. One day, he got an idea for making a toy that could squirt water a long way. Johnson built his water squirter. The toy could squirt water almost 50 feet! Johnson sold his design to a toy company. Millions of the water toys have since been sold. Johnson used the money he made to start his own company. Johnson's company has made other toys. But the company also works on products that help conserve energy and protect the environment.

∧ Water squirter

Sir Isaac Newton (1642–1727)

Isaac Newton was an English scientist. He was one of the greatest scientists that ever lived. Newton wrote some of his most important discoveries in three books known as *Principia*. The books contain Newton's three laws of motion. These laws describe how forces and motion are related. *Principia* also has Newton's laws of gravity. These laws explain how gravity works. They also explain why things fall to Earth and why planets and moons travel in orbits. Newton also showed that white light, such as sunlight, is made up of many different colors. Newton used a piece of glass called a *prism* to separate sunlight into a rainbow of light.

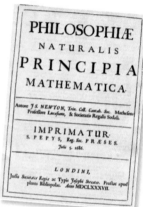

⋀ *Principia*

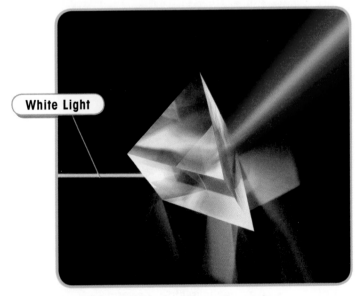

White Light

⋀ White light going through a prism

See Also

Planets Around the Sun
pages 204–205

Light and Color
page 270

Forces Cause Motion
pages 282–283

Gravity and Motion
page 284

Science Word Parts

Many science words can be broken down into word parts. Each word part has a special meaning. Word parts that go at the beginning of words are called *prefixes*. Word parts that go at the end of words are called *suffixes*. Word roots are parts that can go at the beginning, middle, or end of a word. The table below lists word parts that you might see in science.

Word Roots	Meaning	Examples
flect	bend back	reflect, reflection
morph	shape, form	metamorphic
therm	heat	thermometer, geothermal

Prefixes	Meaning	Examples
amphi-	both	amphibian
arthr, arthro-	joint	arthropod
bio-	life	biology, biography
carn-, carni-	meat	carnivore
centi-	one hundred, 1/100	centipede, centimeter
com-, con-	together, with	community, condense
de-	opposite of	decomposer
eco-	environment	ecology, ecosystem
equ-, equi-	even, evenly divided	equator, equal
exo-, ex-	outside, out of	exoskeleton, expand

Prefixes continued	Meaning	Examples
geo-	earth	geology, geothermal
herb-, herbi-	plant	herbivore
ign-	fire	igneous, ignite
in-	not	inactive, invertebrate
inter-	between	Internet
kilo-	one thousand	kilometer, kilogram
micro-	small	microscope
milli-	1/1,000	milliliter, millimeter
non-	not	nonrenewable, nonliving
omni-	all	omnivore
photo-	light	photosynthesis
pre-, pro-	before	predict
re-	again	recycle, reuse
tele-	distant	telescope, television

Suffixes	Meaning	Examples
-graph	write, draw, record	telegraph, biography
-logy	study	biology, geology
-meter	measure	thermometer
-saur	lizard	dinosaur
-scope	view	telescope, microscope
-sphere	ball, globe	atmosphere
-vore	eat	carnivore, herbivore

Glossary of Science Words

abdomen: the third body part of an insect; in other animals it is the middle or belly

absorb: to take in **(270)**

acid rain: a kind of air pollution that can harm living things **(331)**

adaptation: a body part or behavior that helps a living thing survive **(134)**

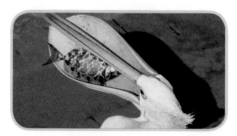

∧ A pelican's pouch is an adaptation.

adult: an animal that is all grown up **(119)**

∧ Adult butterfly

almanac: a book full of information about different topics **(399)**

amphibian: an animal that has a backbone and moist skin; it lives in water when it is young and on land when it is an adult **(101, 108)**

∧ A frog is an amphibian.

animal: a living thing that can move on its own and must eat plants or other animals for food **(83, 98)**

arthropod: an animal without a backbone that has jointed legs **(114)**

∧ A crab is an arthropod.

ash: a material that is made when wood burns **(249)**; a material volcanoes put out when they erupt **(325)**

asteroid: a piece of rock that orbits the sun **(204)**

astronaut: a scientist who goes into space in order to study it **(233, 404)**

∧ An astronaut on the moon

astronomer: a person who studies space

astronomy: the study of space

atmosphere: the air that surrounds a planet, such as Earth

atom: a tiny particle of matter **(240)**

attract: to pull together **(303)**

∧ Magnets attract some metal objects

axis: an imaginary line that goes through Earth's North and South Poles; Earth rotates on its axis **(215)**

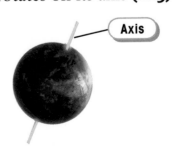

Axis

backbone: a row of bones along the backs of some animals **(100)**

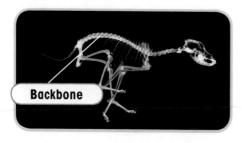

Backbone

bacteria: tiny living things made of only one cell **(148)**

balance: a tool used to measure mass **(62)**

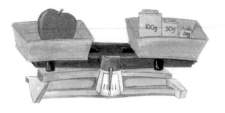

∧ Pan balance

bar graph: a graph that uses bars to show the same kind of data for different things **(32)**

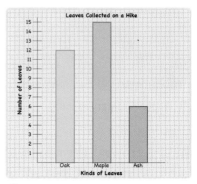

∧ Bar graph showing leaves collected on a hike

battery: an object that stores chemical energy **(258)**

beaker: a container for measuring liquids **(60)**

behavior: something an organism does to get the things it needs to live **(134)**

∧ Using a twig to get food is a kind of behavior.

Big Dipper: a group of stars that some people think looks like a scoop, or dipper **(229)**

biography: the story of a person's life **(391)**

bird: an animal that has a backbone, feathers, and wings **(101, 104)**

boil: to change from a liquid to a gas very quickly **(247)**

∧ Boiling water

bone: a hard structure inside some animals; part of the skeleton

breathe: to move air in and out of the lungs **(99)**

burning: a kind of chemical change that gives off heat energy; burning happens when something reacts with gases in the air **(249)**

calculator: a tool that adds, subtracts, multiplies, and divides numbers

calendar: a tool that measures days **(65)**

JUNE

Sunday	Monday	Tuesday	Wednesday	Thursday	Friday	Saturday
1	2	3	4	5	6	7
8	9	10	11	12	13	14
15	16	17	18	19	20	21
22	23	24	25	26	27	28
29	30					

canyon: a deep and narrow valley **(166)**

∧ The Grand Canyon

carbon dioxide: a gas that plants use to make food **(148)**; both plants and animals give it off

carnivore: an animal that eats only other animals for food

cast: a fossil that forms when a living thing leaves a hollow shape in mud and the shape fills with minerals that then turn to rock **(186)**

∧ Cast fossil

caterpillar: a young butterfly or moth; also called a *larva* **(125)**

∧ Butterfly caterpillar

cell: a tiny part that makes up living things **(81)**

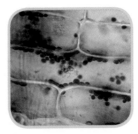

∧ Plant cells

Celsius (°C) scale: the temperature scale used in other countries and by scientists **(52)**

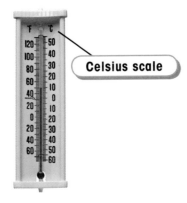

centimeter (cm): the metric unit for measuring short lengths **(55)**

Ceres: a dwarf planet **(205)**

characteristic: a quality that describes a living thing or an object; see *trait*

chart: a grid used to organize data into rows and columns; also called a *table* **(27)**

Time	Temperature (°F)
8:00 A.M.	58
9:00 A.M.	60
10:00 A.M.	62
11:00 A.M.	65
12:00 noon	68
1:00 P.M.	72
2:00 P.M.	74
3:00 P.M.	71

∧ Chart showing temperature data at different times of the day

chemical change: a change of one kind of matter into another kind of matter **(249)**

chemical energy: energy stored in food, fuel, and batteries **(256)**

chemical property: a property that describes how matter can react with other kinds of matter **(248)**

chrysalis: a hard covering around a butterfly pupa **(125)**

∧ Butterfly chrysalis

circle graph: a graph that divides up a circle to show parts of a whole; also called a *pie chart* **(33)**

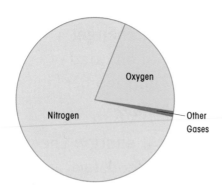

∧ Circle graph showing the gases that make up air

circuit: the path that electrical current takes **(272)**

cirrus cloud: a high, thin, cloud made of ice **(195)**

∧ Cirrus clouds

classify: to put things in groups by the way they are alike **(83)**

clay: the smallest rock particle found in soil **(184)**

climate: the general weather conditions in an area over a long period of time **(198)**

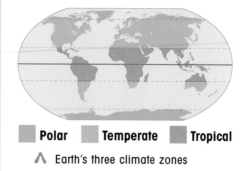

■ **Polar** ■ **Temperate** ■ **Tropical**
∧ Earth's three climate zones

clock: a tool used to measure minutes and hours **(66)**

closed circuit: a circuit that has a complete path that an electrical current can flow through **(273)**

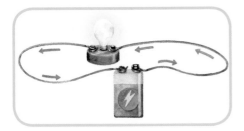

cloud: a clump of tiny water drops that hangs in the air **(163, 194)**

coal: a black, solid fossil fuel that is found underground; it can be burned to produce electricity **(319)**

∧ Lump of coal

cocoon: a soft covering around a moth pupa **(125)**

comet: an object that orbits the sun; when close to the sun it forms a long tail **(204)**

community: all the living things in an ecosystem **(129)**

compass: a tool that uses a magnetic needle to find north, south, east, and west **(305)**; a symbol on a map that shows north, south, east, and west **(382)**

compete: to work against other living things for the same resources **(133)**

∧ Wolves compete for food.

concept map: a diagram that shows how ideas connect **(371)**

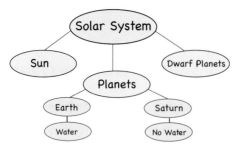

conclusion: a statement that explains the pattern you see in an investigation **(22)**

condensation: the change from a gas to a liquid **(163)**

condense: to change from a gas to a liquid **(247)**

∧ Water drops condense on grass.

cone: a plant part that has scales, is not colorful, and is used to make seeds **(91)**

∧ Pine cone

conifer: a plant that has cones **(95)**

conservation: the wise use of natural resources **(332)**

constellation: a group of stars that looks like it forms a picture in the sky **(228)**

∧ Leo is a constellation that looks like a lion.

consumer: an animal that gets food by eating plants or other animals **(149)**

core: the center of Earth **(159)**

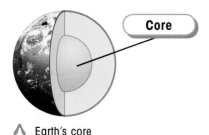

∧ Earth's core

crater: a round dent with high sides formed when an object from space hits a moon or planet **(220)**

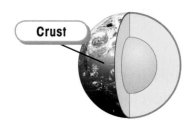

∧ Craters on the moon

crust: the rocky layer on the outside of Earth **(159)**

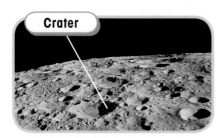

∧ Earth's crust

cumulonimbus cloud: a large, heavy dark cloud that brings thunderstorms **(195)**

∧ Cumulonimbus clouds

cumulus cloud: a thick white cloud that has a puffy top and a flat bottom **(194)**

∧ Cumulus clouds

current: the flow or movement of water, air, or electricity **(271)**

customary system: the units of measure used in the United States **(388)**

dam: a wall across a stream or river that holds back water **(145, 322)**

data: the information you collect in an investigation **(18)**

How the Plants Grew				
Day and Date	Plant in Sunlight		Plant in the Dark	
	How tall	What it looks like	How tall	What it looks like
Monday May 5	9 cm		9 cm	
Friday May 9	11 cm		9 cm	
Monday May 12	12 cm		9 cm	
Friday May 16	14 cm		9 cm	

∧ Data from a plant investigation

day: the time it takes for a planet to turn around once; on Earth, one day is 24 hours **(217)**

DDT: a chemical once used to kill insects; DDT is harmful to animals **(329)**

decomposer: a living thing that gets energy from breaking down once-living things **(150)**

degree (°): a unit used to measure temperature **(52)**

desert: a large area that has very little rain and few plants **(130)**

develop: to change; living things develop as they grow **(82)**

dew: drops of water that form on grass when water vapor condenses **(163)**

dinosaur: a kind of reptile that lived millions of years ago and is now extinct

∧ Tyrannosaurus rex was a kind of dinosaur.

direction: the path a moving object follows **(286)**

∧ The car changes direction when it turns.

dissolve: to mix evenly into a mixture **(251)**

∧ Salt dissolves into water.

distance: a measure of how far an object moves **(287)**

∧ Measuring distance

drought: a long period of time with too little rain **(145)**

dwarf planet: a round object that orbits the sun and is not big enough to be called a planet **(205)**

Earth: the third planet from the sun in the solar system; the planet we live on **(208)**

Earth science: the study of planet Earth and other objects in the sky **(157)**

earthquake: a sudden movement of Earth's crust **(172)**

∧ This building was damaged in an earthquake.

echo: a sound that repeats when sound waves bounce off of a surface

ecosystem: all of the living and nonliving things that are found in one place **(129)**

egg: the first stage in the life cycle of many animals

∧ Bird egg

electrical circuit: the path that electrical current takes **(272)**

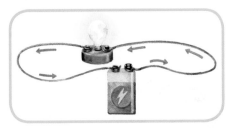

electrical current: the flow, or movement, of charged particles **(271)**

electrical energy: the energy of charged particles **(271)**

electricity: electrical current **(271)**

∧ Toasters use electricity.

endangered: at risk of becoming extinct **(118)**

∧ Manatees are endangered animals.

energy: something that living things use to live, grow, and move **(81)**; the ability to cause movement or create change **(254)**

∧ Mice get energy from the food they eat.

energy of motion: the energy an object has because it is moving; also called *kinetic energy* **(256)**

energy resource: anything in nature that people can use for energy **(316)**

∧ Coal is an energy resource.

engineer: a person who designs technology **(69)**

environment: everything that is around a living thing **(128, 307)**

equator: an imaginary line around Earth halfway between the North Pole and the South Pole **(199, 382)**

Eris: a dwarf planet; also a plutoid **(205)**

erosion: when weathered material is moved from one place to another **(168)**

∧ The Grand Canyon was formed by erosion.

erupt: to put gases, ash, and lava into the air or onto Earth's surface **(173)**

estimate: a number close to an exact amount **(352)**

ethanol: a fuel made from corn that can be mixed with gasoline and used to run cars **(320)**

evaporate: to change from a liquid to a gas **(247)**

evaporation: the change from a liquid to a gas **(162)**

exoskeleton: a hard outer covering on arthropods that protects soft body parts inside **(114)**

Exoskeleton

⋀ Crayfish have thick exoskeletons.

expand: to take up more space, or get bigger **(171)**

experiment: an investigation that tests a hypothesis

extinct: when there are no more living members of a kind of organism **(116)**

⋀ Dinosaurs are extinct.

Fahrenheit (°F) scale: the temperature scale used in the United States **(52)**

Fahrenheit scale

fish: an animal that has a backbone, fins, and gills, and lives in water **(101, 110)**

⋀ Clown fish

flood: an event that happens when a body of water overflows onto dry land **(174)**

∧ A flood left these houses under water.

flower: a plant part that has petals, is often colorful, and makes seeds **(91)**

flowering plant: a plant that uses flowers to make seeds **(91)**

food: something an animal eats or drinks, or a plant makes, that the animal or plant uses for energy

food chain: the path of energy from one living thing to another in an ecosystem **(152)**

∧ A simple food chain

food web: a drawing that shows the different ways energy flows through an ecosystem; it is made up of many different food chains **(155)**

foot (plural: feet): a customary unit of length; 12 inches equals 1 foot

force: a push or a pull **(280)**

forest: a large area covered by trees and other plants **(130)**

forest ranger: a person who helps protect the plants and animals that live in a refuge, or protected area **(339)**

fossil: the remains of an animal or plant that lived long ago **(116, 186)**

∧ Fossil of an animal shell

fossil fuel: an energy resource that formed from dead plants and animals **(317)**

fraction: a number that stands for part of something **(348)**

∧ Each half of the sandwich is $\frac{1}{2}$.

freeze: to change from a liquid to a solid **(246)**

∧ Water freezes to form ice.

fresh water: water that does not contain salt **(160)**

friction: a force that slows objects down **(285)**

fruit: a plant part that forms around the seed of a flowering plant **(91)**

fungus (plural: fungi): a kind of decomposer that cannot move around **(150)**

∧ Fungi growing on a dead log

galaxy: a very large group of stars **(404)**

∧ A galaxy

garbage: any kind of solid waste **(326)**

gas: a state of matter that can change its shape and the amount of space it takes up **(245)**

∧ The balloon is full of air, a gas.

gasoline: a liquid fuel that is made from oil and is used by cars **(318)**

geothermal energy: heat that comes from inside Earth; it is used as an energy resource **(321)**

∧ Geothermal energy can be used to heat water.

germ: a tiny living thing that makes other living things sick **(83)**

germinate: to begin sprouting a plant from a seed

gill: a structure that fish have for breathing under water **(110)**

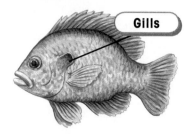

Gills

glacier: a thick layer of ice that stays frozen all year **(160, 170)**

globe: a round model of Earth **(384)**

graduated cylinder: a container used for measuring liquid **(61)**

∧ Reading a graduated cylinder

gram (g): the metric unit for measuring small masses **(63)**

graph: a picture that shows data **(30)**

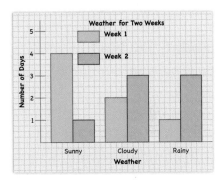

∧ Graph showing weather data

grassland: a large area covered mostly by grass **(130)**

gravity: a force that pulls objects toward each other **(284)**

groundwater: water found in the ground **(164)**

habitat: the kind of ecosystem where an organism lives **(131)**

hail: solid water that falls from clouds; it forms when falling rain bounces around in a cold cloud and turns into balls of ice **(192)**

∧ Hail stones on grass

hand lens: a tool used to make objects look bigger **(51, 241)**

heat energy: the energy of moving particles **(276)**

height: how tall an object is **(242)**

herbivore: an animal that eats only plants for food

hibernate: to go into a deep sleep to stay alive during the winter **(142)**

Hubble Space Telescope: a telescope that orbits Earth and takes pictures of things in space **(231)**

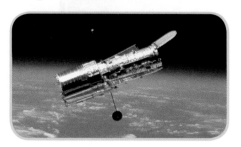

humidity: the amount of water vapor in the air **(191)**

humus: the broken down parts of plants and animals in soil **(182)**

hypothesis: an idea that can be tested **(11)**

igneous rock: a kind of rock that forms when melted rock cools and hardens **(179)**

∧ Obsidian is a kind of igneous rock.

imprint: a fossil that shows the shape of part of an animal or plant **(186)**

∧ Imprint fossil

inch (in.): the customary unit for measuring short lengths **(55)**

inclined plane: a simple machine made of a slanted surface; also called a *ramp* **(295)**

inexhaustible resource: a natural resource that can never be used up

infer: to come up with an explanation using information but not direct observation

insect: an animal that has three body parts, six jointed legs, two feelers, and a hard covering **(112)**

International Space Station: a large structure that orbits Earth; a place where scientists from around the world can do investigations **(233, 397)**

Internet: a worldwide network of computers **(364)**

inventor: a person who uses what they know about the natural world to make useful things or solve problems **(390)**

invertebrate: an animal that does not have a backbone

∧ An octopus is an invertebrate.

investigation: a way to find out the answer to a question **(8)**

iron: a kind of metal found in Earth's crust **(300)**

jointed legs: legs that bend in certain places **(114)**

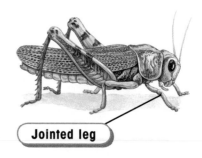

Jointed leg

Jupiter: the fifth planet from the sun in the solar system; the largest planet in the solar system **(211)**

key: see *map key*

kilogram (kg): the metric unit for measuring large masses **(63)**

kilometer (km): the metric unit for measuring long distances; 1,000 meters equals 1 kilometer

kinetic energy: the energy of motion

∧ The skateboarder has kinetic energy as she moves down the ramp.

lake: a large body of water surrounded by land

landfill: a place to bury garbage **(326)**

landform: a natural land shape on Earth's surface **(166)**

landslide: an event that happens when rocks and mud slide down a hill **(175)**

larva: a young butterfly or moth; also called a *caterpillar* **(125)**

latitude line: a line on a map or globe that circles Earth from east to west **(382)**

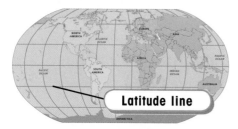

Latitude line

lava: melted rock at Earth's surface; it comes out of volcanoes **(173)**

leaf: a plant part that takes in gases from the air and uses sunlight to turn gases and water into food **(88)**

∧ Tree leaves

length: how long an object is **(242)**

lens: a curved piece of glass that makes things look bigger **(231)**

lever: a simple machine made of a bar that moves around a fixed point **(292)**

∧ A crowbar is a lever.

library: a place with books, magazines, and other materials **(362)**

life cycle: the changes that a living thing goes through during its life **(93, 119)**

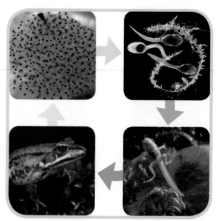

∧ Life cycle of a frog

life science: the study of living things **(79)**

light energy: energy that you can see **(266)**

lightning: a flash of light in the sky during a storm **(393)**

light wave: a wave that carries light energy; the way that light energy moves from place to place **(266)**

link (on computers): a connection to a Web site that has information about a subject **(365)**

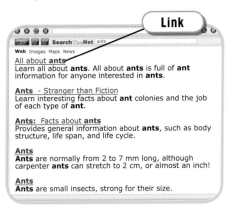

liquid: a state of matter that can change shape but takes up the same amount of space **(245)**

∧ Juice is a liquid.

liter (L): the metric unit for measuring larger volumes, or amounts of space **(59, 60)**

litter: garbage that is not put in a trash can **(326)**

∧ Litter on the side of a road

Little Dipper: a group of stars that some people think looks like a scoop or dipper; Polaris, the North Star, is part of the Little Dipper **(229)**

living thing: something that is alive **(79)**

longitude line: a line on a map or globe that runs through Earth's North and South Poles **(382)**

Longitude line

loudness: how loud or soft a sound is; also called *volume* **(264)**

lungs: sacs inside the bodies of some animals that take in air **(102)**

machine: a tool that makes work easier, usually by letting you use less force

magnet: an object that pulls on some metal objects **(298)**

⋀ Different kinds of magnets

magnetic: can be pulled by magnets **(300)**

⋀ Iron nails are magnetic.

magnetic field: the space around a magnet where the force of magnetism acts **(304)**

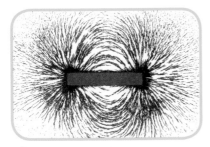

∧ Magnetic field around a bar magnet

magnetism: the pulling force between an object and a magnet **(299)**

magnify: to make an object look larger **(230, 241)**

∧ A hand lens is used to magnify objects.

mammal: an animal that has a backbone and hair or fur; it feeds its young with milk **(101, 102)**

∧ Dogs are mammals.

mantle: the middle layer of Earth; much thicker than the crust **(159)**

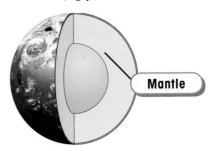

∧ Earth's mantle

map: a picture that shows Earth's surface **(380)**

map key: a guide that explains what the symbols on a map mean **(380)**

Mars: the fourth planet from the sun in the solar system **(210)**

mass: the amount of matter in something **(62, 243)**

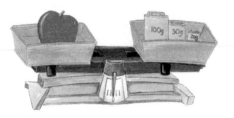

∧ Mass is measured using a balance.

material resources: materials in nature that people use to make things **(310)**

matter: anything that takes up space and has mass **(236)**

measure: to find out how much there is of something **(6)**

measurement: how much there is of something **(6)**

measuring cup: a container for measuring liquids **(59)**

melt: to change from a solid to a liquid **(246)**

∧ Melting popsicle

Mercury: the closest planet to the sun in the solar system **(206)**

metamorphic rock: a kind of rock that forms when other kinds of rock are heated and squeezed deep underground **(181)**

meter (m): the metric unit for measuring longer lengths **(56, 57)**

meter stick: a tool for measuring length **(56)**

metric system: the units of measure used by scientists; most countries use the metric system **(386)**

microscope: a tool used to make objects look bigger; it can magnify more than a hand lens can **(241)**

migrate: to move from one place to another in search of food, water, or warmer temperatures

∧ Caribou migrate south for the winter.

milliliter (mL): the metric unit for measuring smaller volumes; there are 1,000 milliliters in 1 liter **(59, 60, 61)**

millimeter (mm): the metric unit for measuring very small lengths; there are 10 millimeters in 1 centimeter, and 1,000 millimeters in 1 meter **(55)**

mineral: a solid material found in nature that has never been alive **(176)**

∧ Graphite is a mineral.

mining: digging coal, metals, and other valuable materials out of Earth's crust **(327)**

mirror: an object with a smooth, shiny surface; you can see yourself in a mirror **(268)**

mixture: two or more substances mixed together **(250)**

mold (fossil): a fossil that forms after a living thing dies and is buried in sand or mud; it is shaped like the outside of the living thing that made it **(186)**

∧ Mold fossil

mold (fungus): a kind of fungus that grows on old fruit or bread **(150)**

moon: a round body that orbits around a planet **(204)**

motion: a change in position **(281)**

∧ This boy is in motion.

mountain: a large landform that pokes up toward the sky **(166)**

mushroom: a part of a fungus **(150)**

nectar: a sweet liquid made by some flowers; many insects and birds drink nectar **(151)**

∧ Bees drink nectar.

Neptune: the eighth and most distant planet from the sun in the solar system **(214)**

nonliving: not alive **(81)**

nonmagnetic: cannot be pulled by magnets **(301)**

nonrenewable resource: a natural resource that nature cannot replace fast enough for people to use again **(309)**

north pole (of a magnet): one of two places on a magnet where it is strongest **(302)**

North pole

∧ North pole of a bar magnet

North Pole (of Earth): the northern end of the imaginary line that Earth rotates around

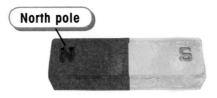

North Pole

nutrient: a material that living things use to grow and develop; it does not provide energy **(86)**

observation: something you notice with your senses **(2)**

observe: to gather information using your senses **(2)**

ocean: a very large body of salt water **(160)**

∧ Ocean life

offspring: a living thing that is made when a plant or animal reproduces **(126)**

oil: a liquid fossil fuel that is found underground; it can be turned into other kinds of fuel **(318)**

omnivore: an animal that eats both plants and animals for food

open circuit: a circuit that has an opening in its path so electrical current cannot flow through it **(273)**

orbit: *(n.)* the path an object takes around another object in space; *(v.)* to move around something **(204, 215)**

∧ Earth's orbit around the sun

organism: a living thing **(80)**

oxygen: a gas that both plants and animals use to get energy from food **(99, 148)**

pan balance: a tool that has one or two moving platforms and is used to measure mass **(62)**

particle: a very tiny part of matter **(271)**

phase: the way the moon looks on a given night **(222)**

∧ Last quarter phase of the moon

physical change: a change in a physical property of matter **(244)**

physical property: a characteristic of matter that you can observe **(238)**

physical science: the study of matter, forces, motion, and energy **(235)**

pictograph: a diagram that uses pictures instead of numbers to show data **(31)**

Chocolate Chip	🍪 🍪 🍪 🍪 🍪 🍪		
Peanut Butter	🍪 🍪		
Key	🍪 = 2 students	🍪 = 2 students	

∧ Pictograph showing what cookies students like best

pie chart: see *circle graph*

pitch: how high or low a sound is **(262)**

plain: a very large, flat landform **(167)**

planet: a large object in space that moves around the sun **(204)**

plant: a living thing that cannot move from place to place and uses energy from sunlight to make its own food **(85)**

plateau: a large, flat area that is higher than the land around it and often has steep sides **(167)**

Pluto: a dwarf planet that orbits the sun; also known as a *plutoid* **(205)**

plutoid: a dwarf planet that orbits the sun beyond Neptune **(205)**

polar climate: a climate that has long cold winters and short cool summers **(200)**

∧ Polar bears live in polar climates.

pole: a place on a magnet where magnetism is the strongest **(302)**

pollen: a powdery material made by flowers; it helps make seeds **(91)**

pollution: any harmful material that is added to the environment **(146, 325)**

∧ Water pollution

population: all organisms of the same kind living in a place at the same time **(129)**

position: an object's location; where it is **(281)**

potential energy: the energy an object has because of its position

∧ The skateboarder has potential energy as she stands at the top of the ramp.

power plant: a factory where other forms of energy are used to produce electricity **(274, 319)**

precipitation: water or ice that falls to Earth; rain, snow, sleet, and hail are all different kinds of precipitation **(164, 192)**

predator: an animal that hunts and eats other animals for food **(149)**

∧ A predator chases its prey.

prediction: an idea about what will happen in the future **(360)**

prefix: a word part that goes at the beginning of a word **(410)**

prey: an animal that another animal eats for food **(149)**

prism: a piece of glass that splits white light into colors **(409)**

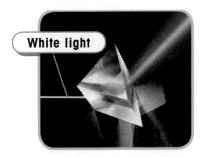

probability: the chance that something will happen **(356)**

producer: an organism that makes its own food **(148)**

property: a characteristic of matter

pull: a force that moves an object closer to another object **(280)**

∧ You pull on objects when you pick them up.

pulley: a simple machine made of a rope that goes around a wheel **(294)**

pupa: the stage of life of a butterfly or moth between a caterpillar and an adult **(125)**

∧ Butterfly pupa

push: a force that moves an object away from another object **(280)**

∧ You push on objects when you kick them.

question: something that leads to an investigation; questions are based on observations **(7, 8)**

R

rain: liquid water that falls from clouds **(192)**

ramp: a simple machine made of a slanted surface; also called an *inclined plane* **(295)**

recycle: to use a material to make something new instead of throwing it away **(337)**

∧ Sorting objects for recycling

reduce: to use less of something, such as a resource **(335)**

reflect: to bounce off **(221, 268)**

refract: to bend as a wave moves from one material to another **(269)**

refuge: a protected area where plants and animals live **(339)**

renewable resource: a natural resource that nature can replace **(308)**

repel: to push away **(303)**

reproduce: to make more living things of the same kind **(82, 91, 119)**

reptile: an animal that has a backbone and skin covered with dry scales **(101, 106)**

∧ A lizard is a reptile.

resource: something that an organism gets from its habitat to meet its needs **(132)**; any material that people can use

reuse: to use something again instead of throwing it away **(336)**

revolve: to move around something else; to orbit

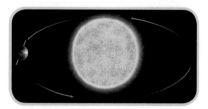

∧ Earth revolves around the sun.

river: a large stream of fresh water than runs into an ocean or lake

rock: a solid material made up of minerals **(178)**

root: a plant part that takes in water and nutrients from the soil, supports the plant, and holds the plant in the soil **(89)**

∧ Plant roots underground

rotate: to spin around an imaginary line called an axis **(215)**

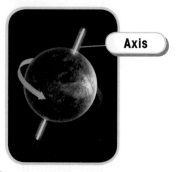

∧ Earth rotates around its axis.

ruler: a tool for measuring length **(55)**

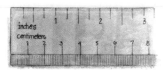

runoff: water that flows along Earth's surface **(164)**

rusting: a chemical change that happens when iron reacts with gases in the air **(248)**

salt water: water that contains salt (160)

sand: a small rock particle found in soil and on beaches (184)

satellite: any object that orbits a planet (71, 221)

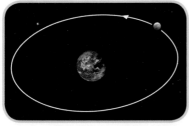

∧ The moon is a satellite of Earth.

Saturn: the sixth planet from the sun in the solar system; known for its large rings (212)

scale: a tool for measuring weight (243)

science: the study of the natural world (1)

scientist: a person who studies the natural world (1, 390)

screw: a simple machine made of a rod with an inclined plane wrapped around it (297)

∧ A screwdriver is used to drive a screw into wood.

search engine: a Web site that lets you find other Web sites by typing in a subject (364)

season: a time of year that shows a certain weather pattern **(196)**

∧ Four seasons

sediment: tiny pieces of sand, rock, and shells carried by moving water **(180)**

sedimentary rock: a kind of rock that forms from hardened layers of sediment **(180)**

seed: a plant part that contains a tiny plant and stored food **(91)**

∧ Seeds from a bean plant

seedling: a young plant that grows from a seed **(94)**

∧ Bean plant seedling

senses: what you use to make observations; the five senses are seeing, hearing, smelling, tasting, and touching **(2)**

separate: to take apart, or divide into groups

shadow: a dark spot that forms when something blocks light **(267)**

Shadow

shelter: something that protects an animal from heat, cold, and danger **(99)**

simple machine: a tool that makes work easier **(291)**

skeleton: all the bones in an animal's body **(100)**

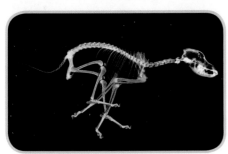

∧ Dog skeleton

sleet: solid water (ice) that falls from clouds; it is formed when falling snow melts and then freezes again **(192)**

smog: harmful gases trapped close to the ground **(331)**

snow: solid water that falls from clouds; it forms as tiny crystals **(192)**

soil: the loose material that covers Earth's surface; it is made of small pieces of rock, minerals, and bits of dead plants and animals **(182)**

solar cells: objects that change the sun's energy into electricity **(324)**

solar collectors: large panels made up of many solar cells **(324)**

∧ Solar collectors on the roof of a house

solar energy: energy from sunlight

solar system: the sun and all the objects that move around it **(204)**

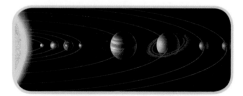

solid: a state of matter that keeps the same shape and takes up the same amount of space when it is moved **(245)**

solution: a kind of mixture in which the substances are spread out evenly; also means the answer to a problem **(251)**

sound energy: energy you can hear; energy made when matter vibrates **(260)**

sound wave: a wave that carries sound energy through matter; the way that sound energy moves through matter **(260)**

∧ Radios make sound waves that travel through air.

south pole (of a magnet): one of two places on a magnet where it is strongest **(302)**

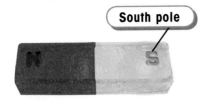

∧ South pole of a bar magnet

South Pole (of Earth): the southern end of the imaginary line that Earth rotates around

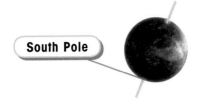

space: the area in all directions beyond Earth **(202)**

space probe: a space craft that carries tools but not people **(232)**

∧ A rover is a kind of space probe.

space shuttle: a space craft that carries astronauts into orbit around Earth **(233)**

∧ The Space Shuttle

speed: a measure of how fast an object is moving; it is found by dividing distance traveled by time **(289)**

spider: an animal that has two body parts, eight jointed legs, and a hard covering **(112)**

spring scale: a tool used to measure force

sprout: (*v.*) to grow from a seed to a seedling; (*n.*) the young plant that comes out of a seed **(94)**

star: a big ball of hot gases that gives off light **(224)**

states of matter: the forms that matter can be in; three states of matter are solid, liquid, and gas **(245)**

stem: a plant part that supports the plant and moves water, food, and nutrients around inside the plant **(90)**

∧ A sunflower has a very long stem.

stopwatch: a tool for measuring minutes, seconds, and parts of a second **(67)**

stored energy: the energy an object has because of where it is; also called *potential energy* **(259)**

stream: a small body of moving water

stratus cloud: a cloud that is flat and layered **(195)**

∧ Stratus clouds

substance: a single kind of matter **(250)**

subsoil: the layer of soil beneath the top layer **(183)**

suffix: a word part that goes at the end of a word **(410)**

sun: the closest star to Earth and the center of the solar system **(204)**

∧ The sun at sunset on Earth

table: a grid used to organize data into rows and columns; also called a *chart* **(27)**

Time	Temperature (°F)
8:00 A.M.	58
9:00 A.M.	60
10:00 A.M.	62
11:00 A.M.	65
12:00 noon	68
1:00 P.M.	72
2:00 P.M.	74
3:00 P.M.	71

∧ Table showing temperature data at different times of the day

tadpole: a young amphibian that has a tail and gills but no legs **(123)**

tally chart: a chart used to count things **(27)**

Season	Tally	Number
Spring	///	3
Summer	### ////	9
Fall	////	4
Winter	//	2

∧ Tally chart showing what season students like best

tape measure: a tool for measuring length; also called *measuring tape* **(57)**

technology: any tool that people find useful **(68)**

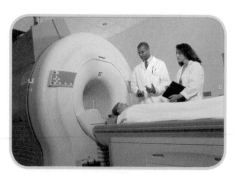

∧ Doctors use technology to help people be healthy.

telegraph: a machine that sends information through wires **(402)**

telescope: a tool that makes far-away objects look larger and clearer **(230)**

∧ Using a telescope to observe the sky

temperate climate: a climate that has cold or cool winters and hot or warm summers **(201)**

∧ Some trees in temperate climates lose their leaves for winter.

temperature: a measure of how hot or cold something is **(52, 190, 277)**

thermometer: a tool used to measure temperature **(52, 190, 277)**

thorax: the second body part of an insect

time: a measure of how long it takes an object to move a certain a distance **(288)**

time line: a list of important events in the order they took place **(391)**

tool: an object that helps you make observations that go beyond your senses **(6)**; something you use to make work easier **(290)**

topsoil: the top layer of soil; most plants and animals are in topsoil **(183)**

trait: a characteristic that may be passed from parent to offspring **(96, 126)**

∧ This foal has many of her mother's traits.

tropical climate: a climate that is very warm and wet for most of the year **(200)**

∧ Many trees grow in tropical climates.

tundra: a large, flat area that is cold all year and has no trees and little rain **(131)**

United States customary system: the units of measure used in the United States **(388)**

units of measure: words or symbols that tell what a number stands for **(386)**

Unit: 1 millimeter (mm)		
10 mm	equals	1 (cm)
100 cm	equals	1 (m)
1000 m	equals	1 (km)

∧ Units of length and distance for the metric system

Uranus: the seventh planet from the sun in the solar system **(213)**

vaccine: medicine given to a person to keep them safe from one kind of sickness; there are vaccines for many different kinds of sicknesses **(393, 396)**

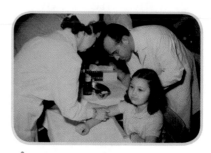

∧ This girl is getting a vaccine for the sickness polio.

valley: the low land between mountains **(166)**

vapor: see *water vapor*

variable: something in an investigation that can change **(16)**

Venn diagram: a diagram made of two or more circles that shows how things are grouped **(36, 371)**

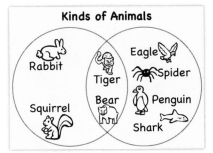

Λ A Venn diagram showing how different kinds of animals are alike.

Venus: the second planet from the sun in the solar system **(207)**

vertebrate: an animal that has a backbone

Λ A snake is a vertebrate.

vibrate: to move back and forth quickly **(260)**

vibration: a fast back-and-forth motion; vibrations make sounds **(264)**

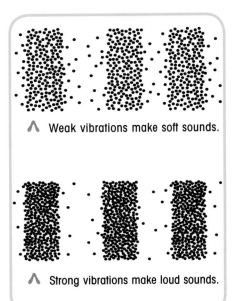

Λ Weak vibrations make soft sounds.

Λ Strong vibrations make loud sounds.

virus: something that makes living things sick

volcano: a mountain with an opening that lets out material from deep inside Earth **(173)**

∧ Erupting volcano

volume: the amount of space matter takes up **(58, 242)**; also means how loud or soft a sound is **(264)**

∧ The volume of a liquid can be measured using a measuring cup.

water: a substance all living things need to survive **(160)**

water cycle: the movement of water between the air and Earth **(164)**

water vapor: water in the gas state **(162)**

∧ Water vapor enters the air.

wave: movement of some kinds of energy from one place to another

weather: a description of the outside air in a certain place at a certain time **(189)**

∧ A rainy day

weathering: the breaking down of rock into tiny pieces **(168)**

Web site: a place on the Internet that has information about a certain subject **(364)**

wedge: a simple machine made of two inclined planes that are stuck together **(296)**

∧ An ax is a wedge.

weigh: to measure the weight of an object

weight: a measure of how hard gravity pulls on an object; it depends on how much mass an object has **(243)**

∧ Weight is measured using a scale.

wetland: a large area that is very wet; it is often found where land and water meet **(131)**

wheel and axle: a simple machine made of a wheel stuck to a rod **(293)**

∧ A door knob is a wheel and axle.

width: how wide an object is **(242)**

wilt: to become limp; plants wilt when they do not get enough water **(87)**

wind: moving air **(193, 323)**

∧ A wind vane shows what direction wind is coming from.

wind energy: the energy of moving air; wind energy is a renewable resource **(323)**

wind farm: a large group of wind turbines **(323)**

∧ A wind farm

wind turbine: a machine that changes the energy of moving air into electricity **(323)**

wood: the hard stem of a tree that can be burned as fuel **(320)**

∧ Wood is burned in a campfire.

word root: a word part that can go at the beginning, middle, or end of a word **(410)**

work: what is done when a force is used to move an object **(290)**

World Wide Web (www): see *Internet*

worm: an animal that has a soft, long body and usually no arms or legs **(113)**

∧ An earthworm

yard (yd): the customary unit for measuring longer lengths **(56, 57)**

year: the time it takes for a planet to finish one trip around the sun; on Earth, one year is about 365 days **(215)**

yolk: the yellow part of a bird or reptile egg; it is food for the animal that grows inside the egg

Index

Credits

COVER PHOTOGRAPHY
Front cover
bees: © iStockphoto.com/Florin Tirlea
wind turbine: ©Stockbyte/Getty Images
rainbow: ©imagewerks/Getty Images
earth: ©Photodisc/Getty Images
girl on bike: © Jonathan Kirn/The Image Bank/
Getty Images
frog: ©Tom Brakefield /Stockbyte/Getty Images
dandelions: ©Photodisc/Getty Images

Back cover
dinosaur fossil: © iStockphoto.com/Linda Bucklin
bees: © iStockphoto.com/Florin Tirlea
pyrite: © Visuals Unlimited/Corbis
vortex: ©Photodisc/Getty Images
running boy: © Bob Thomas/Corbis/©Eyewire
fern: ©/iStockphoto.com/Nancy Nehring
tornado: ©Photodisc/Getty Images
school of fish: © James Forte /National Geographic/
Getty Images

PHOTOGRAPHY
Table of Contents
iv   (b)   © Photodisc/Getty Images
v   (t)   © Mode Images Limited/Alamy
v   (b)   ©North Wind Picture Archives / Alamy

Doing Science
2   © Jupiter Images/Comstock Images/Alamy
4   © image100/CORBIS
5   (t)   © D. Hurst/Alamy
5   (b)   © blickwinkel / Alamy
6   (bl)   ©iStockphoto.com/Tatiana Popova
6   (bc)   © Photodisc/Alamy
6   (br)   © D. Hurst/Alamy
10   (bl)   © AbleStock.com/Jupiter Images
10   (bc)   © Bruce Edwards/Getty Images
10   (br)   © imagebroker/Alamy
13   (t)   © Jupiter Images/Brand X/Alamy
13   (c)   © WoodyStock/Alamy
13   (b)   © Photodisc/Alamy
24   © iStockphoto.com
25   © Dr. Merlin D. Tuttle/Photo
          Researchers, Inc.
38   © Imagehit Inc./Alamy
40   © iStockphoto.com/Tatiana Popova
45   © Jupiter Images/Brand X/Alamy

47   (tl)   © Gail Jankus/Photo Researchers, Inc.
47   (tc)   © Betty B. Derig/Photo Researchers, Inc.
47   (tr)   © Gwen Kirtley Perkins/Photo
          Researchers, Inc.
47   (br)   © USDA/Nature Source/Photo
          Researchers, Inc.
48   © iStockphoto.com/Florin Tirlea
49   (t)   © D. Hurst/Alamy
49   (b)   © JUPITERIMAGES/ Brand X / Alamy
52   © Jupiter Images/Brand X/Alamy
53   (bl)   © image100/CORBIS
53   (r)   © iStockphoto.com/Martin McCarthy
54   © iStockphoto.com/Günay Mutlu
64   (bl)   © PhotoSpin, Inc./Alamy
64   (bc)   © iStockphoto.com/Muharrem Oner
64   (br)   © Image Source Black/Alamy
66   (tl)   © WoodyStock/Alamy
66   (tr)   © WoodyStock/Alamy
68   © David Hay Jones/Photo Researchers, Inc.
69   © Thinkstock/Corbis
70   (b)   © Steve Bly/Alamy
70   (t)   © Enigma/Alamy
71   © NASA/CORBIS
72   (c)   © NOAA, U.S. Department of Commerce
72   (br)   © Nick Koudis/Photodisc/Getty Images
73   © Pete Saloutos/Corbis
75   © Digital Vision/Photolibrary
76   (t)   © image100/Corbis
76   (b)   © Jason Edwards/National Geographic/
          Getty Images
77   © David R. Frazier Photolibrary, Inc./
          Photo Researchers, Inc.

Life Science
81   (b)   © iStockphoto.com/Cathryn Thomas
81   (c)   © blickwinkel / Alamy
81   (t)   © Peter Arnold, Inc. / Alamy
82   (l)   © Michael & Patricia Fogden/CORBIS
82   (r)   © DLILLC/Corbis
84   (l)   © Image Source Black/Jupiter Images
84   (r)   © Stockbyte/Getty Images
85   © Mike Grandmaison/CORBIS
90   (cr)   © Dorling Kindersley/Getty Images
90   (l)   © Photographer's Choice/Getty Images
90   (cl)   © Digital Vision/Getty Images
90   (r)   © Robert Landau/CORBIS
91   (b)   © Geoff Brightling/ Dorling Kindersley/
          Getty Images
91   (l)   © Bruce Edwards/Getty Images
91   (r)   © De Agostini Picture Library/CORBIS
92   © CORBIS

232 (l)   © NASA
232 (r)   © NASA
233   © NASA

Physical Science

236   © John Giustina/Photodisc/Getty Images
237 (b)   © Sean Justice/CORBIS
237 (tr) © Radius Images/Jupiter Images
238 (bl) © Image Source/Jupiter Images
238 (br) © C Squared Studios/Photodisc/
          Getty Images
238 (t)   © ballyscanlon/Photodisc/Getty Images
240 (bl) © Eye of Science/Photo Researchers, Inc
240 (br) © Michael A. Keller/CORBIS
240 (tl) © iStockphoto.com/Gary Alvis
240 (tr) © iStockphoto.com
241 (bl) © JGI/Blend Images/Getty Images
241 (br) © E.R. Degginger/Alamy
241 (tl) © Pascal Goetgheluck/Ardea
241 (tr) © Meg Takamura/IZA Stock/Getty Images
246 (b)   © Envision/CORBIS
246 (t)   © David Chasey/Photodisc/Getty Images
247 (b)   © image100/Jupiter Images
247 (t)   © David Chasey/Photodisc/Getty Images
248 (b)   © RubberBall Selects/Alamy
248 (t)   © imagebroker/Alamy
249 (br) © Burke/Triolo Productions/Brand X/
          CORBIS
249 (cl) © Martial Colomb/Photodisc/
          Getty Images
249 (cr) © iStockphoto.com/Amanda Smith
254   © UpperCut Images/Alamy
255 (bl) © Stockbyte/Getty Images
255 (br) © D. Hurst/Alamy
255 (t)   © Creatas Images/Jupiter Images
258 (bl) © Stocksearch/Alamy
258 (br) © Alex Cao/Digital Vision/Getty Images
258 (t)   © Lorcan/Digital Vision/Getty Images
261 (br) © RubberBall/Alamy
261 (cr) © iStockphoto.com/Lee Pettet
261 (tr) © Corbis/Jupiter Images
266 (b)   © Adam Taylor/Digital Vision/
          Getty Images
266 (t)   © Darren Greenwood/Design Pics/
          CORBIS
269 (b)   © S. Meltzer/PhotoLink/Getty Images
269 (tr) © Keith Leighton/Alamy
270   © D. Hurst /Alamy
276 (cl) © iStockphoto.com/Christine Balderas
276 (cr) © Foodcollection/Getty Images
277 (bl) © Digital Vision/Getty Images
277 (tr) © iStockphoto.com/Hélène Vallée
279   © Gail Mooney/CORBIS
282 (b)   © Tom Prettyman / PhotoEdit
282 (t)   © rubberball/Jupiter Images
283 (l)   © Hemera Technologies/Jupiter Images
283 (r)   © Hayman/Digital Vision/Getty Images
285   © Corbis/Jupiter Images
288   © Dennis MacDonald/PhotoEdit

289   © Creatas Images/Jupiter Images
290 (b)   © Sky Bonillo/PhotoEdit
290 (t)   © Somos/Veer/Getty Images
291 (b)   © David Young-Wolff/PhotoEdit
291 (t)   © iStockphoto.com
292 (b)   © Pixonnet.com/Alamy
292 (t)   © Tetra Images/CORBIS
293 (b)   © C Squared Studios/Photodisc/
          Getty Images
293 (c)   © Cindy Charles/PhotoEdit
294 (b)   © Michael Newman/PhotoEdit
294 (t)   © Travel Ink/Getty Images
296 (b)   © fStop/Alamy
296 (t)   © Stockbyte/Getty Images
297   © Pixland/Jupiter Images
298   © Tony Freeman/PhotoEdit
299   © iStockphoto.com/Justin Horrocks
304   © Cordelia Molloy / Photo
          Researchers, Inc
305 (b)   © David Young-Wolff/PhotoEdit
305 (c)   © iStockphoto.com/Marcus Clackson
305 (t)   © Amy Etra/PhotoEdit

Natural Resources
and the Environment

308   © Montiauk/Eastcott/The Image works
309   © Creatas Images/Jupiter Images
312   © Photodisc/Getty Images
313 (b)   © Emily Lai/Alamy
313 (c)   © iStockphoto.com/Wilson Valentin
313 (t)   © iStockphoto.com/Jeremy Edwards
314   © Wayne G. Lawler/Photo
          Researchers, Inc.
315   © Silverstock/Getty Images
316 (b)   © iStockphoto.com/Andrej Kropotov
316 (t)   © iStockphoto.com/Skip Odonnell
317 (b)   © Steve McCutcheon/Visuals Unlimited/
          Alamy
317 (tl) © Chris Cheadle/Alamy
317 (tr) © The Irish Image Collection/Corbis
318 (b)   © Image Source Black/Jupiter Images
318 (t)   © Bill Bachmann/PhotoEdit
319 (b)   © Brand X Pictures/Jupiter Images
319 (t)   © Thinkstock Images/Jupiter Images
321   © Richard Nowitz/Getty Images
322 (b)   © iStockphoto.com/Stephen Rees
322 (t)   © iStockphoto.com//Kevin Tavares
323   © Comstock Images/Jupiter Images
324 (b)   © iStockphoto.com/Jasmin Awad
324 (t)   © iStockphoto.com/Richard
          Schmidt-Zuper
325   © Photodisc/Getty Images
326 (b)   © Corbis Premium RF/Alamy
326 (t)   © Kevin M. Law/Alamy
327   © Purestock/Getty Images
328 (br) © Pixoi Ltd/Alamy
328 (c)   © Index Stock/Alamy
329   © Klaus Nigge/National Geographic/
          Getty Images

330 (l) © iStockphoto.com
330 (r) © iStockphoto.com/Timothy Hughes
331 (b) © iStockphoto.com
331 (t) © iStockphoto.com/Sander Kamp
336 (l) © iStockphoto.com/Dmitry Goygel-Sokol
336 (r) © South West Images Scotland/Alamy
337 (b) © David Young-Wolff/PhotoEdit
337 (t) © Mark Boulton/Alamy
338 (l) © Darwin Wiggett/Getty Images
338 (r) © Brand X Pictures/Jupiter Images
339 © Andre Jenny/Alamy
340 (b) © Louise Heusinkveld/Alamy
340 (t) © Comstock Images/Jupiter Images
341 (bl) © iStockphoto.com/Greg Christman
341 (t) © Stockbyte/Getty Images
343 © Rubberball/Getty Images

Almanac
346 © iStockphoto.com/Olga Lyubkina
347 © iStockphoto.com/Piotr Skubisz
349 (b) © Filaphoto/Alamy
349 (c) © Burke/Triolo Productions/Brand X/
Corbis
349 (t) © zefa royalty free/Jupiter Images
350 (bc) © iStockphoto.com/Ian McDonnell
350 (bl) © iStockphoto.com/Ian McDonnell
350 (br) © iStockphoto.com
353 © DLILLC/Corbis
356 (b) © BLOOMimage/Getty Images
356 (c) © iStockphoto.com
358 © Goodshoot/Jupiter Images
360 (bl) © Creatas Images/Jupiter Images
360 (br) © iStockphoto.com
360 (c) © iStockphoto.com
361 © iStockphoto.com
363 © Thinkstock/Corbis
366 © Carlos Davila/Getty Images
367 © Jupiter Images
368 (bl) © iStockphoto.com/Oleg Prikhodko
368 (br) © iStockphoto.com/Ivan Stevanovic
368 (t) © Somos Images/Corbis
370 © Blend Images/Alamy
373 © Jupiter Images
378 (bl) © Jupiter Images
378 (br) © Comstock Images/Jupiter Images
382–383 © stockmaps.com/GeoNova
Publishing, Inc.
384 (bl) © Mode Images Limited/Alamy
384 (br) © Photodisc/Getty Images
385 (b) © stockmaps.com/GeoNova
Publishing, Inc.
385 (t) © stockmaps.com/GeoNova
Publishing, Inc.
386 © iStockphoto.com/Martin McCarthy

Yellow Pages
390 © Underwood & Underwood/CORBIS
391 (bc) Courtesy Sandra Faber
391 (bl) © Bettmann/CORBIS
391 (br) © North Wind Picture Archives / Alamy
391 (tl) Library of Congress
391 (tr) © Michael Porro/Getty Image News
392 (r) ©Hulton Archive/Getty Images
393 (bl) Courtesy Alan Shinn
393 (c) © Célio Pedrosa
393 (tl) © NASA
393 (tr) © Bettmann/CORBIS
394 (b) ©Digital Vision,Ltd.
394 (c) © James Randklev/CORBIS
394 (l) From John Dalton A New System of
Chemical Philosophy, 1808. Courtesy
David Darling
395 (bl) © Bettmann/CORBIS
395 (br) © Bettmann/CORBIS
395 (tl) © The Granger Collection, New York
395 (tr) © Bettmann/CORBIS
396 (bl) NASA - digital version©Science Faction/
Getty Images
396 (br) © Ted Soqui/Corbis
396 (c) © CORBIS SYGMA
396 (tl) © Bettmann/CORBIS
396 (tr) © INTERFOTO Pressebildagentur/Alamy
397 (bl) © NASA
397 (br) © Najlah Feanny/CORBIS SABA
397 (tl) Courtesy US Geological Service
397 (tr) © European Space Agency/NASA
398 (bl) ©Pat Morris/ardea.com
398 (br) © Lawrence Lawry / Photo
Researchers, Inc
398 (t) Mary Anning (1799-1847) (oil on
canvas) by English School (19th
century) Private Collection/ The
Bridgeman Art Library
399 (bl) © The Granger Collection, New York
399 (br) © Michael Ventura / Alamy
399 (t) © North Wind Picture Archives / Alamy
400 (bl Courtesy USDA
400 (br) © Burke/Triolo Productions/Brand X/
Corbis
400 (t) © Bettmann/CORBIS
401 (bl) © Chris Lyon/Getty Images
401 (br) © The London Art Archive / Alamy
401 (t) © Stefano Bianchetti/CORBIS
402 (br) Courtesy Edison National Historic Site
402 (c) © Bettmann/CORBIS
402 (t) Courtesy Library of Congress
403 (b) © Bettmann/CORBIS
403 (t) © Bettmann/CORBIS
404 (br) © NASA
404 (c) © NASA
404 (t) Sandra Faber photo with Hubble Deep
Field, courtesy R. R. Jones, Hubble Deep
field Team, NASA

440 (tr) © Pixland/Jupiter Images
441 (br) © Digital Vision/Alamy
441 (tl) © Ralph Lee Hopkins/National Geographic/Getty Images
442 (cl) © Joel W. Rogers/CORBIS
442 (tl) © James Gritz/Robert Harding/Jupiter Images
442 (tr) © Corbis/Jupiter Images
443 (bl) © NASA
443 (br) © Digital Vision/Getty Images
443 (cl) © NASA
443 (cr) © Digtial Vision,Ltd.
443 (tr) ©3B Scientific, www.a3bs.com
444 (bl) © Comstock/Jupiter Images
444 (br) © Photolibrary/Getty Images
444 (tl) © iStockphoto.com/Paul Prescott
445 (bl) © Stuart O'Sullivan/Stone/Getty Images
445 (br) © Jupiter Images/Brand X/Alamy
445 (tl) © Pete Saloutos/Corbis
445 (tr) © Bill Brooks / Alamy
446 (bl) © Workbook Stock/Jupiter Images
446 (br) © Keren Su/Digital Vision/Getty Images
446 (cl) © Frans Lanting/CORBIS
446 (tl) © Lothar Lenz/zefa/CORBIS
446 (tr) © NASA
447 (bl) Courtesy US Geological Service
447 (cl) © Polka Dot Images/Jupiter Images
448 (br) © Altrendo/Getty Images
448 (tr) © Stockbyte/Getty Images
449 (tl) © iStockphoto.com

ILLUSTRATION

Art that appears on the Title page was created by Nomar Perez.

All mascots were created by Nomar Perez.

Doing Science
Burgandy Beam: 66, 67
Sharon Lane Holm: 3, 11, 18, 19, 23(cr), 29(b), 41, 44, 54, 55(tr, b), 56, 58, 59, 60, 62, 63
Nomar Perez: xii–1, 50
Carol Schwartz: 7, 9, 17, 42, 43, 46, 51, 57, 61
© WoodyStock/Alamy: 66 (b)

Life Science
Sharon Lane Holm: 86, 87(l, r), 88, 89(l,r), 92, 94, 95, 148
Nomar Perez: 78–79, 98
Carol Schwartz: 80, 83, 101, 104, 110, 114, 116, 128, 129, 153(tl, ct, tr), 155

Earth Science
Burgandy Beam: 187(cl)
Stephen Durke: 165, 183, 204–205(bl, br), 215(t), 215(b), 218, 228(cl), 229
Sharon Lane Holm: 196(bl), 202

Nomar Perez: 156–157, 161, 177, 182, 208, 216(l,r)
Carol Schwartz: 162, 185, 188(t), 188(b), 193(bl), 217(t)
Robin Storesund: 159, 199, 222

Physical Science
Burgandy Beam: 260(b), 264(b), 265(b), 273(t,c), 279, 300, 301
Sharon Lane Holm: 242(tr, bc), 243(t), 245(cr, tr), 253, 257, 267(c), 286, 299(bc)
Nomar Perez: 234–235, 239(tr, bl), 244, 259, 264(tr), 265(tr), 270(b), 274, 275(tr, bl), 280(bl, br), 281(bl), 284(b), 288, 289
Carol Schwartz : 243(cr), 245(br), 250, 251(cr), 252(c), 252(br), 260(tr), 262(tr), 263(tr), 267(tr), 268(bl, br), 27(b), 272(b), 276, 278, 287(t, b), 295(c, bl), 298, 299(tr),
Robin Storesund: 297, 303(c, b)

Natural Resources and the Environment
Sharon Lane Holm: 317, 320(br)
Nomar Perez: 306–307, 312, 315, 320(c), 334
Carol Schwartz: 310, 311, 329, 332(bl, br), 333(cl, cr), 336

Almanac
Burgandy Beam: 345(tr, cr, br), 352
Stephen Durke: 357(br), 359
Sharon Lane Holm: 354(c), 355(c), 387 (tr, cr, br), 388 (cr, br)
Nomar Perez: 353, 354(br), 357(c), 358, 364, 372(bl), 343
Carol Schwartz: 348, 350(c), 362, 363(c), 369, 371(t),
Robin Storesund: 351, 351, 365, 374(c), 375(c), 376(c), 377(c), 379(c), 380(c), 381(tr, b),

Glossary
Burgandy Beam:413 (cr), 419 (tl), 425 (tl), 443 (cr), 444 (cr),
Stephen Durke: 413 (br), 443 (br), 444 (br)
Sharon Lane Holm:
414 (bl, cr, br), 422 (bl), 423 (bl), 437 (tr), 440 (cl, tr), 441 (cl), 445 (cl)
Nomar Perez: 435 (bl), 447 (cl), 448 (cl, br), All letter mascots
Carol Schwartz: 415 (bl), 423 (cl), 423 (tr), 423 (br), 424 (cr), 425 (bl), 427 (bl), 428 (tr), 430 (br), 431 (bl), 433 (cr), 434 (cr), 438 (br), 442 (cl)
Robin Storesund: 414 (tr), 416 (cl), 417 (cr), 418 (bl, br), 421 (tl, bl), 426 (bl), 431 (cr), 437 (bl), 439 (cr), 445 (br)